Southern Secrets

a collection of recipes

Unique Features

Party Menus with Recipes and Plans
Quick and Easy Recipes
Low Calorie Menus and Recipes with Calorie Count
All Recipes Twice Tested

Published By
THE EPISCOPAL DAY SCHOOL MOTHERS' CLUB
Jackson, Tennessee

COVER AND ILLUSTRATIONS BY PATSY WHITE CAMP

First Printing	10,000 Copies	October 1979
Second Printing	5,000 Copies	March 1981
Third Printing	5,000 Copies	January 1983
Fourth Printing	5,000 Copies	August 1986
Fifth Printing	1,000 Copies	December 2009

Copies of SOUTHERN SECRETS may be obtained by writing to:

SOUTHERN SECRETS
University School of Jackson
232 McClellan Road
Jackson, Tennessee 38305

International Standard Book Number 978-0-918544-30-8

Copyright © 1979

All rights reserved. No part of this book may be reproduced or utilized in any form or by any means, including photocopying and recording, or by any information storage and retrieval system, without permission from the publisher.

Printed in the United States of America

FOREWORD

"Secrets shared are the leaven of life...increasing joy and expanding knowledge..."

Every successful endeavor has a secret ingredient.

In pursuing the secret of educating children, we at the Episcopal Day School have found a special recipe. The intangible key to this recipe is a loving Christian atmosphere which provides the leaven for academic excellence and fosters the development of human potential.

In 1970 we began supporting this philosophy through the annual Antique Show and Sale, which has grown through the years into a popular event featuring antiques, lectures, and delicious food. Our involvement in this project led to the discovery that we were dedicated to the pursuit of excellence in the kitchen as well as the classroom.

Our tearoom, which had modest beginnings as a snack bar at the 1970 show in the old Lambuth College Gym, mushroomed into a gourmet delight at the Jackson Civic Center. The elegant Antique Show Preview Party provided another creative outlet for our culinary interests. As requests for our recipes increased, we began exchanging our cooking ideas with others, a process which resulted in the publication of this book.

With pleasure, we share our Southern Secrets with you.

THE EPISCOPAL DAY SCHOOL MOTHERS' CLUB

TABLE OF CONTENTS

PARTY SECRETS 7
   Easter Fare (A Brunch) 9
   Super Super Bowl Party (Informal Supper) 12
   "Around-the-clock" Luncheon 14
   Sew and Lunch 17
   Soup Kitchen 20
   Country Fair Picnic 22
   An Affair to Remember (Late night Supper) 26
   Passport to an International Supper 29
   Over-the-Limit Duck Supper 32
   A Trip on the Orient Express (Dinner Party) 35
   We Wish You A Merry Christmas (Caroling Party) 38
   Kentucky Derby Party (Southern-Style Buffet) 41
   Over the Hill Supper (Surprise Birthday) 44
   Afternoon Sherry Party 48
   Midsummer Night's Dream (Large Cocktail Party) 51
   Rose Garden Tea for a Bride-to-be 57

QUICK AND EASY SECRETS 63
   Appetizers and Beverages 65
   Main Dishes 67
   Vegetables 77
   Breads 81
   Desserts 82

BEST KEPT SECRETS 85
   Appetizers and Beverages 87
   Salads and Salad Dressings 101
   Soups, Sauces and Marinades 113
   Main Dishes 122
   Eggs and Cheese 142
   Vegetables 144
   Breads 156
   Desserts 174
LOW CALORIE SECRETS 199

COOK'S GUIDE 233

INDEX 239

Party Secrets

EASTER FARE (A BRUNCH)

MENU
VICHYSSOISE
BAKED CRABMEAT SALAD
TART ASPIC
EASY QUICK ROLLS
STRAWBERRY TORTE

Let happy Easter holidays begin with your brunch for friends and relatives. For invitations, paint tiny yellow chicks parading across a white note. Inside say, "I couldn't let Easter parade by without seeing you! Brunch—11:00—etc."

To produce smiles as guests arrive, attach a straw hat decorated with fresh flowers and satin bows to your door knocker. Be sure to set a pot of new spring blossoms in a large Easter basket beside the front door. This is a day for bunches of fresh flowers around the house, gingham tablecloths and napkins tied with satin ribbons. The centerpiece can be as simple as a basket of brightly colored eggs mixed with French buns or something more elaborate like pots of tulips, ceramic lambs and rabbits. As a favor for each friend, put a hand-painted egg on a tiny stand at each place. An egg tree (branch sprayed white) is always a charming conversation piece and specially decorated eggs can be added to it year after year.

VICHYSSOISE

½ cup boiling water
2 chicken bouillon cubes
2 11-ounce cans potato soup
Garlic salt
2 cups milk
¼ cup chopped tops of green onions
1 8-ounce carton whipped, whipping cream

Dissolve bouillon cubes in boiling water. Combine the bouillon, the potato soup and the milk in a blender and mix until smooth. Add garlic salt to taste and fold in the whipped cream. Refrigerate until well-chilled, about 4 hours. Serve in champagne glasses with green onions sprinkled on top. Serves 6 to 8.

MRS. JERRY (MARTHA) KIZER

PARTY SECRETS

BAKED CRABMEAT SALAD

3 cups crabmeat
3 cups softened bread crumbs
3 cups milk
3 cups mayonnaise
18 chopped boiled eggs
3 tablespoons parsley

3 teaspoons dried onion flakes
1½ teaspoons salt
1 teaspoon black pepper
1 teaspoon red pepper
2 cups buttered bread crumbs

Combine all ingredients. Top with buttered bread crumbs. Bake at 350 degrees for 45 minutes. Serves 24.

MRS. SIMPSON (CONNIE) RUSSELL

TART ASPIC

1 3-ounce box lemon gelatin
1⅔ cups tomato juice
½ teaspoon black pepper
½ teaspoon salt
½ teaspoon ground cloves

½ teaspoon celery salt
¼ teaspoon red pepper
¼ teaspoon Tabasco
¼ cup vinegar

Heat tomato juice. Dissolve lemon gelatin in hot liquid. Add all other ingredients. Pour into small individual molds. Artichoke hearts can be added for variety. Serves 8.

MRS. DON (PATTY) LEWIS

EASY QUICK ROLLS

1 cup self-rising flour
½ cup milk
1 tablespoon sugar

2 heaping tablespoons mayonnaise

Mix in a bowl and spoon into cold, greased muffin tin. Bake at 350 degrees until brown, about 25 minutes. To make clover-leaf rolls, spoon 3 small spoonfuls in tins. Makes 8 rolls.

MRS. GARY (CATHY) DUNAWAY, RALEIGH, NC

STRAWBERRY TORTE

PASTRY:

2⅔ cups flour
1 teaspoon salt
1 cup shortening

7 or 8 tablespoons cold water
Sprinkles of granulated sugar

Preheat oven to 450 degrees. Prepare pastry and divide into 6 equal parts. Roll each into a 7-inch circle; place on ungreased cookie sheet. Prick each with fork and sprinkle each with granulated sugar. Bake 6 to 8 minutes. Cool.

FILLING:

1 pint fresh strawberries, washed and capped
½ cup powdered sugar

2 cups chilled whipping cream
½ teaspoon vanilla

Chop all berries except a few for garnish. In a cold bowl, beat whipping cream, powdered sugar and vanilla until stiff. Fold in berries. Stack all 6 circles of pastry, putting about ¾ cup filling between each layer. Frost top with remaining filling and garnish with reserved berries. Refrigerate at least 2 hours before serving. Sprinkle with powdered sugar. Serves 8.

MRS. DAVID (CATHY) FARMER

PARTY SECRETS

SUPER SUPER BOWL PARTY
MENU
DILL DIP SERVED WITH FRESH VEGETABLES
BEEF AND CHEESE SPREAD WITH CRACKERS
CHILI
SMORGASBORD OF MEATS, CHEESES, BREADS
FOR MAKE-YOUR-OWN SANDWICHES
OATMEAL-CARMELITOS

This is to be a casual gathering, a day for enjoying football and friends. Whether his team wins or loses, this party will raise everyone's spirits. Pompons and pennants of appropriate team colors will greet guests at your door along with pots of colorful chrysanthemums.

Have plenty of hors d'oeuvres and drinks at easy reach. When the crowd gets hungry, lead them to a buffet table laden with a crock of chili and a "deli" spread of meats, cheeses and breads. Coffee and a delicious pick-up dessert complete the meal.

DILL DIP

1 pint mayonnaise
1 pint sour cream
2 tablespoons dried parsley
2 tablespoons dried minced onion
3 tablespoons dried dill weed
1½ teaspoons Lawry's seasoned salt

Mix and serve. Makes 4½ cups.

MRS. CARL (ALICE) KIRKLAND

BEEF AND CHEESE SPREAD

½ of 2.5-ounce jar dried beef, finely chopped
2 8-ounce packages cream cheese, softened
¼ cup chopped green onions, tops only
2 teaspoons Worcestershire sauce

Mix well. Form into a ball and serve with crackers. Serves 18 to 20.

MRS. JERRY (MARTHA) KIZER

CHILI

- 2 pounds ground beef
- 3 large chopped onions
- 2 15-ounce cans kidney beans
- 1 large can tomatoes (1 pound 12 ounces)
- ½ teaspoon garlic salt
- ½ teaspoon oregano
- 2 teaspoons salt
- 2 tablespoons chili powder
- ¼ cup catsup
- 3 tablespoons Worcestershire
- 2 teaspoons sugar
- 1 teaspoon red wine vinegar

Brown meat. Drain off fat. Add onions and cook until tender. Add other ingredients. Simmer covered about 2 hours, stirring occasionally. Serves 6.

OATMEAL-CARMELITOS

- 1 14-ounce package Kraft caramels
- ½ cup milk
- 2 cups flour
- 2 cups quick-cooking oats
- 1½ cups brown sugar
- 1 teaspoon soda
- ½ teaspoon salt
- 1 cup (2 sticks) melted oleo
- 1 6-ounce package semi-sweet chocolate chips
- 1 cup nuts, chopped

Preheat oven to 350 degrees. Melt caramels in milk; cool slightly. Combine remaining ingredients except chocolate chips and nuts. This will be of a crumbly consistency. Press half of this mixture in a greased 9 x 13-inch pan. Bake 10 minutes. Remove from oven and sprinkle with chips and nuts. Spread caramel mixture on carefully. Spread with remaining crumb mixture. Bake 20 minutes; cool. Cut into squares before chilling. Makes 28 to 32 squares.

MRS. JOHN (LEEBA) CURLIN

PARTY SECRETS

"AROUND-THE-CLOCK" LUNCHEON FOR A MOTHER-TO-BE

MENU
COLD AVOCADO SOUP
(CAN BE SERVED IN TINY PAPER CUPS WHILE GUESTS CHAT)
HOT CHICKEN SALAD
ORANGE ASPIC
BRAN MUFFINS
CHOCOLATE ICEBOX TARTS

Having a luncheon in honor of a new mother-to-be? This party gives the expectant mother an idea of how much of her time baby will take when he arrives. Each guest is given a particular time of day or night to represent, when first invited. Then she is instructed to buy a little gift for mother or baby that could be used at that time. Example: time—1:00 a.m., gift—pacifier.

Dwell on the "time" theme for decorations such as clocks, schedules, tiny wrist watches as napkin rings. All manner of baby things plus fresh flowers will make a fine centerpiece. Greet the honoree with a lollipop corsage. After lunch it will be fun to open the gifts and read the notes attached.

AVOCADO SOUP

1 large avocado
½ cup half and half

1½ cups chicken broth
Garlic salt and pepper to taste

Place all ingredients in a blender and purée. Chill. When serving, garnish with a teaspoon of sour cream and a dash of paprika. Serves 4.

MRS. TOM (SALLY) RAINEY

HOT CHICKEN SALAD CASSEROLE

¾ cup Hellmann's mayonnaise
¼ cup water
1 10¾-ounce can cream of chicken soup
2 cups diced cooked chicken
2 tablespoons grated onion
½ cup chopped almonds
¼ cup green pepper, finely cut
1½ cups cooked rice (⅓ cup uncooked)
½ teaspoon salt
2 cups crushed potato chips

Mix mayonnaise, water and undiluted soup together; stir in chicken, onion, almonds, pepper, rice and salt. Place all in greased 2-quart casserole; top with potato chips and bake 30 minutes at 350 degrees. Serves 10. Almonds can easily be omitted if children dislike them, but they add good crunch.

MRS. COOPER (GAIL) EDMONSON, FRANKLIN, TN

ORANGE ASPIC

2 11-ounce cans mandarin oranges
Juice of mandarin oranges plus enough orange juice to make 2 cups
2 3-ounce packages orange gelatin
1 pint orange sherbet

Drain oranges into 2-cup measuring cup and fill to top with more orange juice. Heat and dissolve gelatin. Beat sherbet into 2 cups of liquid. Add mandarin oranges and pour mixture into mold. Refrigerate until set. Serves 8.

MRS. COOPER (GAIL) EDMONSON, FRANKLIN, TN

PARTY SECRETS

BRAN MUFFINS

1 cup shortening
2½ cups sugar
4 eggs
5 cups flour
5 teaspoons soda

½ teaspoon salt
1 quart buttermilk
6 cups Kellogg's All Bran
2 cups boiling water

Cream shortening and sugar together. Add eggs 1 at a time. Sift dry ingredients together and add alternately with buttermilk to shortening mixture. Add cereal and boiling water. Fill muffin tins ¾ full and bake at 400 degrees for 20 to 25 minutes. Batter can be stored in covered bowl in refrigerator 8 to 10 weeks. Yields 5½ dozen great muffins.

MRS. PAUL (PEGGY) WALKER

CHOCOLATE ICEBOX TARTS

2 dozen ladyfingers
1 teaspoon vanilla
1½ cups powdered sugar or
   1 cup plain sugar

1 stick butter
3 eggs
½ cup cocoa

Soften butter and cream with sugar. Add eggs 1 at a time, beating well. Add cocoa and flavor with vanilla. Line muffin tins with split ladyfingers and fill each with mixture. Freeze. Top with whipped cream when ready to serve. Makes 18 tarts.

MRS. ROBERT (BLANCHE) EMERSON

SEW AND LUNCH
MENU
HOT CINNAMON MOCHA
EGGPLANT AND SHRIMP CASSEROLE
FRESH FRUIT SALAD WITH POPPY SEED DRESSING
HOMEMADE ROLLS
FRENCH MINT FRANGO PIES

In October or November send scissor or thimble-shaped invitations accented with colored yarn to friends who thrive on needlework. Invite them to bring their Christmas sewing projects, enjoy lunch and spend the afternoon sewing and chatting. If the party date is close enough to Christmas, hang a green wreath on the front door with a few tomato pincushions attached for color. Fill a basket with balls of yarn and coordinated Christmas tree balls for a unique centerpiece. Greet each guest with a cup of hot mocha stirred with a cinnamon stick. After an afternoon of good fun and friendship, don't forget to send the group home with handmade tree ornaments.

HOT CINNAMON MOCHA

1 6-ounce package semi-sweet chocolate chips
1¼ cups strong coffee or 2 teaspoons instant coffee in 1¼ cups boiling water
2 teaspoons ground cinnamon
⅛ teaspoon salt
6 cups milk
2 tablespoons sugar (optional)
½ teaspoon vanilla

Measure chocolate, coffee, cinnamon and salt in a saucepan. Heat and stir until chocolate is melted and mixture is smooth. Stir in milk. Heat through. Stir in sugar and vanilla. Beat chocolate mixture with mixer or blender until foamy. Makes 2 quarts. Serve hot in mugs.

MRS. TOM (FAITH) HADLEY, HUMBOLDT, TN

PARTY SECRETS

EGGPLANT AND SHRIMP CASSEROLE

1 large eggplant, cooked and mashed
¾ cup milk
2 tablespoons melted butter
1 small green pepper, chopped
1 small onion, chopped
Dash of minced garlic

Pinch of thyme
Salt and pepper to taste
Dash of cayenne
2 eggs, beaten
1 4½-ounce can shrimp
¾ cup grated sharp cheese
Bread crumbs

Combine all ingredients and top with bread crumbs. Bake at 350 degrees for 25 minutes. Serves 4 or 5.

MRS. AUGUSTUS (ANN) MIDDLETON

POPPY SEED DRESSING

1¼ cups sugar
2 teaspoons dry mustard
2 teaspoons salt
1 small grated onion

⅔ cup vinegar
1 pint salad oil
1 tablespoon celery seed
1 tablespoon poppy seed

Combine sugar, salt, mustard and onion with *half* the vinegar. Blend well in blender. Add oil gradually. Add remaining vinegar in small amounts and beat until thick. Add seeds. To be used over mixed fruit. Serves 25.

MRS. PAUL (PEGGY) WALKER

HOMEMADE ROLLS

1 cup shortening
½ cup sugar
1 cup boiling water
1 cup cold water

2 packages dry yeast
2 eggs, well-beaten
6 cups sifted flour
1 teaspoon salt

Cream the shortening and sugar. Add boiling water slowly. When shortening is dissolved, add cup of cold water. When this mixture is lukewarm, add yeast and stir to dissolve. Add eggs, salt and flour. Place in refrigerator overnight. Roll out. Allow to rise. Bake 10 minutes in a 450-degree oven. Makes 50 rolls.

MRS. COOPER (GAIL) EDMONSON, FRANKLIN, TN

FRENCH MINT FRANGO PIES

1 cup butter or margarine
2 cups powdered sugar
4 1-ounce squares Baker's unsweetened chocolate, melted and cooled
1 teaspoon peppermint flavoring
2 teaspoons vanilla flavoring
12 to 18 vanilla wafers, crushed
4 whole eggs
18 4-ounce paper cups

Combine butter and sugar; beat until light and fluffy. Add chocolate and beat thoroughly. Add eggs, 1 at a time, beating for several minutes after each. Add peppermint and vanilla flavorings; beat again. Place paper cups on tray; cover bottom of cups with half the wafer crumbs. Spoon in chocolate mixture. Top with remaining crumbs or nuts, if preferred. Freeze. Remove from freezer about 10 minutes before serving. May be topped with whipped cream, if desired. May also be topped with cherry, if desired. Keeps 3 months. Serves 18. This is a *good* recipe to be prepared ahead and makes a big hit with children.

MRS. JOE (NANCY) GOOD

PARTY SECRETS

SOUP KITCHEN

MENU
OLD-FASHIONED SOUP POT
MEXICAN CORN BREAD
CARAMEL BARS

If you can't keep your guests out of the kitchen, stop trying! Here's a meal served right from the range. This party is a great one for busy holiday shoppers who need a moment to relax and a quick lunch. Write the invitations on your personalized recipe cards. "A Recipe For a Good Time—Join the Grand Opening of Carol's Soup Kitchen—Come Anytime Between Eleven and Two, etc."

You might plan your party for a Saturday to include your working friends. Decorations are simple arrangements of fresh vegetables in copper pots accented with dried pasta and kitchen utensils. Be sure to greet your friends in a chef's hat.

OLD-FASHIONED SOUP POT

1 tablespoon cooking oil
1 pound lean stew meat
2 quarts water
1 14½-ounce can tomatoes, mashed
1 envelope dry onion soup
4 stalks celery sliced in ½-inch pieces
2 carrots sliced in ½-inch pieces
1 pound package frozen sliced okra
1 pound package mixed vegetables
4 Oscar Mayer smoked sausage links
1 bay leaf
Worcestershire sauce and salt to taste

Brown stew meat in oil and add 2 quarts of water. Bring to a boil and add tomatoes, onion soup, celery, carrots, okra, mixed vegetables, sausage, bay leaf, Worcestershire sauce and salt to taste. Return to boiling; then simmer for 3 hours. Serves 12.

MRS. WILLIAM (DELORIA) HAYNES

MEXICAN CORN BREAD

6 slices bacon, fried and crumbled
1½ cups corn bread mix
¾ cup milk
½ cup salad oil
2 eggs
1 large onion, grated
1 tablespoon sugar
1 17-ounce can yellow cream-style corn
4 ounces grated sharp cheese
½ pimiento, chopped
½ teaspoon garlic salt
1 hot cherry pepper (may substitute 1 Jalapeño pepper or 3 dashes Tabasco)

Mix all ingredients and bake 35 minutes at 375 degrees. Serves 8 to 12. This is excellent on a cold day with hot vegetable soup for lunch.

MRS. CHARLES (CARMEN) BRUER

CARAMEL BARS

1 stick oleo
2 cups light brown sugar
2 eggs
1 cup self-rising flour
1 teaspoon vanilla
1 cup pecans
Powdered sugar

Melt stick oleo in 8 x 10-inch pan. Slosh around to butter pan; then pour into bowl. To butter, add brown sugar, eggs, flour, vanilla and pecans. Line pan with waxed paper; then pour mixture into pan. Bake at 325 degrees for 30 minutes or until it rises and falls in the center. Let partially cool. Turn out; cut into bars and roll in powdered sugar. Serves 15 to 20. This recipe is requested every year at the Antique Show. It is usually bagged and sold several pieces together.

MRS. BENTLEY (JUDI) RAWDON

PARTY SECRETS

COUNTRY FAIR PICNIC

MENU
BOX LUNCH
GLORIOUS FRIED CHICKEN
HALF GREEN PEPPER FILLED WITH POTATO SALAD
INDIVIDUAL CHEESE BALL AND CRACKERS
WHOLE WHEAT OATMEAL BREAD
WITH STRAWBERRY BUTTER
STUFFED EGGS
PICKLES
PARMESAN CHEESE STICKS
LEMON SPONGE PIE

A country fair is as American as the Fourth of July; so why not celebrate this great holiday with a fair theme? This can be a party for the whole family and would be a good way to entertain a big group of relatives or neighbors.

American flags and pots of geraniums line the walkway to the yard used for the festivities. Set the stage with red-checked tablecloths on tables and bales of hay to sit on. The centerpieces can be baskets of fresh vegetables, fruits and eggs along with jars of pickles marked with blue ribbons. Set out plenty of lawn games such as volleyball, horseshoes and croquet. Plan races, relays and a "Best Decorated Bike" parade for the young. What a sparkle a country music group would add to the affair.

During the games, let guests help themselves to peanuts, pretzels and cheese cut from a big wheel. To cool the contestants, have a child's pool filled with ice and beer and large pitchers of lemonade close at hand. The adults will enjoy drawing numbers for partners, picking up a box lunch for two and finding just the right spot to settle. The children will prefer helping themselves to picnic treats by filling their own baskets.

Ask each lady to bring her favorite pie to serve for dessert. A panel of judges might select the "Fairest of the Fair" among the home-baked desserts.

An evening display of fireworks plus a small jar of your special jelly or relish sent home with each family will make this party one to remember.

GLORIOUS FRIED CHICKEN

3 fryers, cut into serving pieces
1 tablespoon salt
½ teaspoon pepper
¾ cup flour
2 eggs, beaten
2 tablespoons water
1½ cups fine dry bread crumbs
½ cup grated Parmesan cheese
2 sticks butter or margarine

Combine salt, pepper and flour. Put in shallow dish. Beat eggs with water in second dish. Mix bread crumbs and Parmesan cheese in third shallow dish. Roll chicken in flour, then in egg mixture, then in crumb mixture. Divide butter between 2 large skillets; melt. Place chicken pieces, skin side down, in butter and cook until browned on both sides. Place chicken on foil lined baking sheet. Bake in 400-degree oven for 30 or 40 minutes. Delicious served with corn on the cob and sliced tomatoes. Serves 12.

MRS. JOHN (LINDA) WOMACK

MARTHA'S INDIVIDUAL CHEESE BALLS

1 8-ounce package sharp Cheddar cheese, grated
1 8-ounce package medium Cheddar cheese, grated
2 8-ounce packages cream cheese, softened
½ cup mayonnaise
1 tablespoon Roquefort cheese
1 teaspoon garlic salt

Mix above ingredients well. Roll into small cheese balls about the size of golf balls. Roll in chopped nuts or paprika. Wrap each in plastic wrap and serve with crackers in a box lunch. Makes 16 to 18 balls.

MRS. JERRY (MARTHA) KIZER

PARTY SECRETS

WHOLE WHEAT OATMEAL BREAD

1¼ cups whole wheat flour
1 cup brown sugar
1 teaspoon salt
1 teaspoon baking powder
1 teaspoon baking soda
½ teaspoon cinnamon
½ teaspoon nutmeg

1 cup quick-cooking oats
½ cup raisins
1½ cups canned sweetened
   applesauce
⅓ cup Wesson oil
2 large eggs
¼ cup milk

Grease and flour a 9 x 5 x 3-inch loaf pan. In a large mixing bowl sift together dry ingredients. Stir in oats and raisins. Beat applesauce, oil, eggs and milk together. Make a well in center of flour mixture. Pour applesauce mixture into the well and stir only until dry ingredients are thoroughly moistened. Pour batter in prepared pan and bake in a preheated 350-degree oven for about 1 hour. Makes 1 loaf. OPTIONAL: May sprinkle batter with a mixture of 2 tablespoons brown sugar, 2 tablespoons chopped nuts and ¼ teaspoon cinnamon before baking.

MRS. DAVID (JANIS) FITE

STRAWBERRY BUTTER

1 pint fresh strawberries or 10
   ounces frozen, drained
½ pound unsalted butter

1 cup powdered sugar (If using
   fresh berries, add ½ cup
   sugar.)

Put ingredients in blender in order given. Blend until creamy and smooth. If the mixture appears to curdle, continue blending until creamy. Chill. Serve with toast, biscuits, muffins, pancakes or waffles. Makes 2½ cups.

MRS. TOM (FAITH) HADLEY, HUMBOLDT, TN

PARMESAN CHEESE STICKS

Canned potato sticks **Parmesan cheese**

Sprinkle potato sticks lavishly with Parmesan cheese. Spread on cookie sheet and bake at 300 degrees for 10 minutes. Place individual servings in Baggies and tie for picnic.

MRS. JACK (ANNE) GARDNER, SEARCY, AR

LEMON SPONGE PIE

1 cup sugar
3 tablespoons all-purpose flour
1 teaspoon grated lemon rind
2 tablespoons lemon juice
1 large egg, separated
2 tablespoons butter or
 margarine, melted
1 cup milk
¼ teaspoon salt
1 unbaked pie shell

Combine sugar and flour in a medium-sized mixing bowl. Stir in lemon rind and juice; beat in egg yolk, then melted butter. Stir in milk. Beat egg white with salt until fairly stiff peaks form; then fold into lemon mixture until no streaks of white are visible. Pour into unbaked pie shell. Bake at 350 degrees for 35 to 40 minutes or until crust is lightly browned and filling is puffy and touched with brown. Cool 15 minutes before cutting. Good warm or cold. Serves 6.

MRS. DUANE (LOIS) SPIESE

PARTY SECRETS

AN AFFAIR TO REMEMBER
(LATE NIGHT SUPPER)

MENU
BEEF CREPES
SPINACH SALAD AND DRESSING
REFRIGERATOR ROLLS
CHERRY BERRIES ON A CLOUD

Watch for an upcoming special event such as a symphony concert, ballet or a play by the local theater guild. Encourage a congenial group of friends to attend the performance and invite them all to your house afterwards for a late evening supper. If you send invitations to this party, make them resemble handbills from a theater; complete with opening date, curtain time and producers for *your* performance. To set a festive mood, attach a bouquet of fresh flowers plus toy horn or toe shoes or masks to the front door.

CREPES

1 cup sifted flour
¼ teaspoon salt
1 teaspoon sugar

3 eggs
1½ cups milk

Sift together flour, salt, sugar. Add eggs 1 at a time, beating thoroughly. Gradually add milk a little at a time. Mix until smooth. Let batter stand 1 to 2 hours before cooking crepes to be sure all the bubbles have settled. Makes about 18.

BEEF FILLING FOR CREPES

1 pound ground chuck
1 medium onion, chopped
1 10¼-ounce can beef gravy
1 4-ounce can sliced mushrooms, drained
1 teaspoon Worcestershire
½ teaspoon salt

½ teaspoon seasoned salt
¼ teaspoon pepper
¼ teaspoon garlic salt
1 tablespoon catsup
½ teaspoon celery salt
2 tablespoons dry sherry or red wine

Lightly cook meat; drain; add onion and cook 5 minutes. Add gravy and mushrooms and all other ingredients. Stir well and simmer, uncovered, for 1 hour. Use about ⅓ cup filling for each crepe. Should fill about 12 crepes.

MRS. PAUL (PEGGY) WALKER

DRESSING FOR SPINACH OR LETTUCE SALAD

½ cup salad oil
¼ cup wine vinegar (red or white)
1½ teaspoons sugar
2 teaspoons dry mustard
1 teaspoon salt
½ teaspoon paprika
1 tablespoon chives
1 teaspoon parsley
1 tablespoon grated onion
Freshly ground or cracked pepper
1 ice cube

Combine all ingredients in a jar. Shake well to blend. This is good on any mixed green salad with hard-boiled eggs, bacon and sliced fresh mushrooms. Makes about 1 cup for 8 individual salads.

MRS. CARL (ALICE) KIRKLAND

REFRIGERATOR ROLLS

1 cup Crisco
½ cup sugar
1 tablespoon salt
2 cups hot water
2 eggs, beaten
1 package or cake yeast
½ cup warm water
7 cups flour

In a large bowl mix the Crisco, sugar, salt and water with an electric mixer. When this cools to lukewarm, add eggs, yeast dissolved in warm water and flour. Cover and let rise until doubled in bulk. Refrigerate overnight. Roll into approximately 1½-inch balls. Place in buttered muffin tins. Brush with melted butter and let rise for 2 hours. Bake at 400 degrees until brown. Extra dough can be kept in refrigerator for a week or 2.

MRS. STANFORD (HELEN) WHITE

PARTY SECRETS

CHERRY BERRIES ON A CLOUD

6 egg whites
¼ teaspoon cream of tartar
1 teaspoon vanilla
1½ cups sugar
2 3-ounce packages cream cheese
1 cup sugar
2 cups cream, whipped

2 cups miniature marshmallows
1 21-ounce can cherry pie filling
1 teaspoon lemon juice
2 cups fresh sliced strawberries or 1 10-ounce package frozen strawberries, thawed and undrained

Beat egg whites, cream of tartar and vanilla until frothy. Slowly add 1½ cups sugar and beat until stiff and glossy. Bake in greased 13 x 9 x 2-inch pan for 1 hour at 275 degrees. Turn off oven and leave in oven for 12 hours.

FILLING:
Soften cream cheese with 1 cup sugar; fold in cream, whipped; add marshmallows. Spread on meringue and refrigerate 12 hours.

TOPPING:
Mix together cherry pie filling, lemon and strawberries. Spread over top. Serves 10 to 12.

MRS. WILLIAM (LAURA) BURNETT
MRS. ROBERT (PEGGY) MANDLE

PASSPORT TO AN INTERNATIONAL SUPPER

MENU
QUICHE LORRAINE
CHICKEN CURRY
BAKLAVA

This International Party is fun as a progressive supper given by three couples or can be done at one house with the three courses representing different countries. For invitations, guests receive small notebooks made to resemble passports. Listed inside are the countries or homes they will visit, the names of the "tour guides" and the menu for the evening. Guests are greeted by banners made similar to the country's flag at each front door. The first port will be France where wine and a hearty slice of quiche are served. Centerpieces can be assembled from folk art objects, souvenirs, globes, toys and maps mixed with flowers and candles. Torches will guide your friends to the next house, representing India, where they will enjoy a delicious chicken curry. To top off this special affair, the group will move to Greece for traditional Baklava, coffee and live music.

QUICHE LORRAINE

1 9-inch pie shell
4 slices bacon, cooked and crumbled
½ cup diced ham
½ cup diced Swiss cheese
4 eggs
1 cup half and half
½ teaspoon salt
¼ teaspoon nutmeg (maybe a touch more)
¼ teaspoon white pepper

Sprinkle bacon in bottom of unbaked pie shell. Cover with ham and Swiss cheese. Put eggs, cream and spices in blender and blend until mixed. Pour over ham, cheese and bacon in pie shell and bake at 350 degrees for 45 minutes or until mixture is set. Serve hot. Serves 6.

PARTY SECRETS

CHICKEN CURRY

1 tablespoon curry powder
1 tablespoon butter
1 onion, minced
2 stalks celery, diced
½ cup diced apple
½ cup beef broth
½ cup sliced mushrooms
1 cup light cream
1 cup milk

2 tablespoons cold water
1 teaspoon cornstarch
¼ teaspoon monosodium
  glutamate
¼ teaspoon salt
2 cups diced cooked chicken
Kumquats and parsley for garnish
3 cups cooked rice

Sauté curry powder in butter until nicely browned; stir in vegetables and apple; mix thoroughly. Add beef broth. Bring to a boil; then stir in cream and milk. Bring just to a boil again. Combine cornstarch and cold water. Add to the above mixture and cook, stirring constantly until it thickens. Stir in chicken, mushrooms, monosodium glutamate and salt. Trim with preserved kumquats and parsley. Serve over rice. Offer the following condiments: watermelon pickles, chutney, salted peanuts, coconut and raisins. Makes 5 or 6 servings.

MRS. RICHARD (SUSAN) DAVIDSON

BAKLAVA

3 pounds chopped pecans
3 teaspoons cinnamon
2 teaspoons cloves
1 cup sugar

1 pound unsalted butter
1 pound fillo (Greek strudel leaves)

Combine pecans, cinnamon, cloves, sugar and mix well. Grease a 17½ x 12½ x 2-inch pan with melted butter. Place 8 filla in pan. Brush each with butter. Sprinkle top fillo with layer of nut mixture. Cover with 3 filla, brushing each with butter and sprinkling top fillo with nut mixture. Continue the 3-filla procedure until all nut mixture is used. Finish with 6 filla on top, brushing each with butter. With a sharp-pointed knife cut into small squares. Keep knife moistened with cold water to make cutting easier. Bake in preheated oven at 300 degrees for 1½ hours. Remove from oven. Cool and pour hot syrup over baklava.

SYRUP:

2 cups sugar
4 ounces honey
1 cup water

Juice of ½ lemon
2 or 3 cloves
1 teaspoon cinnamon

Mix all ingredients; bring to boil and pour over baklava. Makes about 2 dozen squares.

MRS. GEORGE (JANIE) THOMAS

PARTY SECRETS

OVER-THE-LIMIT DUCK SUPPER

MENU
DELICIOUS DUCKS WITH WILD RICE
BAKED ASPARAGUS DISH
CORN PUDDING
ICEBOX ROLLS
STRAWBERRY SHERBET

This supper will appeal to all duck hunters and hopefully to their wives who will be celebrating the close of duck season. Serve the hunters with "subpoenae" to appear at your house on the appointed night to testify on their own behalf to the charge of going "over the limit". Gather decoys, duck calls, dried grasses, feathers and you will certainly come up with handsome arrangements for the front door and tables.

After this hearty meal, it would be fun to call on the wives to recount humorous experiences they have had with the sport of duck hunting. Needless to say, the hunters themselves will fill the rest of the evening with their favorite anecdotes.

DELICIOUS DUCKS

2 good-sized ducks (i.e. mallards)
2 tablespoons orange marmalade
1 orange, whole
1 small can (6 ounces) frozen orange juice concentrate, thawed

1 cup water
½ cup melted butter
¼ cup soy sauce
Salt and pepper

Wash and dry ducks. Salt and pepper liberally inside and out. Brush with melted butter and soy sauce. Put ½ orange and 1 tablespoon marmalade in each body cavity. Place both ducks in pressure cooker or crock pot. Pour remaining butter and soy sauce over ducks. Pour 1 cup water in bottom. Pour orange juice concentrate (undiluted) over ducks. Cook 45 minutes in pressure cooker; 45 minutes on high for crock pot, then 3 to 4 hours on medium heat. After cooking is complete, remove duck meat from bones, saving juice in pan. Thicken juice with small amount of flour and water paste. Mix with duck meat. Serve over rice. Garnish with orange slices and parsley. Freezes well. Serves 4.

MRS. LINDA RICE FORBES

BAKED ASPARAGUS DISH

2 cans asparagus tips (10½-ounce size)
1 can cream of celery soup (10½ ounces)
3 hard-boiled eggs, sliced
⅛ teaspoon red pepper
¼ teaspoon salt
⅓ cup slivered almonds
1 cup cheese cracker crumbs
2 tablespoons butter

Mix all ingredients except cracker crumbs and butter together gently. Place in 1½-quart casserole. Cover with crumbs and dot with butter. Bake at 350 degrees for 30 minutes or until bubbly. Serves 6. May be combined and refrigerated ahead of time to be baked later.

MRS. THOMPSON (SALLY) DABNEY

CORN PUDDING

2 17-ounce cans yellow cream-style corn
3 tablespoons flour
2 sticks oleo, melted
1⅓ cups sugar (may use less)
4 large eggs, beaten

Mix all ingredients and pour into a greased 2-quart casserole. Bake for 1 hour at 325 degrees. This is a good recipe with turkey and dressing at Thanksgiving. Serves 6 to 8.

MRS. JERRY (RUTH ANN) SMITH

PARTY SECRETS

ICEBOX ROLLS

5 tablespoons sugar
1 teaspoon salt
1 package yeast

2 cups lukewarm water
¾ cup shortening
5 cups flour

Mix sugar, salt, shortening and yeast (which has been dissolved in warm water). Then add flour to the mixture. Set in icebox for at least 4 hours. Make out rolls and let rise 1 hour. Bake at 400 degrees for 20 minutes. Dough will keep in refrigerator for up to 1 week. Makes at least 3 dozen rolls.

MRS. DAVID (BETSY) FAVARA

STRAWBERRY SHERBET

⅓ cup ice water
¼ cup Cointreau
¼ teaspoon lemon juice

2 10-ounce packages frozen, sweetened strawberries

Combine water, Cointreau and lemon juice in blender. Spoon frozen berries into blender and whirl at high speed for 3 or 4 seconds. Turn off and scrape down sides. Repeat process until mixture is smooth and thick. Spoon into dishes and serve immediately or put in a covered plastic container and freeze. Serves 6.

MRS. ROBERT (BLANCHE) EMERSON

A TRIP ON THE ORIENT EXPRESS
(DINNER PARTY)

MENU
FRIED WONTONS WITH SAUCES
CHOP SUEY SERVED WITH RICE
ALMOND BARS
MANDARIN ORANGES SOAKED IN TRIPLE SEC

Here's your chance to entertain and to celebrate the Chinese New Year all in one. Invitations are made like Oriental scrolls on rice paper or the thinnest stationery. Copy a few Chinese letters down the left side of the paper and invite your friends to an evening in the Orient. They will be delighted when they first sight Japanese lanterns hung on the porch. A large paper parasol will add to the spirit of the party as will the Chinese kite attached to the front door.

As is the custom, each guest must leave his shoes in the entrance hall. The buffet table should be centered with a simple branch decorated with small paper fans or tiny tissue flowers. Set this centerpiece on a brocade table runner. Remember to use any lacquer ware, bamboo accessories, Imari, or Oriental statues for accent. Serve the meal at low tables or on trays with a votive candle and a fresh cut blossom at each place.

Ring a bell to alert guests that a new course is being served at the buffet table. For a sweet ending, serve almond bars with mandarin oranges, chilled and soaked in Triple Sec.

Perhaps this is the night for some old-fashioned parlor games: Chinese checkers, parcheesi, backgammon. A lovely favor for each lady would be a delicate rice paper wallet or an Oriental fan.

FRIED WONTONS

- 1 package wonton skins
- ¼ pound cooked pork or chicken, chopped
- ¼ pound cooked shrimp, chopped
- ¼ pound water chestnuts, minced
- 1 teaspoon cooking oil
- 1 teaspoon sherry or wine
- 1 tablespoon soy sauce
- ¼ teaspoon ground ginger
- ⅓ teaspoon sugar

Mix all ingredients except skins. Blend well. Place about 1 teaspoonful of mixture in center of wonton skin. Fold diagonally. Join 2 extreme ends together. May need to moisten to hold together. Deep fry to golden brown. Serve hot with sweet-sour sauce or sauce for wonton or egg rolls. Serves about 42.

MRS. BRUCE (MARY) FISCHER, SACRAMENTO, CA

PARTY SECRETS

SWEET AND SOUR SAUCE

½ cup brown sugar
½ cup vinegar
3 tablespoons cornstarch
1½ cups pineapple juice
2 tablespoons soy sauce

Bring brown sugar and vinegar to a boil. Combine cornstarch and pineapple juice; add to hot mixture and cook until thickened. Stir in soy sauce. Yields 2 cups.

MRS. JOHN (JANICE) RIDDLER

SAUCE FOR WONTON OR EGG ROLLS

¼ cup soy sauce
¼ cup white vinegar
1 tablespoon sesame oil
2 tablespoons minced fresh ginger
1 tablespoon minced garlic
½ teaspoon sugar
2 tablespoons hot oil (optional)

Stir all ingredients in a mixing bowl to blend well. Either pour over or dip wonton into this sauce. This is also a great marinade for chuck roast to grill as steak. Makes ¾ cup.

MRS. JIM (ANN) AVENT

CHOP SUEY

6 butterfly pork chops, cubed (any cut of pork may be used)
Small amount of flour
2 tablespoons oil
2 cups onion, chopped
2 cups celery, chopped
1 clove garlic, pressed
1 cup water
2 cans fancy Chinese vegetables, drained
Soy sauce to taste
Cooked rice

Roll pork cubes in flour and brown in oil. Add onion, celery, garlic and water. Simmer until tender. Add Chinese vegetables and soy sauce. Heat through. Serve over rice. Serves 6.

MRS. R. B. (NORMA) MARTINDALE, JR.

ALMOND BARS

CAKE:
1 box Betty Crocker pound cake mix
1 stick melted butter
2 eggs
1 teaspoon almond flavoring

TOPPING:
1 8-ounce package cream cheese
1 pound box powdered sugar
2 eggs
1 teaspoon almond flavoring

Mix the pound cake mix, butter, 2 eggs and almond flavoring together and spread in a greased and floured 9 x 13-inch pan. Mix cream cheese, sugar, 2 eggs and almond flavoring and pour over cake dough. Sprinkle with almonds; press into mixture. Bake at 350 degrees for 35 to 40 minutes. Slice into "fingers". Can be frozen. Slice, put in container, wrap well and freeze. Makes 16 squares.
VARIATION: Use 1 teaspoon vanilla in batter.

MRS. LINDA RICE FORBES

PARTY SECRETS

"WE WISH YOU A MERRY CHRISTMAS" CAROLING PARTY
(A SUPPER FOR SEVERAL FAMILIES)

MENU
HOT MULLED WINE
CHEESE WREATH
(FAVORITE CHEESE BALL RECIPE
MOLDED IN WREATH SHAPE AND SERVED WITH CRACKERS)
SAINT PAUL'S HEAVEN
BLANCHE'S BROCCOLI
FRENCH BREAD
EASY ICE CREAM BALLS
SUGARED PECANS

CHILDREN'S MENU
HOT CHOCOLATE
HOT DOGS
CHILI
GARNISHES
KRAUT
POTATO CHIPS
GINGERBREAD MEN

Here's a Christmas tradition for the whole family to look forward to year after year. Let young and old help plan this caroling party for close friends and neighbors. It can be a bring-a-dish gathering or "your treat" as we've planned here. Let the children make the invitations with a Christmas theme or if you have access to small pamphlets of carols, hand deliver one to each family with a note of invitation attached. Be sure to star those songs you'll be singing so the families can practice.

Gather the group as soon as it's dark with extra flashlights and a guitarist, if possible. It's a good idea to warn the neighbors that you'll be coming to their houses to sing between certain hours. Let the children deliver a little gift to each door as you carol, perhaps a miniature pound cake. Return to a roaring fire at your house before the little ones get too cold. Children can be fed right away while adults enjoy hot mulled wine and the cheese wreath. At the end of this relaxed and special evening, send each family home with a small remembrance, perhaps a sack of sugared pecans to hang on their tree and to enjoy on the day they take the tree down.

It would be ideal to set up for children in the kitchen or playroom. Use paper Christmas plates, cups and napkins. Serve yourself and create your own favorite hot dog.

HOT MULLED WINE

1 cup boiling water
½ cup sugar
1 lemon, sliced
1 orange, sliced
12 whole allspice
12 whole cloves
4-inch stick cinnamon
1 fifth dry red wine

In large saucepan combine the boiling water, sugar, sliced lemon, sliced orange, allspice, cloves and stick cinnamon. Bring to a boil. Reduce heat and simmer 5 minutes. Add the wine. Bring to boiling point. Do not boil, but simmer 10 minutes. Pour the hot mulled wine into thick glasses or mugs. Place a slice of lemon, a slice of orange and a few whole spices in each glass. Makes 6 to 8 drinks.

MRS. GLENN (KAREN) BARNETT
MRS. KING (LUANNE) BOND

ST. PAUL'S HEAVEN

3 pounds sausage
4 boxes Lipton's chicken noodle soup (8 packages)
6 cups water
3 chopped peppers
3 chopped onions
1 stalk celery, chopped
2 cups uncooked rice
2 cups mushrooms, drained
2 cups sliced almonds

Cook sausage and drain. Cook soup in water. Combine ingredients and top with almonds. Bake at 350 degrees for 1½ hours. Serves 25.

MRS. JIM (ANN) AVENT

BLANCHE'S BROCCOLI

1 10-ounce box broccoli spears (frozen)
Boiling water
Salt

SAUCE:
1 cup mayonnaise
Juice of 1 lemon
2 teaspoons grated onion
Dash of Tabasco

Cook broccoli according to package directions in boiling, salted water. Drain and arrange on serving platter. Combine sauce ingredients and pour over hot or cold broccoli. Serves 6.

MRS. ED (MONA) HICKS

PARTY SECRETS

PARTY SECRETS

FRENCH BREAD

1¼ cups warm water
1 package dry yeast
1 tablespoon Wesson oil (heaping)
1 tablespoon sugar (heaping)
1 teaspoon salt
Flour for a stiff dough (about 4 cups)
Cornstarch
Water
Sesame seeds

Mix all ingredients well. Knead dough for 5 minutes. Place dough in greased bowl, turning enough to grease lightly. Cover and let rise in a warm place for 1½ hours. Punch down and let rise again for 1 hour. Divide dough into 3 parts and roll each piece like a jelly roll. Grease baking sheet and sprinkle with meal lightly. Brush mixture of cornstarch and water on top of each loaf. Sprinkle sesame seeds on top of each loaf. Let loaves rise for 1½ hours. Bake at 425 degrees for 10 to 15 minutes. Yields 3 loaves that freeze beautifully.

MRS. THOMAS (NANCY) CRENSHAW, HUMBOLDT, TN

EASY ICE CREAM BALLS

½ gallon vanilla or peppermint ice cream
1 package Oreo cookies
2 squares semi-sweet chocolate
1 small can evaporated milk (5.33 ounces)
1 stick butter
2 cups confectioners sugar

Scoop out ice cream balls. Roll in Oreo crumbs that have been crushed in blender. Place on cookie sheet in freezer. In double boiler heat chocolate squares, milk, butter and confectioners sugar. Pour over ice cream balls and serve. Whipped cream and cherry on top, optional. Very easy and *so* good. Makes about 18 balls.

MRS. ALLEN (CAROL) STRAWBRIDGE, DRESDEN, TN

SUGARED PECANS

1 pound pecans
1 egg
1 tablespoon water
1 cup sugar
1 teaspoon salt
1 teaspoon cinnamon

Dip pecans into a mixture of egg and water. Then dip into a mixture of sugar, salt and cinnamon. Bake at 250 degrees for 30 or 40 minutes.

MRS. TOM (FAITH) HADLEY, HUMBOLDT, TN

KENTUCKY DERBY PARTY
(SOUTHERN-STYLE BUFFET)

MENU
TO BE SERVED BEFORE THE BUFFET
ASSORTED CHEESE AND CRACKERS
HOT CLAM DIP

BUFFET
COUNTRY HAM AND EASY ANGEL BISCUITS
CHEESE GRITS CASSEROLE
FRIED CHICKEN LEGS
BAKED APRICOTS
STUFFED MUSHROOMS
PECAN TARTS
MINT JULEPS
BLOODY MARYS
FRESH ORANGE JUICE

For a special gathering in May, invite a group of horse racing enthusiasts to watch the Kentucky Derby on T.V. with a Southern-style buffet to be served afterwards. Make the invitations like a ticket to the race itself. Decorate with horseshoes, strips of colored silk, red roses and plenty of magnolia. Open a betting booth for quarter, half-dollar and dollar bets. (Win tickets only, to avoid confusion.) Have a blackboard handy.

Greet guests with mint juleps, bloody Marys and fresh orange juice. Serve hors d'oeuvres and drinks during the race from a tea cart. After the race and your "winners" are congratulated, lead the guests to this prize-winning buffet.

HOT CLAM DIP

12 ounces cream cheese
1 8-ounce jar Old English cheese
½ large onion, chopped
2 3¾-ounce cans minced clams, drained
3 tablespoons Worcestershire sauce
¼ teaspoon black pepper
¼ teaspoon Tabasco sauce

Mix cheeses in double boiler. Dice onion and combine with cheeses, clams and other ingredients; refrigerate. On day of party allow dip to come to room temperature (6 to 8 hours). Serve warm in chafing dish. Makes less than 1 quart.

PARTY SECRETS

QUICK AND EASY ANGEL BISCUITS

½ pint whipping cream
2 cups Bisquick

Yellow corn meal

To Bisquick add whipping cream, reserving 1 tablespoon. Roll out ¼-inch thick and cut with small biscuit cutter. Brush tops with cream and sprinkle with yellow corn meal. Bake at 400 degrees until brown. Serves 8.

MRS. DON (PATTY) LEWIS
MRS. JACK (ANNE) GARDNER, SEARCY, AR

CHEESE GRITS CASSEROLE

1 cup quick cooking grits
1 6-ounce roll garlic cheese
1 stick butter or margarine

2 eggs, beaten
¾ cup milk

Cook grits according to package directions. Add cheese and butter or margarine. Cool. Add eggs and milk. Pour into a 6 to 8 cup casserole and bake uncovered for 1 hour at 375 degrees. If this recipe is doubled, bake in 2 separate casseroles as baking takes much longer if doubled. Excellent with country ham and biscuits. Serves 6.

MRS. MIKE (BETTY) POWERS

BAKED APRICOTS

2 16-ounce cans apricot halves, drained well
1½ boxes light brown sugar

1 12-ounce box Ritz crackers, crushed
1 stick butter

In a greased 2½-quart dish layer apricot halves, brown sugar and Ritz crackers. Dot with butter. Bake at 300 degrees for 45 minutes to 1 hour. Serves 16.

MRS. BILL (SANDRA) PERKINS

STUFFED MUSHROOMS

12 large, fresh mushrooms
1 10-ounce package frozen chopped spinach or broccoli
3 tablespoons butter
1 clove garlic
Dash Tabasco
Juice of 1 lemon
3 tablespoons Parmesan cheese
3 tablespoons mayonnaise
½ teaspoon Worcestershire sauce
1 teaspoon seasoned salt

Cook spinach or broccoli and drain well. Sauté garlic in butter. Dip mushrooms in this butter and place in buttered pan. Mix green vegetables with remaining ingredients and stuff mushrooms. Bake at 350 degrees for 20 minutes. Serves 4. Can use smaller mushrooms and serve as hors d'oeuvres.

MRS. RUFFIN (JENNY) CRAIG

PECAN TARTS

2 sticks margarine
½ pound cream cheese
2¼ cups flour
¼ teaspoon salt
¾ cup pecans, ground

SYRUP:
1 pound box brown sugar
2 tablespoons butter, melted
3 eggs, beaten
¾ teaspoon vanilla

Mix softened margarine and cream cheese. Add salt and flour. Mix and chill dough ½ hour. Roll into balls (walnut size) and put in small muffin tins. Press with thumb to make tart shell. Place ¼ teaspoon ground nuts on bottom of each tart shell. Add 1 teaspoon syrup to each. To prepare syrup, combine brown sugar, butter, eggs and vanilla and put in each tart. Bake at 350 degrees for 20 minutes. Remove shells from muffin tins immediately after taking from oven. Sprinkle with powdered sugar when cool. Makes 60 small tarts or 30 larger ones.

SALLY MITCHELL

OVER THE HILL COCKTAIL SUPPER
(SURPRISE BIRTHDAY)

MENU
PLATTER OF SLICED HAM WITH RYE BREAD
MUSTARD SAUCE
LOW-COUNTRY OYSTERS
SPINACH MADELEINE
MUSHROOMS DIVINE
FRESH VEGETABLES AND HIDDEN VALLEY DIP
PINEAPPLE CHEESE BALL
BIRTHDAY CAKE AND CHAMPAGNE

Why not give your spouse or a friend a surprise birthday party with a "This Is Your Life" flair? Ask the guests to prepare a humorous anecdote or toast about the honoree to be given when the cake and champagne are brought out. Tombstone-shaped invitations can say, "A Wake Will Be Held In Memory Of John Smith Whose Youth was Spent in Most Wasteful Fashion For The Past 39 Years".

If you get carried away with this theme, have all guests wear black, light the walkway with torches, put a funeral wreath on the front door and serve a tombstone shaped cake lit with sparklers instead of candles. Give the honoree a T-shirt or football jersey with his age on it. Perhaps guests will bring amusing gifts, too.

HAM

6 to 8-pound semi-boneless ham
Jam or jelly to cover ham
1 teaspoon cinnamon
1 teaspoon dry mustard
1 teaspoon ginger
1 teaspoon allspice

Remove skin if ham has skin. Rub with jam or jelly and sprinkle with spices and cook at 250 degrees for 4½ hours to cook out water.

MUSTARD SAUCE

MUSTARD MIXTURE:
1 cup dry mustard   1 cup white vinegar

ADDED LATER:
3 whole eggs   Dash salt
1 cup sugar

Mix mustard and vinegar and allow to sit in refrigerator overnight. Mix eggs, sugar, salt and the mustard mixture. Cook over medium heat to thin white sauce stage using electric mixer. It will thicken as it cools. Makes about 1½ pints.

MRS. BARNETT (MAY) SCOTT
MRS. HORACE (NANCY) GEYER

LOW-COUNTRY OYSTERS

1 pound fresh mushrooms   2 small cans pimientos (sliced)
  (sliced)   4 cups cream
1½ quarts oysters   8 tablespoons flour
8 tablespoons butter   Salt and pepper to taste

Saute' mushrooms and pimientos in butter. After mushrooms have cooked a few minutes, sift flour over mixture and when it begins to thicken, add cream, salt and pepper. Let oysters simmer in their own liquor in another pan until the edges curl. Add oysters to mushroom sauce and add more cream if too dry. Serve from chafing dish or on a platter surrounded by toast triangles. Very good Sunday night supper. Serves 8.

MRS. AUGUSTUS (ANN) MIDDLETON

SPINACH MADELEINE

2 10-ounce packages frozen chopped spinach
4 tablespoons butter
2 tablespoons flour
2 tablespoons chopped onion
½ cup evaporated milk
½ cup vegetable liquor
½ teaspoon black pepper
¾ teaspoon celery salt
¾ teaspoon garlic salt
Salt to taste
6-ounce roll Jalapeño cheese
1 teaspoon Worcestershire
Red pepper to taste

Cook spinach according to directions on package. Drain and reserve liquor. Melt butter in saucepan over low heat. Add flour, stirring until blended and smooth, but not brown. Add onion and cook until soft, but not brown. Add liquid slowly, stirring constantly to avoid lumps. Cook until smooth and thick; continue stirring. Add seasonings and cheese which has been cut into small pieces. Stir until melted. Combine with cooked spinach. This may be served immediately or put into a casserole and topped with buttered bread crumbs. The flavor is improved if the latter is done and kept in refrigerator overnight. This may also be frozen. Serves 5 to 6. This can be used as a dip and is very good. Heat in a saucepan and put in chafing dish. Serves 20.

MRS. BILL (BECKY) BAIN
MRS. TYLER (KATHRYN) SWINDLE

MUSHROOMS DIVINE

2 pounds fresh mushrooms
3 pounds onions, chopped
1 stick butter
1½ teaspoons salt
1½ teaspoons freshly ground black pepper
Juice of 2½ lemons
Freshly ground nutmeg to taste

Wash mushrooms, but do not soak. Remove stems (freeze and save for soup or other use). Over low heat, saute' onions in ½ stick butter. Place mushrooms, cap side down, on top of onions in large skillet. Fill cavities of mushrooms with pats of butter. Sprinkle with remaining ingredients. Cover and simmer about 12 to 15 minutes. Serve in chafing dish as hors d'oeuvres or as vegetable with steak or chicken. Serves 8 to 10 as a vegetable dish.

LINDA HAWS

PINEAPPLE CHEESE BALL

- 2 8-ounce packages cream cheese, softened
- 1 8¼-ounce can crushed pineapple, well drained
- 2 cups chopped pecans
- ¼ cup finely chopped bell pepper
- 2 tablespoons finely chopped onion
- 1 tablespoon seasoned salt
- Canned pineapple slices
- Maraschino cherries
- Parsley sprigs

In medium bowl, with fork, beat cream cheese until smooth. Gradually stir in pineapple, 1 cup pecans, pepper, onion and salt. Shape into a ball. Roll in remaining nuts. Wrap in plastic wrap. Refrigerate until chilled. To serve, place on tray and garnish with pineapple slices, cherries, and parsley. Serve with assorted crackers. Serves 20.

MRS. MIKE (BETTY) POWERS
MRS. CHUCK (LINDA) CLARK

PARTY SECRETS

PARTY SECRETS

AFTERNOON SHERRY PARTY
"WEAR SOMETHING TO TRADE"

MENU
CRABBIES
CHICKEN ALMOND SPREAD
SPICED PINEAPPLE CHUNKS
BUTTERSCOTCH BROWNIES
MOCK OYSTERS ROCKEFELLER
ARTICHOKE HEARTS AND MUSHROOM BUTTONS
(MARINATED IN ITALIAN DRESSING)
CHEESE PUFFS
SHERRY OR COLD DUCK, COFFEE

Treat the ladies to a late afternoon sherry party. The guest list should include a thoughtful mixture of your younger and older friends. The beginning of a new year is a good time to stage this party or after the snowy season when people are ready to get out and mix again. Give each guest a humorous "fortune", telling her what to expect in the new year. As a conversation starter and lots of fun too, invite every lady to wear something to trade. Who knows, one person's trash may be another's treasure.

January and February are months to turn your interests in new directions, so why not invite a professional to give the group some new make-up and hair-styling pointers. Or perhaps you could ask someone to give short reviews of several of the newest self-help books.

All that's really needed to make this party a success is a group of merry people, delicious food and plenty of wine or sherry.

CRABBIES

1 7½-ounce can crabmeat
1 stick sweet butter
1 teaspoon mayonnaise
1 5-ounce jar Kraft Old English cheese spread

1 teaspoon garlic powder
½ teaspoon seasoned salt
6 English muffins

Soften butter to room temperature and mix with cheese, crab, mayonnaise, garlic powder and salt. Spread on split English muffins. Cut into one-fourths or one-sixths and broil until bubbly and crisp. These may be frozen up to 1 week. Makes 2 or 3 dozen.

JUNE GAJEWSKI, ST. LOUIS, MO

CHICKEN ALMOND SPREAD

1 3-ounce package cream cheese
½ teaspoon celery salt
½ teaspoon onion salt
1 teaspoon seasoned salt
1 teaspoon Worcestershire
Dash Tabasco
⅓ cup sour cream
¼ cup toasted almonds
Snipped parsley
1 cup cooked chicken
1 can mushrooms (3 ounces)
Paprika

Soften cream cheese and blend seasonings, sour cream, chicken, parsley and mushrooms, all chopped finely. Mold in serving dish and refrigerate at least 1 day before using. Serve with Melba toast rounds. Serves 12 to 14.

MRS. ROBERT (JAN) KILBURN

SPICED PINEAPPLE CHUNKS

1 1-pound 12-ounce can pineapple chunks (reserve ¾ cup syrup)
¾ cup vinegar
1½ cups sugar
Dash salt
6 to 8 whole cloves
1 4-inch piece cinnamon stick

Drain syrup from pineapple. To ¾ cup syrup add vinegar, sugar, salt, cloves and cinnamon. Heat 10 minutes. Add pineapple and bring to a boil. Put in jars and refrigerate 2 days before serving. To serve, drain and serve cold with toothpicks. Serves 8.

MRS. BRUCE (MARY) FISCHER, SACRAMENTO, CA

BUTTERSCOTCH BROWNIES

1½ sticks butter
Pinch salt
2 cups flour (all-purpose)
3 cups brown sugar (1 box)
3 eggs
1 cup chopped nuts
1 teaspoon vanilla

Melt butter; add sugar and beat in the eggs. Sift in flour and salt. Add vanilla and nuts. Bake at 325 degrees for 30 minutes in a 13 x 9-inch Pyrex dish. Makes about 2 dozen. Good pick up for party.

FAIRFAX HALL SCHOOL, WAYNESBORO, VA

PARTY SECRETS

MOCK OYSTERS ROCKEFELLER

2 10-ounce packages frozen chopped broccoli
1 medium onion, grated
1 stick margarine
1 10½-ounce can mushroom soup
1 4-ounce can chopped mushrooms, drained
1 roll garlic cheese
Sliced almonds, optional

Boil chopped broccoli and drain. Saute' onion in margarine until soft. Combine soup, onion, mushrooms and mix with broccoli and crumbled cheese in pan. Keep hot and allow cheese to melt. Add almonds and stir well. Serve hot from a chafing dish. May be made ahead of time and refrigerated. Reheat before serving. Serves 25 as a cocktail dip.

CHEESE PUFFS

1 stick butter
1 8-ounce package cream cheese
8 ounces sharp Cheddar cheese
2 egg whites, beaten well
1 loaf unsliced salt-rising bread

Melt in double boiler the butter and 2 cheeses. Add 2 well-beaten egg whites. Cube the bread in 1-inch cubes; dip in cheese mixture. Put on cookie sheet and freeze. After they've hardened, put them in a plastic bag and use as needed. When ready to serve, cook in 350-degree oven for 15 minutes. Makes about 3 to 3½ dozen.

MRS. CHARLES (BETSY) COX

MIDSUMMER NIGHT'S DREAM
(LARGE COCKTAIL PARTY)

MENU
ROAST BEEF ON ROLLS
WITH HORSERADISH SAUCE
MUSHROOM CRESCENTS
PICKLED SHRIMP
EASY CHEESE BALL
FRESH STRAWBERRIES WITH POWDERED SUGAR
FROSTED GRAPES
CHESS SQUARES
WINE, NON-ALCOHOLIC FRUIT PUNCH

ALTERNATE MENU FOR COCKTAIL SUPPER
COUNTRY HAM WITH HOMEMADE ROLLS
CHEESE TRIANGLES
MINIATURE FRIED CHICKEN DRUMSTICKS
SEAFOOD MOLD WITH CRACKERS
SPINACH ORIENTAL WITH TRISCUITS
FRESH FRUIT WITH GINGER APRICOT SAUCE
INDIVIDUAL CHEESE CAKES

Turn a large cocktail party into a summer spectacular. Select the loveliest part of your yard and have your husband string tiny white Christmas lights in various small trees. The more you use, the more fantasy you put into the affair. Rent a striped tent and engage musicians for the evening, if you can. Spread lovely quilts, tablecloths or printed sheets on the grass with assorted cushions for comfortable seating. In the middle of each tablecloth will go a hurricane lamp, a wine cooler with iced wine, loaves of French bread and a basket of fresh fruit. Cover the long serving table with your best tablecloths, straw hats filled with fresh flowers and plenty of candles.

HORSERADISH SAUCE

1 quart Hellmann's mayonnaise   1 5-ounce jar Kraft horseradish

Mix and refrigerate overnight. Makes 37 ounces.

MUSHROOM CRESCENTS

PASTRY:
3 3-ounce packages cream cheese
½ cup butter or oleo
1½ cups unsifted all-purpose flour

FILLING:
2 tablespoons butter or oleo
1 medium onion, chopped
1 3-ounce package cream cheese
½ teaspoon salt
¼ teaspoon thyme
⅛ teaspoon freshly ground pepper
1 egg beaten with 1 teaspoon water for glaze
1 4-ounce or 6-ounce can chopped mushrooms and juice

For pastry, soften cream cheese and butter at room temperature. Stir flour, cream cheese and butter until well-combined and smooth. Wrap and chill 30 minutes. To prepare filling, melt butter in a skillet. Add onion and saute' until lightly browned. Add mushrooms and heat for about 3 minutes. Lower heat and add cream cheese a bit at a time, stirring until it has melted. Stir in salt, thyme and pepper. Remove dough from refrigerator. On a lightly floured board roll into ⅛-inch thickness. Cut into circles with 2½-inch round cookie cutter. Place ½ teaspoon filling on each circle. Fold in half and press together with tines of fork. Make a small slit in the top of each crescent to let steam through. Repeat with remaining dough and scraps. Brush with egg glaze. Bake on ungreased baking sheet for 15 minutes at 350 degrees. This freezes well in airtight container. Keeps 1 month frozen. Warm in 300-degree oven for 20 minutes. Makes 40 crescents.

MRS. WILLIAM (LAURA) BURNETT
MRS. RUSSELL (PEGGY) ROBBINS

PICKLED SHRIMP

5 pounds shrimp
7 teaspoons salt
1 cup celery tops
½ cup pickling spice
4 cups sliced onions
A few bay leaves

2½ cups salad oil
1½ cups white vinegar
5 teaspoons celery seed
3 teaspoons salt
¼ cup capers (1 jar)

Drop shrimp into boiling water to which 7 teaspoons salt, celery tops and pickling spices have been added. Boil 8 minutes. Drain and cool. Peel shrimp (devein if desired). Using a large bowl, alternate shrimp with sliced onions and bay leaves. Mix salad oil, vinegar, celery seed, 3 teaspoons salt and capers. Pour over shrimp; cover and place in refrigerator for at least 3 days. One week is better. Turn once or twice a day. To serve, drain, reserving liquid in case you have some left over. Put in serving dish with onion slices and capers. Serves 20.

MRS. AUGUSTUS (ANN) MIDDLETON

EASY CHEESE BALL

1 8-ounce package cream cheese
1 5-ounce jar Old English sharp cheese spread

¼ teaspoon garlic salt
½ teaspoon Worcestershire
1 cup chopped pecans, optional

Let cheeses soften at room temperature. Combine cheeses with garlic salt and Worcestershire. Blend with electric mixer. Chill for ease of handling; then shape into a ball and roll in chopped pecans. May also be rolled in chopped parsley or paprika instead of nuts. Serve with party crackers. This is quick and easy to make. It spreads on crackers easily. Serves 25 to 30.

MRS. COLLINS (SUZANNE) BONDS, MILAN, TN

PARTY SECRETS

FROSTED GRAPES

1 egg (white only)   ½ cup sugar
Plump purple or white grapes

Beat egg white until stiff; dip small bunches of grapes into egg white and let stand on waxed paper until nearly dry. Sprinkle with sugar and refrigerate until dry. Better to keep them in a tightly closed container. Use as a garnish.

MRS. MIKE (BETTY) POWERS

CHESS SQUARES

CAKE:
1 box pound cake mix   2 eggs
1 stick melted butter

TOPPING:
1 8-ounce package cream cheese   2 eggs
1 pound confectioners sugar   Nuts or coconut (optional)

Combine cake mix, butter and 2 eggs. Spread in greased and floured 13 x 9 x 2-inch pan. Blend cream cheese, sugar and 2 eggs. Spread over top of cake mixture. Add nuts or coconut across top. Bake 35 minutes at 350 degrees. Middle will be shaky when removed from oven, but will set up when cooled. Cut into squares. Makes about 2 dozen.

MRS. CHARLES (BETSY) COX

CHEESE TRIANGLES (TIROPETES)

1 3-ounce package cream cheese
½ pound Feta cheese
½ pound butter, melted
½ pound cottage cheese
3 eggs, well-beaten
1 pound fillo or pastry sheets

Combine the cheeses and stir. Add eggs and mix well. Cut each pastry sheet into 3-inch strips. Brush with melted butter. Place 1 teaspoon of the filling on 1 end of strip and fold over to make a triangle. (Fold as you would a flag). Continue folding from side to side. Proceed this way for length of strip for each triangle. Place the triangles on a buttered cookie sheet. Brush tops with melted butter. Bake at 325 degrees until lightly browned. May be frozen before baked. Makes approximately 120 triangles.

MRS. GEORGE (JANIE) THOMAS

SEAFOOD MOLD

1 pound can salmon (or tuna)
1 8-ounce pack cream cheese (softened)
2 tablespoons grated onion
1 tablespoon horseradish (drained)
¼ teaspoon salt
¼ teaspoon liquid smoke
½ cup chopped pecans
3 tablespoons parsley

Drain, flake and remove bones and skin from fish. Combine first 7 ingredients and mix well. Chill. Shape into mold or ball. Cover with nuts and parsley. Serve with crackers. Serves 12 as single hors d'oeuvre. This may be frozen if wrapped well.

MRS. LINDA RICE FORBES

SPINACH ORIENTAL

2 10-ounce boxes chopped spinach
1 8-ounce carton sour cream
1 pack Lipton's onion soup mix
1 tablespoon lemon juice

Put all of this in a casserole dish in the oven for 1 hour at 350 degrees. Stir once or twice before serving. Serve with Triscuits. Serves 6 in a casserole and 8 to 10 as a dip.

PARTY SECRETS

GINGER APRICOT SAUCE

½ cup sugar
2 tablespoons cornstarch
¼ teaspoon nutmeg
½ teaspoon ginger

½ teaspoon lemon rind (freshly grated)
1¼ cups pineapple juice
1 12-ounce can apricot nectar
1 teaspoon lemon juice

Mix sugar, cornstarch, spices and rind in saucepan. Stir in juices until smooth. Bring to boil. Lower heat and simmer about 10 minutes, stirring constantly until thick. Let cool. Stir occasionally. Makes 3 cups sauce. Use over any type fruit, canned or fresh and well-drained. This can be pineapple chunks, mandarin oranges, banana slices, strawberries, green grapes, etc. It can be served as a salad or light dessert. Makes 4½ cups.

MRS. LINDA RICE FORBES

INDIVIDUAL CHEESE CAKES

FILLING:
2 8-ounce packages cream cheese, softened
¾ cup sugar

2 eggs
1 teaspoon vanilla
1 tablespoon lemon juice

24 vanilla wafers

1 20-ounce can cherry pie filling

Beat all filling ingredients together until light and fluffy. Line each muffin cup with a paper baking cup containing a vanilla wafer, flat side down. Spoon in filling mixture, filling cups ⅔ full. Bake at 375 degrees for 15 to 20 minutes. Cool. Remove paper and put a tablespoon cherry pie filling on top of each cake. Chill. Serves 24.

MRS. WILLIAM (LAURA) BURNETTE

ROSE GARDEN TEA
FOR A BRIDE-TO-BE

MENU
CARROT AND CUCUMBER SANDWICHES
SHRIMP MOLD WITH MELBA ROUNDS
TROPICAL FRUIT FLUFF
SILVER TIP BLOSSOMS
HOT CHEESE PUFFS
LUSCIOUS SQUARES
CHICKEN SALAD SANDWICHES
QUANTITY FRUIT PUNCH
COFFEE AND TEA

Is there a better way to honor a spring bride-to-be than with a garden tea? A bouquet of fresh flowers with satin ribbons blowing in the breeze will greet guests as they arrive. Large pots of daisies lead the way to the party. Set up round tables with pastel gingham cloths under the trees. Wicker baskets filled with fresh flowers will make lovely centerpieces. Your best china, silver and crystal is the order of the day. Serve the festive spread on a large round table in the middle of the others. Ask a few friends to help pass flat baskets brimming with party food from group to group. Music from a strolling violinist would add a romantic flair to the party. Send each guest home with a gingham sachet made with rose petals from your own garden.

CARROT AND CUCUMBER SANDWICHES

1 3-ounce package cream cheese, softened
5 tablespoons grated carrots
2 tablespoons prepared horseradish, drained
1 tablespoon mayonnaise
1 medium cucumber, peeled and sliced
Salt to taste
Cayenne pepper to taste
20 to 25 bread rounds (about 2 inches in diameter)
Mayonnaise for bread rounds

Peel cucumber and cut into very thin slices. Mash softened cream cheese; add carrots, horseradish, mayonnaise, salt, cayenne pepper. Spread each bread round with mayonnaise. Place slice of cucumber in center and flute around edges of bread with carrot mixture using cookie press, if possible. (Without cookie press, just spread carrot mixture around edge and top with cucumber). Serves 20 to 25.

MRS. JAMES (SHARON) MATTHEWS

SHRIMP MOLD

6 ounces cream cheese, softened
1 10¾-ounce can tomato soup, undiluted
2 envelopes unflavored gelatin
½ cup cold water
¾ cup finely chopped green pepper
¾ cup finely chopped celery
½ cup finely chopped onion
1 cup mayonnaise
1 3-ounce can small shrimp

Dissolve gelatin in water. Add cream cheese, tomato soup and bring to a boil. Cool. Add pepper, celery, onion, mayonnaise and shrimp. Chill in mold in refrigerator until firm. Serve with cocktail crackers or Melba rounds. Serves 20.

MRS. ROBERT (SYLVIA) JELKS

TROPICAL FRUIT FLUFF

2 tablespoons apricot preserves
1 cup sour cream
¼ cup flaked coconut
1 pecan half
Milk

Cut up any large pieces of apricot preserves in 16-ounce bowl. Combine sour cream plus coconut; mix well. If necessary, thin the sauce with small amount of milk. Chill. Turn into a 14 to 16-ounce serving bowl and garnish top with pecan half. Serve as a dip with mandarin oranges, seedless green grapes, pineapple wedges, sliced banana, or melon balls. Yields 1½ cups dip. Serves 12.

MRS. BLAIR (SALLY) ERB

SILVER TIP BLOSSOMS

1 ¾ cups flour
1 teaspoon soda
½ teaspoon salt
½ cup sugar, white
½ cup firmly packed brown sugar
½ cup shortening
½ cup peanut butter

1 egg
2 tablespoons milk
1 teaspoon vanilla
1 package milk chocolate kisses (48)
Enough sugar to roll dough in (about ¾ cup)

Combine all ingredients except candy and last sugar in large bowl. Mix on low speed until dough forms. Shape dough into balls about size of rounded teaspoonfuls. Roll balls in white sugar and place on ungreased cookie sheet. Bake at 375 degrees for 10 to 12 minutes. Top each with chocolate kiss and press into dough. Good pick up for party. Makes 48 pieces.

MRS. TOM (FAITH) HADLEY, HUMBOLDT, TN

HOT CHEESE PUFFS

2 5-ounce jars Old English cheese spread
1½ sticks margarine, softened

1 egg at room temperature
35 slices white bread

Cream cheese spread, margarine and egg together, using a mixer. Cut small circles of white bread using a 2-inch biscuit cutter. (You will have 70 circles out of 35 slices of bread.) Spread a thin amount of cheese spread on a bottom circle. Stack another on top and ice like a cake. Brown at 350 degrees for 10 minutes. Makes 35 puffs.

MRS. CHUCK (PATSY) CAMP

LUSCIOUS SQUARES

PASTRY:

1 cup flour
2 tablespoons light brown sugar
1 stick margarine
½ teaspoon baking powder

Sift together flour and sugar. Work into this 1 stick margarine. Pat into lightly greased 9 x 12-inch pan. Bake in 325-degree oven until brown.

FILLING:

3 beaten eggs
1½ cups light brown sugar
2 tablespoons flour
½ teaspoon salt
1 teaspoon vanilla
1 3½-ounce can Angel Flake coconut
½ to 1 cup pecans, chopped

Mix dry ingredients together and add to beaten eggs. Add vanilla. Fold in flaked coconut and pecans. Spoon over pastry. Do not spread. Bake 325 degrees for 25 minutes. Top will be light brown. When cool, spread with butter icing.

BUTTER ICING:

1 stick margarine
3 tablespoons milk
1 16-ounce box confectioners sugar
Dash salt
1 teaspoon vanilla

Place margarine and milk in saucepan and bring to boil. Pour this mixture over sugar and salt. Stir until dissolved. Add vanilla. Spread over cake. Chill approximately 1 hour before cutting. Makes 60 squares.

MRS. THOMAS (JEAN) HOUSER

QUANTITY FRUIT PUNCH

3 quarts pineapple juice
1½ cups lemon juice
3 cups orange juice
⅓ cup lime juice
2½ cups sugar
4 28-ounce bottles carbonated water
1 cup lightly packed fresh mint leaves
1 pint fresh strawberries, quartered

Combine juices, sugar and mint. Chill. Just before serving, add remaining ingredients; pour over cake of ice in punch bowl. Yields 75 4-ounce servings.

MRS. WILLIAM (SUSIE) OLD

CHICKEN SALAD

1 stewed chicken, boned and cut up
2 or 3 stalks of celery, chopped
½ small onion, minced
3 hard-boiled eggs, chopped
1 tablespoon pickle relish
1 tablespoon parsley
½ teaspoon thyme
½ teaspoon oregano
½ teaspoon dry mustard
½ teaspoon salt
½ teaspoon pepper
Dash Worcestershire sauce
Dash curry powder
About 1 cup mayonnaise

Mix all ingredients and prepare a day ahead if possible. Makes about 8½ cups. Spread on party bread for sandwiches.

Quick and Easy Secrets

EASY EASY BOILED CUSTARD

3 3-ounce packages instant vanilla pudding
3 quarts milk
¾ cup sugar
1 teaspoon vanilla
1 pint Cool Whip

Mix enough milk with pudding to make it smooth, about 2 cups. Beat this 5 minutes; add sugar, vanilla and Cool Whip, also the remaining milk. Beat this 5 minutes more. Cool overnight. This is especially good for people who are allergic to eggs. It is delicious. Serves 20.

MRS. A. M. (RUBY NELL) BURKETT, TRENTON, TN

SUPER EGGNOG

1 quart boiled custard
1 quart eggnog
½ pint whipping cream
Fresh nutmeg
4 ounces rum (or brandy)

Mix boiled custard and eggnog in large mixing bowl. Whip ½ pint whipping cream (unsweetened). Add cream and rum. Stir and serve with freshly grated nutmeg. Serves 8 to 10.

MRS. T. O. (CAROL) LASHLEE, HUMBOLDT, TN

SHRIMP DIP

½ cup milk
1½ cups mayonnaise
1½ tablespoons Worcestershire sauce
½ teaspoon garlic salt
4 drops Tabasco sauce
1 small onion, quartered
2 5-ounce cans shrimp
1 pound Cheddar cheese, grated

Place all ingredients in blender and blend thoroughly. Yields 3 cups. This recipe is extra easy and extra good.

MRS. JOHN (LINDA) WOMACK

QUICK AND EASY SECRETS

SWISS OLIVE CANAPÉS

1 cup shredded Swiss cheese
¼ cup mayonnaise
¼ cup bacon bits
1 tablespoon dried chives
¼ cup chopped ripe pitted olives
Party-sized rye bread

Mix cheese, mayonnaise, bacon bits, chives and olives. Spread thinly on rye bread. Broil until bubbly. These may be made ahead and frozen. Makes 18 to 24 canapés.

MRS. LARRY (MANDY) WILLIAMS
MRS. ROBERT (BRENDA) HILL

CRAB DIP

6½ ounces claw crabmeat, drained
9 ounces horseradish sauce

Mix together and serve with Ritz crackers, Fritos, etc. Serves 10.

MRS. BILL PURNELL, OXFORD, MS

FANTASTIC SHRIMP DIP

4 heaping tablespoons mayonnaise
2 heaping tablespoons creole mustard
1 4½-ounce can shrimp, drained

Mix mayonnaise and mustard. Add drained shrimp to sauce. Serve with Fritos, potato chips, or crackers. Serves 10. For best results, prepare 6 to 8 hours ahead.

MRS. JAMES (ANNE) BARKER

CHEESE DIP

1 pound Velveeta cheese
1 5-ounce jar horseradish
1 cup mayonnaise

Melt cheese in a double boiler. Add horseradish and mayonnaise, blending well. Pour into serving bowl and refrigerate. Serve with Triscuit. It has a very tangy flavor and spreads easily with a cheese knife. Makes about 2 soup-sized bowls and serves 10 to 12.

MRS. JOHN (CARROLL) MOSS

HAM BARBECUE

1 cup cubed, cooked ham
1 teaspoon salad oil
1 8¾-ounce can pineapple tidbits
¼ cup bottled barbecue sauce
1½ teaspoons cornstarch
½ cup cold water
½ medium green pepper, cut in small strips
Hot cooked rice for 2 to 4 people

Brown ham in oil in skillet. Drain pineapple, saving syrup. Stir syrup and barbecue sauce into the meat. Cover and let simmer for 10 minutes. Blend cornstarch with cold water and stir into meat. Cook and continue stirring until thick and bubbly. Add the pineapple and the green pepper to the skillet and let it heat thoroughly. Serve at once with cooked rice. Serves 3 to 4.

MRS. JOHN (LEEBA) CURLIN

CHICKEN ALMONDINE

6 chicken breasts (boned)
1 10½-ounce can cream of chicken soup
1 10½-ounce can cream of mushroom or celery soup
½ cup cooking wine
⅓ cup slivered almonds
Salt and pepper
Parsley for garnish

Arrange chicken breasts in a 1½-quart casserole, tucking edges under to form small mounds. Salt and pepper to taste. Bake covered for 1 hour at 325 degrees. Mix together soups and wine and pour over chicken. Return to oven and cook 30 to 45 minutes until mixture bubbles. Remove chicken and place on a platter. Sprinkle with almonds and garnish platter with parsley. Remove sauce to gravy boat and serve with chicken. A very easy dinner for any guests. It allows you much time for visiting and little kitchen time. Serves 6.

MRS. JAMES (SALLY) LANE

SWEET AND SOUR CHICKEN

8 chicken breasts (or other chicken pieces), salted and peppered
1 8-ounce bottle Russian dressing
1 10-ounce jar peach preserves
1 package onion soup mix (dry)

Mix dressing, preserves and soup mix. Pour over chicken in 13 x 9 x 2-inch casserole dish. Bake for 1 hour at 350 degrees. May cover with foil during part of baking time if chicken begins to get too brown. Serves 8. Unbelievably delicious!

MRS. LINDA RICE FORBES

CHEROKEE CHICKEN

¼ cup vegetable oil
2 tablespoons butter or oleo
1 frying chicken or 6 breasts
1 green pepper, minced
1 garlic clove, minced
2 tablespoons onion, minced
2 tablespoons cooking sherry
1 10½-ounce can whole cranberry sauce
Salt and pepper to taste

Heat oil and butter in skillet. Add chicken and cook until golden brown on all sides. Pour off all but 2 tablespoons fat. Add green pepper, garlic and onion and cook until soft. Add sherry, cranberry sauce, salt and pepper. Cover and simmer 30 to 45 minutes. Serves 4 to 5.

MRS. MICHAEL (JUDY) STILES

CHICKEN EXCELSIOR

6 chicken breasts
Dash garlic salt
¼ pound butter
1 teaspoon paprika
3 tablespoons lemon juice
1 8-ounce carton sour cream
¼ cup sherry wine
1 4-ounce can mushrooms and stems
Dash of cayenne pepper

Sprinkle chicken with garlic salt. Melt butter; add paprika and lemon juice. Roll chicken breasts in mixture and place on baking sheet. Bake at 375 degrees 1 hour or until tender. Make sauce of sour cream, wine and mushrooms. Pour over chicken and bake 15 minutes more. Serves 6.

MRS. ALLEN (BEVERLY) FAIL

ROUND STEAK ROYALE

1 pound round steak
1 clove of garlic, cut
½ cup sliced onion
1 3-ounce can mushrooms

1 cup sour cream
Flour
Oil
Salt, pepper, seasoned salt

Rub round steak with cut clove of garlic. Dredge with flour; brown in hot oil. Sprinkle with salt, pepper and seasoned salt. Place in skillet with *cover;* top with sliced onions and mushrooms. Add ½ cup water (more later if necessary). Cover and cook 2 hours on low heat. Remove steak to platter. Add sour cream to drippings, thinning with water if necessary. Pour over steak. Garnish with spiced crabapples and parsley. A nice way to dress up an inexpensive cut of meat. Serves 4.

MRS. LINDA RICE FORBES

ROUND STEAK CASSEROLE

2 pounds round steak, cut into bite-sized pieces
2 tablespoons cooking oil
1 cup sliced or chopped onion
1 cup uncooked rice (Uncle Ben's)
1 10½-ounce can beef broth soup

1 10½-ounce can water
3 tablespoons soy sauce
½ green pepper, chopped
1 2-ounce jar sliced pimiento, drained

Brown meat in oil in a 10-inch skillet. Stir in onion, rice, broth, soy sauce and 1 can water. Bring to a boil. Reduce heat. Cover and simmer about 25 minutes. Stir in green pepper and pimiento. Heat 5 more minutes and serve. Serves 4 to 6.

MRS. JONATHAN (JO) BUTLER

QUICK AND EASY SECRETS

OLD FAITHFUL

4 to 6 medium-thick pork chops
6 tablespoons raw rice
1 10½-ounce can chicken broth or onion soup
1 large onion, sliced

2 tomatoes, sliced
1 bell pepper, sliced in rings
2 tablespoons oil or garlic salt
Salt and pepper

Brown chops in oil or in garlic salt, omitting oil. Meanwhile put rice in bottom of greased casserole dish. Lay the browned pork chops on rice and top with vegetable slices, seasoning as you go. Pour broth over entire mixture. Cover and cook at 350 degrees for 1 hour. Serves 4 to 6.

MRS. BRUCE (MARY) FISCHER, SACRAMENTO, CA

BARBECUED PORK CHOPS

4 loin chops
¼ cup chili sauce
3 tablespoons lemon juice
¼ cup chopped onion
½ teaspoon salt

½ teaspoon Worcestershire sauce
½ teaspoon chili powder
1 teaspoon prepared mustard
⅓ cup water

Brown chops. Combine chili sauce, lemon juice, onion, salt, Worcestershire sauce, chili powder, mustard and water. Pour over chops and bake 45 minutes at 325 degrees; turn and bake 45 minutes more. Serves 4. NOTE: These are simple to prepare and may be made early in the day and refrigerated until baking time.

MRS. ROBERT (JAN) KILBURN

SWEET 'N SOUR CHOPS

6 butterfly (boneless) pork chops
1 10½-ounce can beef consommé
½ cup drained pineapple chunks
¼ cup chopped green pepper
¼ cup ketchup
2 tablespoons wine vinegar
1 tablespoon brown sugar
1 teaspoon soy sauce
½ teaspoon dry mustard

Brown chops in fry pan; pour off excess fat. Arrange chops in 13 x 9 x 2-inch casserole. Combine consommé, pineapple, chopped pepper, ketchup, wine vinegar, brown sugar, soy sauce and dry mustard. Pour over chops and bake uncovered in 400-degree oven for 45 minutes. Serves 6.

MRS. JOHN (LINDA) WOMACK

HUSBAND'S DELIGHT

1½ or 2 pounds lean ground beef
1 cup chopped onion
8 ounces cream cheese
1 10½-ounce can cream of mushroom soup
¼ cup milk
¼ cup catsup
⅓ cup ripe olives, sliced
8 to 10 uncooked biscuits

Brown beef and onions together. Pour off excess fat. Mix cheese, soup, milk, catsup and olives together in a bowl. When meat is browned, mix soup mixture with meat and pour into a 2-quart casserole dish. Bake for 10 minutes at 375 degrees. Then top casserole with biscuits and bake 15 to 20 minutes more. Serves 5 or 6.

MRS. THOMAS (LINDA) HAYES

QUICK AND EASY SECRETS

LITTLE LAMBLESS LOAVES

1½ pounds ground chuck
2 cups soft French bread crumbs
¼ teaspoon oregano
1 10½-ounce can condensed onion soup

Mix together until just blended. Spoon mixture into 12 ungreased muffin tins, pressing lightly. Bake at 400 degrees for 15 to 20 minutes or until well-browned. Serves 12. NOTE: Original recipe is called "Little Lamb Loaves", calling for 1 pound ground lamb and ½ pound ground chuck. If you can get ground lamb, you might try it.

MRS. BRUCE (MARY) FISCHER, SACRAMENTO, CA

HAMBURGER-CHEESE CASSEROLE

1 8-ounce package noodles
1 pound ground beef
1 tablespoon margarine
1 tablespoon green pepper
2 8-ounce cans tomato sauce
¼ cup sour cream
1 cup cream-style cottage cheese
1 8-ounce package cream cheese
⅓ cup chopped onions
Seasoned salt to taste

Cook noodles. Brown meat in margarine; then add green pepper and tomato sauce. Let simmer 10 minutes. Mix sour cream, cottage cheese and cream cheese together. Put ½ of noodles in a layer on bottom of 3-quart casserole and put all of the cheese mixture over noodles. Put chopped onions over cheese layer, and then ½ of meat sauce. Put last of noodles on meat sauce and follow with remainder of meat sauce. Bake in 400-degree oven for 40 to 50 minutes or until bubbly. Serves 8.

MRS. AUGUSTUS (ANN) MIDDLETON

SEVEN LAYER CASSEROLE

1 cup raw rice
1 15½-ounce can whole kernel corn, drained
Salt and pepper lightly
1 8-ounce can tomato sauce with ½ can additional water
½ cup chopped onion and ½ cup chopped bell pepper, mixed together
1 pound raw ground beef
Salt and pepper lightly
1 8-ounce can tomato sauce with ½ can additional water
4 strips of bacon, cut in half crosswise

Layer ingredients as listed above, and in that sequence, into a 2-quart casserole dish. Cover and bake 1 hour at 350 degrees. Uncover and bake 30 minutes longer or until bacon is crisp. Serves 6.

MRS. BRUCE (MARY) FISCHER, SACRAMENTO, CA

QUICK-GOOD SLOPPY JOES

1 pound ground beef
2 tablespoons salad oil
1 cup chopped onion
1 16-ounce can pork and beans
1 cup barbecue sauce
2 tablespoons brown sugar
1 teaspoon dry mustard

Sauté meat and onions in oil. Add remaining ingredients; mix well. Simmer covered for 10 minutes. Serve on hamburger buns. Serves 8.

MRS. LOU (BOBBIE) BOUDREAU, CINCINNATI, OH

CRAB CASSEROLE

1 6-ounce can crabmeat
1 4-ounce can sliced mushrooms, drained
1½ tablespoons chopped chives
1 10½-ounce can cream of mushroom or cream of shrimp soup
Salt and pepper

Mix all ingredients and simmer until thoroughly heated. Serve over hot rice with a salad. Serves 4 to 6.

MRS. AUGUSTUS (ANN) MIDDLETON

QUICK AND EASY SECRETS

COUNTRY FRIED STEAK

4 minute steaks
1 large onion
Flour, salt and pepper

1 10½-ounce can golden mushroom soup
½ soup can water

Brown steaks that have been covered with flour and salt and pepper in hot oil in an iron skillet. Put steaks in a Pyrex dish. Slice onion and place slices over steak. Mix can of golden mushroom soup with ½ can water. Pour over onions and steaks. Bake in 350 degree oven *covered* for 1 hour. Serves 4.

MRS. FRED (LINA) BOWYER

SALMON CAKES WITH TOPPING

2 cups canned salmon
1 egg, beaten
Salmon liquid plus milk to equal ¾ cup
1 cup cracker crumbs

1 tablespoon lemon juice
¼ cup chopped onion, optional
Salt and pepper
1 10¾-ounce can cream of chicken soup

Combine salmon and egg. Stir in remaining Ingredients except soup. Mix well. Spoon mixture into greased muffin pans. Bake at 350 degrees for 30 minutes. Remove from pan. Spoon heated cream of chicken soup over each salmon cake. This recipe fills 9 muffin tins. Serves 6 if men are eating, 9 if ladies are eating.

MRS. TOM (DIANNE) HENSLEY

SALMON SOUFFLE

6 eggs
½ cup heavy cream
1 teaspoon Worcestershire sauce
Dash Tabasco

1 anchovy filet
Salt and pepper (optional)
1 15-ounce can salmon, drained
11 ounces cream cheese
1 tablespoon butter

Preheat oven to 375 degrees. Butter a 1½-quart casserole dish or soufflé dish. Put eggs, cream, Worcestershire, Tabasco and anchovy in electric blender. Blend until smooth. Add salmon and cream cheese in pieces to batter. Blend at high speed for a few seconds. Pour into dish and bake at 375 degrees 45 to 50 minutes. Serves 6.

MRS. WILLIAM (MARCIA) MOSS

POZOLE WITH PORK

1½ pounds cubed pork
1 tablespoon shortening
2 cups chopped onion
3 cups canned hominy, undrained
2 cloves minced garlic
¼ cup Spanish-style tomato sauce
Salt and pepper to taste
Minced parsley (enough to sprinkle over top)

Brown pork in shortening. Add onions; cook until soft. Stir in hominy, garlic and tomato sauce. Add salt and pepper to taste. Cook in 350-degree oven or on top of stove until meat is tender and sauce reduced. Sprinkle with minced parsley before serving. A good casserole or main dish served with salad and hot bread. Freezes well; may be reheated. Serves 6.

MRS. ROBERT (TONI) CONOVER, BRADFORD, TN

SAUSAGE FILLING FOR CREPES

1 pound mild pork sausage
¼ cup chopped onion
½ cup shredded American cheese
1 3-ounce package cream cheese
¼ teaspoon celery salt
Dash garlic powder
¾ cup sour cream
1 tablespoon milk

Brown sausage and onions. Stir in cheeses, celery salt and garlic powder. Remove from heat. Add sour cream and milk. Place 2 tablespoons of mixture in crepe. Place in greased baking dish. This makes enough filling for 12 to 16 crepes.

TOPPING:
4 tablespoons soft butter
¼ cup sour cream

Combine soft butter and cream; spread over crepes. Sprinkle crepes with additional shredded American cheese for garnish. Bake covered at 375 degrees for 20 minutes. Serves 6 to 8. This is a very spicy, filling dish. Manicotti noodles may be used instead of crepes.

MRS. ROLLIE (GAYLE) OLSON, PROVIDENCE, RI

EGG AND SAUSAGE QUICHE

Pastry for 1-crust, 9-inch pie, deep dish
8 ounces bulk pork sausage
4 chopped hard-boiled eggs
1 cup (4 ounces) shredded natural Swiss cheese
1 cup (4 ounces) shredded natural Cheddar cheese
3 beaten eggs
1¼ cups light cream or milk
¾ teaspoon salt
⅛ teaspoon pepper

Line pie plate or quiche dish with crust, do not prick. Bake 7 minutes at 350 degrees. Brown sausage; crumble and drain well. Layer pie crust with eggs, sausage, cheeses and pour combined milk, beaten eggs, salt and pepper over all. Bake 350 degrees for 30 to 40 minutes or until set. Cool 10 minutes before serving. Serves 6 to 8.

MRS. DAVE (MARGE) JORDAN

FLORIDA BRUNCH CASSEROLE (Crustless Quiche)

1 cup diced ham (1½)
2 cups diced Cheddar cheese (3)
3 eggs, beaten (4½)
4 slices cubed bread (6)
2 teaspoons dry mustard (3)
1 teaspoon salt (1½)
2 cups milk (3)

Combine all ingredients. Pour into 9 or 10-inch baking pan or dish. Bake about 45 minutes at 350 degrees. Serves 4. NOTE: To serve 6, use measurements listed in parentheses and bake in a 13-inch pan.

MRS. CHARLES (CARMEN) BRUER

BAKED SCRAMBLED EGGS

6 eggs
⅓ cup milk
1 teaspoon salt
⅛ teaspoon pepper
¼ pound cubed cheese of your choice

Combine all ingredients, except cheese, and beat until frothy with rotary beater. Stir in cheese. Bake in buttered 1-quart casserole dish uncovered about 30 minutes at 350 degrees until golden brown and puffy. Serve immediately. Similar to a souffle. Serves 3 to 4.

MRS. MICHAEL (JUDY) STILES

QUICK AND EASY SECRETS

CHEESE GRITS CASSEROLE

1 cup grits
1 teaspoon salt
4 cups water
1 stick butter
¼ pound Velveeta cheese
¼ pound sharp cheese
3 eggs, slightly beaten
⅓ cup milk

Cook grits in salted water until done. Add butter, cheeses, eggs and milk, stirring until melted and smooth. Place in a 1½-quart casserole and bake for 1 hour at 325 to 350 degrees. Can be made ahead and frozen until ready for use. Serves 6 to 8.

MRS. STEVE (SUSAN) GANNAWAY

POTATOES ANNE

8 ounces Philadelphia cream cheese, softened
4 cups hot mashed potatoes*
1 egg, beaten
⅓ cup chopped onion
¼ cup chopped pimiento
1 teaspoon salt
¼ teaspoon pepper

Blend softened cream cheese, hot mashed potatoes, egg, onion, pimiento, salt and pepper. Bake in a 1½-quart casserole dish at 350 degrees for 45 minutes. This is a good substitute for baked potatoes with steak or chicken. Good for company as it frees you from kitchen. Very easy. Serves 8 to 10.

*(I use 1 5-ounce box Betty Crocker Potato Buds. Follow package directions for making 4 cups. Any instant brand could be used or you could make 4 cups mashed potatoes from scratch.)

MRS. JACK (ANNE) GARDNER, SEARCY, AR

OLD-FASHIONED FARM FRY

4 eggs, lightly beaten
4 slices bacon
1 pound can potatoes, diced
1 tablespoon chopped onion
½ cup grated Cheddar cheese
Salt, pepper

Fry the bacon until crisp; finely chop. Drain all but 2 tablespoons of fat. Add diced potatoes, chopped onion, salt and pepper to fat. Cook on medium to low heat until the potatoes are an ivory color. Return bacon to skillet with potatoes and onions. Sprinkle the cheese over the mixture. Add the eggs. Cook and stir until the eggs are set. Serves 4.

MRS. JOHN (LEEBA) CURLIN

SUPERB SPINACH

2 10-ounce packages frozen, chopped spinach
1 8-ounce package cream cheese
1 cup mushrooms, chopped
1 egg, beaten
½ teaspoon salt
¼ teaspoon garlic salt
¾ cup Ritz cracker crumbs

Cook spinach as package indicates. Drain. Stir in all other ingredients except crumbs. Pour into 1½-quart casserole dish; sprinkle with cracker crumbs and bake at 350 degrees until hot in center. MICROWAVE INSTRUCTIONS: Open ends of boxes of frozen spinach. Set on a platter and microwave on high for 10 minutes. Drain spinach. Mix all other ingredients except cracker crumbs. Pour into a 1½-quart casserole and microwave on high for 12 minutes. Sprinkle cracker crumbs over top and run under browning unit for 3 to 5 minutes. Serves 6 to 8.

MRS. M. S. (BARBARA) SYMMS, BIRMINGHAM, AL

ASPARAGUS CASSEROLE

3 eggs
2 cups canned asparagus and juice
1 teaspoon salt
⅛ teaspoon pepper
1 chopped pimiento
1 cup grated Wisconsin mild cheese
1¼ cups cracker crumbs
1 cup milk
½ stick margarine

Beat eggs in large mixing bowl. Add remaining ingredients to the eggs and mix well. Pour into buttered 1½-quart baking dish. Top with the melted ½ stick margarine. Bake uncovered at 350 degrees for 30 to 35 minutes. Serves 8 to 10.

MRS. JOHN (LINDA) WOMACK

ASPARAGUS WITH CHEESE SAUCE

1 15-ounce can asparagus
2 tablespoons butter
2 tablespoons flour
1 cup milk
Salt and pepper to taste
1 cup grated American cheese

Melt butter; stir in flour and add milk slowly. Cook over medium heat until thick, stirring constantly. Add salt and pepper and grated cheese to sauce. Pour over drained asparagus that has been placed in a casserole dish. May top with crushed Ritz crackers if desired. Bake at 350 degrees 35 to 40 minutes. Serves 8.

MRS. LARRY (WANNA) CASEY

MARINATED CARROTS

5 cups carrots (½-inch slices), cooked until tender

Marinate above carrots for 12 hours in the following:

1 onion, chopped
1 bell pepper, chopped
1 10¾-ounce can tomato
   bisque soup
½ cup salad oil
1 cup sugar
¾ cup cider vinegar
1 teaspoon salt
1 teaspoon pepper
1 teaspoon dry mustard

Drain and serve at room temperature. Serves 8 to 10.

MRS. DON (LINDA) BROOKS, HUMBOLDT, TN

DIRTY RICE

1 cup uncooked rice
1 10½-ounce can onion soup
1 10½-ounce can beef bouillon
1 stick margarine

Mix all ingredients together. Cover and bake at 350 degrees for 1 hour. Serves 5 to 6.

MRS. EDWARD (GAYLE) CROCKER

SWEET POTATO SURPRISE

3 eggs
3 cups grated raw sweet
    potatoes
¾ cup sugar

2 cups scalded milk
¼ cup butter
Salt to taste
Nutmeg to taste

Beat eggs and add sugar, scalded milk, potatoes, butter, salt and nutmeg. Pour into 2½-quart greased dish and bake in 350-degree oven for 1¼ hours. Serves 8 to 10.

MRS. TOM (DIANNE) HENSLEY

GOURMET ONIONS

5 medium onions, sliced in rings
½ teaspoon monosodium
    glutamate
½ teaspoon salt
½ teaspoon pepper

½ teaspoon sugar
⅓ cup butter
½ cup cooking sherry
2 tablespoons Parmesan cheese

Sprinkle sliced onions with monosodium glutamate, salt, pepper and sugar. Cook in butter 5 to 8 minutes or until barely tender, stirring to separate rings. Add sherry and cook quickly 2 to 3 minutes. Sprinkle with cheese. Serves 6.

MRS. BRUCE (MARY) FISCHER, SACRAMENTO, CA

HOLIDAY BROCCOLI

1 medium onion, chopped
3 well-beaten eggs
6 tablespoons margarine
2 tablespoons flour
¾ to 1 cup water

1 8-ounce jar Cheez-Whiz
2 10-ounce packages chopped
    broccoli
Bread crumbs
Butter

Saute' onion in margarine until tender. Add flour and water. Stir until thick. Blend in Cheez-Whiz. Cook broccoli according to directions on package and drain. Combine broccoli and cheese sauce. Add eggs and mix gently. Pour in a 1½-quart buttered casserole dish. Sprinkle bread crumbs on top and dot with butter. Bake in 350-degree oven for 30 minutes. Serves 6.

MRS. TYLER (KATHRYN) SWINDLE

EASY CORN BREAD

1½ cups Hot Rize corn meal
1 cup buttermilk
1 egg
1 tablespoon bacon grease

Mix all ingredients and pour into hot, greased iron skillet or muffin-tins. If you use tins, fill only half-full. Bake at 475 degrees for 20 minutes. Makes 12 muffins.

MRS. EDWARD (GAYLE) CROCKER

MIRACLE MUFFINS

2 cups self-rising flour
2 cups softened vanilla ice cream
6 teaspoons butter

Mix flour and ice cream together well. Fill greased muffin tins halfway. Push ½ teaspoon (or less) of butter into center of each unbaked muffin. Bake 10 to 12 minutes at 450 degrees. Yields 12 muffins.

MRS. EVANS (GYNEL) WILSON

BEER BREAD

3 cups self-rising flour
2 tablespoons sugar
1 bottle or can (12 ounces) beer

Mix all ingredients together and put in greased 9 x 5 x 3-inch loaf pan. Bake 25 minutes at 350 degrees. At this point take bread out of oven and brush with butter. Then bake bread 25 minutes longer. Yields 1 loaf.

MRS. LOU (BOBBIE) BOUDREAU, CINCINNATI, OH

CARAMEL GRAHAMS

Graham crackers to cover cookie sheet	1 stick oleo
	1 stick butter
Pecan pieces to spread over crackers	½ cup sugar

Completely cover a large cookie sheet with graham crackers broken into sections. Sprinkle generously with pecan pieces. Combine in a saucepan oleo, butter, sugar, and cook these ingredients until bubbly (about 3 minutes). Pour evenly over crackers and pecans. Bake in preheated oven 350 degrees for 12 minutes. Remove immediately from baking sheet and cool. Serves 20.

MRS. JIM (BETTY) EMISON, ALAMO, TN

CRUSTLESS COCONUT PIE

4 eggs	2 cups Angel Flake coconut
2 cups sugar	1½ teaspoons vanilla
½ cup self-rising flour	2 cups milk
1 stick margarine	

Beat eggs until frothy; then add sugar, flour, margarine, coconut and vanilla. Mix thoroughly and add milk. Pour into 2 generously greased 8-inch pie tins. Bake at 350 degrees for 30 minutes.

MRS. JOHN (PEGGY) CAMPBELL, PONTOTOC, MS

COCONUT CREAM PIE

1 frozen pie shell, baked as directed	1 teaspoon vanilla
	Sugar to taste
1 3¼-ounce box instant vanilla pudding	½ pint whipping cream
	1 cup coconut

Mix pudding as the box suggests, but add a teaspoon of vanilla. Let this set. Whip cream to a peak. Add sugar to taste. Fold coconut into pudding. Fold whipped cream *gently* into this mixture. Pour into pie shell. Chill and serve. Serves 6 to 8.

MRS. C. I. (BARBARA) CRAIS, BIRMINGHAM, AL

QUICK AND EASY LEMON OR LIME PIE

2 graham cracker crusts
1 6-ounce can frozen lemonade or limeade
1 14-ounce can Eagle Brand milk
1 large size Cool Whip

Mix thawed and undiluted lemonade or limeade with Eagle Brand milk. Then add Cool Whip and mix. Pour mixture into pie crusts and chill. Makes 2 pies; serves 12.

MRS. TOBY (DORA JANE) ROSS

GERMAN CHEESE CAKE

3 8-ounce packages cream cheese
1½ cups granulated sugar
1½ pints sour cream
4 eggs
1 teaspoon vanilla
Crushed graham crackers

Grease springform pan and powder bottom and sides with crushed graham crackers. Set aside. Put softened cream cheese in mixer 1 package at a time and beat until smooth. Add sugar and sour cream and beat well. Add 1 egg at a time and beat until smooth. Add vanilla. Pour into prepared springform pan and bake at 350 degrees for 35 minutes. Turn oven off and leave in oven for 1 additional hour. Do *not* open oven door. May be made a few days ahead of time and can be frozen. Can be served plain or can be topped with fresh fruit and any canned fruit pie filling. Serves 12 to 14.

MRS. JAMES (SALLY) LANE

TIPSY ANGEL FOOD CAKE

1 angel food cake
¾ cup butter
2½ cups confectioners sugar
4 egg yolks
½ cup rum
½ cup slivered almonds, toasted
2 pints whipped cream or Dream Whip

Split angel food cake into 3 layers using a wet knife or a piece of string. Cream butter and eggs well. Gradually stir in rum until smooth. Fold in slivered almonds. Spread between layers of cake. Frost cake with whipped cream or you may just slice and add a dollop of cream to each piece. Refrigerate covered. Serves 10.

MRS. BILL (NANCY JANE) WHITE

FRENCH MINT TEA

3 family-sized tea bags
Enough water to cover well
Handful of fresh, clean mint
Juice of 4 lemons
1 12-ounce can frozen orange juice
2 cups sugar

In a pot bring to a boil, tea bags, water and mint. Cover and remove from heat. Allow to steep 30 minutes. Remove tea bags and mint by strainer. Add lemon juice, orange juice and sugar. Add enough water to make 1 gallon. Refrigerate. This is refreshing on hot summer days and good for parties. Yields 1 gallon or 16 8-ounce servings.

MRS. TOM (FAITH) HADLEY, HUMBOLDT, TN

CHEESE BALL

½ pound sharp cheese
½ pound American cheese
½ pound cream cheese
1 teaspoon chili sauce
2 teaspoons Worcestershire sauce
1 small onion, finely chopped
2 tablespoons mayonnaise

Grate cheeses and soften for half a day. Blend cheeses, chili sauce, Worcestershire sauce, onions and mayonnaise. Roll into a ball and refrigerate 2 to 3 days. Sprinkle with paprika before serving. Serves 20.

MRS. BOBBY (POLLY) CARTER

SHRIMP BALL

1 onion, finely chopped
1 7-ounce can of shrimp
8 ounces cream cheese
1½ teaspoons lemon juice
15 chopped stuffed olives
Dash red pepper
Dash Worcestershire sauce

Mix onion, shrimp, cheese, lemon juice, olives, pepper and Worcestershire sauce well in medium bowl. Chill well. Roll into ball and serve with crackers. Serves 10.

MRS. LLOYD (ARVA) RAY, RED BAY, AL

"OUR FAVORITE" CHEESE BALL

8 ounces Camembert cheese
8 ounces butter
1 tablespoon onion, minced
1 teaspoon paprika
Party rye and pumpernickel bread

Chill Camembert cheese and butter. After chilling, cut into small chunks and combine with onion and paprika just until they hold together. Texture should be chunky. Shape into a mound on serving dish and surround with party rye and pumpernickel. This has an interesting flavor and texture and keeps well in the refrigerator. Serves 12 to 14.

LINDA HAWS

SWISS ALMOND CHEESE MOLD

1 pound grated Swiss cheese
1 pound softened butter
½ cup coarsely ground almonds
½ teaspoon almond extract
Whole almonds for garnish

Mix all ingredients and blend until smooth and creamy. Mold and garnish with whole almonds. Serve as a spread with assorted cocktail crackers. Serves 24.

TOASTED MUSHROOM ROLLS

½ pound mushrooms
¼ cup butter
3 tablespoons flour
¾ teaspoon salt
¼ teaspoon Accent (or MSG)
1 cup light cream
2 teaspoons minced chives
1 teaspoon lemon juice
Thin white sandwich bread

Clean, dry and finely chop mushrooms. Saute' mushrooms in butter for 5 minutes; stir in flour, salt, Accent and cream. Cook until thick; then add chives and lemon juice. Cook a little longer; then set off heat to cool. Meanwhile remove crusts from 12 to 15 slices of thin white sandwich bread and roll each slice with a rolling pin until thin. Spread mushroom mixture on bread and roll up jelly roll fashion. Brush outside with softened butter and place on cookie sheet. *Freeze.* At serving time, slice each roll into thirds and separate slightly. Toast in 400-degree oven 15 to 20 minutes, checking to be sure they don't burn. Makes 3 to 4 dozen appetizers. These are not difficult to make but do require 30 to 45 minutes to prepare.

MRS. LARRY (BARBARA) DOOLEY, EAST GREENWICH, CT

OLIVE CHEESE PUFFS

¼ pound grated sharp Cheddar cheese
¼ cup soft margarine
½ cup sifted plain flour
¼ teaspoon salt
½ teaspoon paprika
24 small stuffed olives

At least 4 or 5 hours ahead, grate cheese and blend with margarine. The cheese and margarine mixture needs to be at room temperature before mixing in other ingredients. Stir in flour, salt and paprika. Mix very well with hands. Wrap each olive with enough dough to cover it completely. Arrange on ungreased baking sheet and refrigerate. About 30 minutes before serving, remove and bake puffs at 400 degrees for 10 to 15 minutes. Serve warm. Yields 24 puffs. These puffs may be frozen prior to baking, but should be allowed to defrost in the refrigerator rather than at room temperature.

MRS. JOHN (LINDA) WOMACK
MRS. BROOKS (LINDA) CLAYTON

CHICKEN PUFFS

2 tablespoons butter (real)
¼ cup all-purpose flour
1 egg
¼ cup shredded processed Swiss cheese
2 cups finely chopped chicken (may also use turkey or tuna)
¼ cup finely chopped celery
2 tablespoons chopped pimiento
2 tablespoons dry white wine or dry sherry
¼ cup mayonnaise
½ teaspoon salt
Dash of pepper

Melt butter in ¼ cup *boiling* water. Add flour and dash salt; stir vigorously. Cook and stir until mixture forms a ball that does not separate. Remove from heat and cool slightly. Add egg and beat vigorously with mixer until smooth. Stir in cheese. Drop dough onto greased baking sheet, using 1 level teaspoon of dough for each puff. Bake at 400 degrees about 20 minutes. Remove puffs from oven; cool and split. Combine chicken, celery, pimiento, wine, mayonnaise, salt and pepper. Fill each puff with 2 teaspoons. Yields 2 dozen small puffs for appetizers. Larger puffs are great for luncheons.

SISSY FRANKLAND

CHEESE PASTRY APPETIZER

1 cup flour
½ cup shredded natural Swiss cheese
½ teaspoon salt
⅓ cup plus 1 tablespoon shortening
2 to 3 tablespoons *cold* water

Heat oven to 475 degrees. Stir flour, cheese and salt together. Cut in shortening. Sprinkle water over mixture, 1 tablespoon at a time, mixing with fork until flour is moistened. Gather into a ball; divide dough in half. Lightly flour a cloth-covered board; roll half of dough into a 9-inch circle. Place on ungreased baking sheet; turn under ½ inch all around. Crimp edge; prick circle with fork. Bake 8 to 10 minutes or until lightly browned. Roll other half of pastry into 7-inch circle; place on baking sheet. Score into 16 sections, cutting only part way through pastry. Cut around rim of each section to form scalloped edge. Cut out a 1-inch circle from center. Bake about 10 minutes or until lightly browned. Cool. Just before serving, spread cheese filling evenly to edge of 9-inch circle. Place scored circle on top. If desired, garnish with olives. To serve, cut into wedges. Serves 16.

CHEESE FILLING:

Soften 4 ounces cream cheese; beat with 2 ounces bleu cheese and 1 tablespoon horseradish until fluffy. Add 1 tablespoon milk; beat until fluffy. Fold in ¼ cup sliced pimiento-stuffed olives.

MRS. DAVID (CATHY) FARMER

FRIED CREPE TIDBITS

Crepes made by any basic recipe
Parmesan cheese
Salt

Make crepes according to any basic recipe. Cut crepes into pieces as large as you choose. Deep fry each piece until golden brown and drain thoroughly. Dust while hot with salt and Parmesan cheese to taste. Serve with soup or salads. Also the fried crepe pieces may be dusted with sugar and cinnamon or powdered sugar. These may be used for dippers for hot fudge sauce or a heated mixture of apricot jam and brandy. These are very easy and most impressive. These may also be served with soup instead of crackers.

MRS. BRUCE (MARY) FISCHER, SACRAMENTO, CA

ROLLED HAM SURPRISE

1 8-ounce package cream cheese
1 tablespoon Worcestershire sauce
1 tablespoon soy sauce
1 tablespoon finely grated onion
3 tablespoons mayonnaise
1 3-ounce package sliced sandwich ham

Mix well cheese, Worcestershire sauce, soy sauce, onion and mayonnaise. Slice ham slices into lengthwise strips. Fill each strip with cheese mixture. Roll up and secure with toothpick. Serves 20.

MRS. JOHN (PEGGY) CAMPBELL, PONTOTOC, MS

SAUSAGE BALLS

1 pound hot sausage
½ pound sharp cheese
3½ cups Bisquick
½ teaspoon red cayenne pepper

Melt sausage and cheese in a double boiler. Add Bisquick and red pepper. Shape into 1-inch balls and bake at 250 degrees for 25 minutes. Makes about 100 balls. They freeze beautifully.

MRS. EDWARD (GAYLE) CROCKER

SPINACH STUFFED MUSHROOMS

1 pound medium-sized fresh mushrooms
1 package Stauffer's Frozen Spinach Soufflé
½ cup sour cream
2 tablespoons lemon juice
3 tablespoons grated onion
⅓ cup grated Parmesan cheese
Salt and pepper to taste

Wash and pull out stems of mushrooms. Prepare spinach soufflé according to package directions. Add all other ingredients to soufflé and mix in a bowl. Chop mushroom stems and add to mixture. This may be prepared a day ahead. About 30 minutes before serving, stuff the mixture into mushrooms and sprinkle with extra cheese. Bake at 350 degrees for 20 to 25 minutes; then broil to brown tops. Serve hot as an appetizer. Makes approximately 4 dozen.

MRS. ROBERT (JAN) KILBURN

BROILED CHEESE APPETIZERS

½ cup Miracle Whip
½ cup Parmesan cheese
½ cup chopped onion
Melba rounds or toast or party rye

Mix Miracle Whip, cheese and onion. Chill at least 2 hours. Spread on rounds, toast or rye. Broil until bubbly. Serves 10.

MRS. BRUCE (MARY) FISCHER, SACRAMENTO, CA

MUSHROOM STRUDELS

1½ cups finely chopped fresh mushrooms
1 tablespoon grated onion
¼ cup sherry
1 cup fresh bread crumbs
1 tablespoon butter
1 pound fillo (Greek strudel leaves)

Mix all ingredients and cook over medium heat until they cook down and turn dark. Set aside. Dampen a dish towel, wring out well, and spread out. Put 1 sheet of fillo pastry on towel; set the others aside covered with wax paper and another damp towel. Brush pastry lightly with melted butter. Spread 4 to 6 tablespoons mushroom filling along the long edge of pastry. Carefully roll up. Put long roll on a baking sheet and brush with butter. Repeat with remaining pastry and mushroom filling. Refrigerate. When long rolls are chilled, trim ends and cut into 1¼-inch pieces. These may be frozen until ready to serve. Bake in a 375-degree oven until pastry is well browned, about 20 minutes if cooked thawed, 25 to 30 minutes if baked when frozen. Makes about 70.

MRS. JIM (BETTY) EMISON, ALAMO, TN

TEXAS DIP

1 pound ground beef
1 purple onion, chopped
1 15-ounce can black olives, chopped
1 medium bottle hot catsup
1 15-ounce can red kidney beans, drained and mashed
8 ounces Cheddar cheese, grated

Brown ground beef and add kidney beans and catsup. Stir and mix well. Layer meat mixture, olives, onions and cheese in a chafing dish and heat at 350 degrees for 30 minutes or until it bubbles. Serve with Doritos. This can be made ahead and frozen. It is a real hit with the men! Serves 15.

MRS. PEGGY BURKETT

BEST-KEPT SECRETS

SHRIMP DIP

8 ounces cream cheese
1 10¾-ounce can tomato soup
2 7-ounce cans shrimp, drained and chopped
1 cup mayonnaise
2 cups celery, chopped
½ to 1 cup onion, chopped

In medium bowl blend cheese and soup until smooth. Add shrimp, mayonnaise, celery and onion. Mix well. Serve with Pringles or Fritos. Serves 10.

MRS. BRUCE (MARY) FISCHER, SACRAMENTO, CA

CLAM CHEESE DIP

1 8-ounce package cream cheese
1 tablespoon lemon juice
½ teaspoon salt
1 teaspoon Worcestershire sauce
1 teaspoon horseradish
1 tablespoon sherry
4 tablespoons clam juice
1 7¼-ounce can minced clams, drained

Mix cream cheese with lemon juice, salt, Worcestershire sauce, horseradish, sherry and clam juice until smooth. If too thick, add more clam juice. Add minced clams. Chill 1 hour or more. Serve with corn chips, crackers, etc. Serves 10.

MRS. FRED (LINA) BOWYER

PRAIRIE FIRE

1 quart red beans, cooked and put through a sieve
½ pound butter
½ pound Cheddar cheese
4 Jalapeños (pickled hot peppers), very finely chopped
1 teaspoon Jalapeño juice
2 tablespoons minced onion
1 clove garlic, very finely chopped

Mix and heat over hot water until cheese is melted. Serve hot from a chafing dish with Fritos. Makes about 3 pints. NOTE: This makes an inexpensive, delicious bean dip. May be frozen.

MRS. ROBERT (JAN) KILBURN

SPINACH DIP

½ cup green onion, chopped
2 cups Hellmann's mayonnaise
1 cup uncooked chopped spinach (10-ounce package)
½ cup chopped parsley
1 teaspoon salt
1 teaspoon pepper

Thaw spinach and press out water. Mix with mayonnaise, onion, parsley, salt and pepper and chill overnight. Makes 3½ cups of dip.

MRS. LARRY (BARBARA) DOOLEY, EAST GREENWICH, CT

GULLAH HOT CRAB DIP

2 6½-ounce cans crabmeat
2 8-ounce packages cream cheese
2 teaspoons horseradish
½ cup onion, chopped very finely
½ teaspoon salt
½ teaspoon pepper
1 tablespoon lemon juice
¼ to ½ cup milk

Drain crabmeat and soften cheese. Mix. Add horseradish, onion, salt, pepper, lemon juice and enough milk to reach desired consistency (you may have to add more milk later). Place in 2-quart baking dish and bake at 350 degrees for 45 minutes or until it bubbles in center. Serve for dinner or luncheon in pastry shells. Serve in a chafing dish with Melba toast rounds as a cocktail food. Serves 6 for dinner or 25 for appetizers.

MRS. AUGUSTUS (ANN) MIDDLETON

WATER CHESTNUT DIP

1 8-ounce can water chestnuts, drained and sliced
1 cup sour cream
1 cup mayonnaise
¼ cup fresh parsley chopped
1 tablespoon white onion, minced
1 teaspoon soy sauce
1 small clove garlic, minced
¼ teaspoon ginger, ground

Mix water chestnuts, sour cream, mayonnaise, parsley, onion, soy sauce, garlic and ginger. Chill thoroughly before serving with carrot sticks, celery and cucumbers. Makes 3 cups.

MRS. LARRY (BARBARA) DOOLEY, EAST GREENWICH, CT

ZIPPY BEEF DIP

1 tablespoon dry sherry
1 teaspoon minced onion
1 8-ounce package cream
  cheese
2 tablespoons mayonnaise
¼ cup chopped green stuffed
  olives
1 3-ounce package smoked
  finely cut chipped beef

Stir onion into sherry in medium bowl. Blend with cream cheese and mayonnaise until smooth. Stir in chipped beef and olives. Chill. Serve with bland cracker. Serves 10.

MRS. JAMES (PAT) CRAIG

CREAMY DIPPING SAUCE

2 8-ounce packages cream cheese
1 cup sour cream
6 whole green minced onions
4 tablespoons minced parsley
2 tablespoons Dijon mustard
¼ cup mayonnaise
1 teaspoon lemon juice
Pinch each of tarragon, basil and marjoram
Salt and freshly-ground pepper to taste

Combine all ingredients in medium mixing bowl and blend until smooth. Cover and chill until ready to serve. Sauce will keep up to three days covered in refrigerator. Serve with assorted fresh vegetables. Serves 10 to 12.

BURGUNDY CHEESE RING

1½ cups water
9 tablespoons butter
2 teaspoons salt
1½ cups sifted flour
6 eggs
2 cups Gruyere or Swiss cheese, grated
1 egg, beaten for glazing

Preheat oven to 400 degrees. Bring the water, butter and salt to boil in a saucepan. When butter has melted, remove from heat and beat in the flour until all is incorporated. Return to heat and continue beating until dough forms a ball and leaves the sides of the pan (about 2 to 4 minutes). Remove from heat and beat in the eggs, 1 at a time, being sure each egg is beaten in well. Gradually add the grated cheese and mix well. With moist hands shape dough into sausage roll and twist into ring. Place ring on greased cookie sheet; make a few slits across top; brush with beaten egg. Bake at 400 degrees for 30 to 35 minutes until golden brown and puffed. *Do not open door while baking!* Slice and serve immediately as an appetizer. Serves 6 to 8. This is delicious and not as difficult to make as it may sound.

MRS. JIM (ANN) AVENT

BEST-KEPT SECRETS

SUGARED PECANS

1 cup sugar
¼ teaspoon salt
6 tablespoons milk

2 teaspoons grated orange zest*
1 teaspoon vanilla
2 cups pecan halves

Combine sugar, salt, milk and orange zest in heavy saucepan. Cook, stirring often, until mixture reaches 238 degrees on a candy thermometer. Remove from heat and blend in vanilla and nuts. Stir until nuts are coated and it looks very grainy. Turn out onto waxed paper and separate each nut. Store in airtight containers. Serves 4.

*Orange zest is just the orange part of the rind (none of the white).

MOCK PATÉ

8 ounces braunschweiger
3 ounces cream cheese
3 teaspoons lemon juice
2 dashes Tabasco

⅛ teaspoon salt
⅛ teaspoon pepper
Dash garlic powder

Let cream cheese soften and cream with braunschweiger. Add lemon juice, Tabasco, salt, pepper and garlic powder, mixing well. Put in small mold and chill. If desired, chilled unmolded paté may be iced with 3 ounces cream cheese mixed with 2 teaspoons mayonnaise, a dash of salt and a dash of Tabasco. Decorate with caviar, paprika or parsley flakes. Serve on Waverly Wafers. Spreads 48 to 50 crackers (approximately 4 crackers per ounce).

MRS. ROBERT (BLANCHE) EMERSON
MRS. MARGARET SULLIVANT, HOLLY SPRINGS, MS

HAM MOUSSE

HAM:
- 2 cups finely ground ham
- ½ cup sour cream
- ½ cup mayonnaise
- ½ cup heavy cream, whipped
- 1 tablespoon onion, grated
- ¾ cup Jezebel Sauce
- ¾ cup water
- 1 ¼-ounce package unflavored gelatin
- 1 teaspoon salt

Sprinkle gelatin over cold water in saucepan. Place over low heat; stir until gelatin dissolves. Gradually add to sour cream and mayonnaise, stirring till smooth. Chill until slightly thickened. Stir in ham, onion, salt and Jezebel Sauce. Fold in whipped cream. Pour into 1-quart mold and chill until firm. Unmold and glaze with chaud-froid and decorate as desired.

CHAUD (HOT)-FROID (COLD) GLAZE:
- 2 ¼-ounce envelopes unflavored gelatin
- ¾ cup chicken broth (canned)
- 2 tablespoons vinegar
- 2 cups mayonnaise

Combine chicken broth and vinegar in saucepan with gelatin. Place over low heat and stir constantly until gelatin is dissolved. With wire whisk, blend in mayonnaise until the mixture is very smooth. Pour ⅓ of this mixture over ham mousse and refrigerate until set (about 10 minutes). Reheat remaining glaze over very low heat until it liquefies. Pour ½ the remaining sauce over the mousse. Refrigerate mousse again. Repeat procedure with the remaining ⅓ of the glaze. Cover with plastic wrap and refrigerate until serving time. Serves 10-12 as an appetizer.

JEZEBEL SAUCE

- 1 16-ounce jar pineapple preserves
- 1 4-ounce jar hot mustard
- 1 16-ounce jar apple jelly
- 1 6-ounce bottle horseradish
- Salt and pepper to taste

Mix all ingredients in blender. Yields approximately three cups, and will keep in the refrigerator for months.

DRUNKEN FRANKS

½ cup catsup
½ cup mustard
Dash of Worcestershire sauce, salt and pepper
½ cup brown sugar
¾ cup bourbon
2 packages franks

Put catsup, mustard, Worcestershire sauce, salt, pepper and brown sugar in a large saucepan and bring to a boil. Cut franks into bite-sized pieces. Add franks and bourbon. Marinate overnight in the refrigerator or 6 hours at room temperature. Preheat and serve in a chafing dish. Serves 30 to 40. This is a hearty appetizer that men enjoy.

MRS. JAMES (CAROL) MANNON, TRENTON, TN

COCKTAIL MEAT BALLS

1½ pounds ground beef or chuck
1 tablespoon Worcestershire sauce
1 egg
Salt and pepper to taste
12 ounces chili sauce
12 ounces red currant jelly

Mix ground beef, Worcestershire sauce, egg, salt and pepper. Roll into bite-sized balls and brown in small amount of vegetable oil until done, turning frequently. Drain on paper towels. If desired, meat balls may be frozen. Before serving, heat chili sauce and jelly in a saucepan. Add meat balls and simmer until heated. Serve in chafing dish with toothpicks. Makes 50 to 60 meat balls and 1½ pints of sauce.

MRS. CHUCK (PATSY) CAMP

SPICED PINEAPPLE

1 28-ounce can pineapple chunks
¾ cup vinegar
1¼ cups granulated sugar
1 4-inch stick cinnamon
6 to 8 whole cloves
Dash salt

To ¾ cup of the pineapple syrup add vinegar, sugar, salt, cloves and cinnamon. Heat 10 minutes. Add chunks and bring to a boil. May be served hot or cold in a 24-ounce bowl with toothpicks. Serves 8-10.

MRS. DAVID (JANIS) FITE

DRESSING FOR PEAR SALAD

4 egg yolks
1 tablespoon sugar
3 tablespoons vinegar
1 tablespoon melted butter
Dash salt
14 large marshmallows, chopped
1 cup whipping cream, whipped
1 cup nuts, chopped
Dash cayenne pepper
1 small jar maraschino cherries with stems

Beat egg yolks and gradually add sugar. Add vinegar slowly; then add melted butter, salt and chopped marshmallows. Cook *slowly* in heavy saucepan until marshmallows have melted and mixture thickens. Cool. Fold in whipped cream and nuts. Place in center of pear halves on bed of lettuce. Top with maraschino cherry with stem. Sprinkle with cayenne pepper. Makes a beautiful salad plate and is delicious! Dressing is enough for 2 large cans of pear halves. If not serving this much, remainder may be kept in jar in refrigerator. Makes approximately 1 quart.

MRS. JACK (CAROLYN) CUNNINGHAM, MILAN, TN

FRUIT SALAD DRESSING

2 3-ounce packages cream cheese
1 cup mayonnaise
1 cup cream, whipped
1½ cups nuts, chopped

Cream the cream cheese and mayonnaise. Fold in whipped cream and nuts. Good mixed with any canned or fresh fruit.

MRS. TOM (FAITH) HADLEY, HUMBOLDT, TN

HOT PINEAPPLE CASSEROLE

1 20-ounce can pineapple chunks
1⅔ cups grated Colby cheese
½ cup flour
½ cup sugar
½ teaspoon salt

Drain juice from pineapple. Mix juice, flour, sugar and salt. Cook until slightly thickened. Do not allow mixture to become too thick. Layer pineapple, cheese and flour mixture. Sprinkle cheese on top. Bake at 375 degrees for 30 minutes. Serves 6.

MRS. GEORGE (ELIZABETH) SMITH

HOT FRUIT SALAD

½ cup white raisins
1 cup canned pears (good quality), cut in bite-sized pieces
1 cup white pitted cherries
1 cup canned apricots or peaches
1 cup pineapple chunks
2 fresh large-sized oranges, peeled and sectioned
Freshly grated orange rind

SAUCE MIXTURE:

¾ cup sugar
¾ cup fruit juices (¼ cup from each of the 3 above cans)
3 tablespoons butter
3 tablespoons flour
¾ teaspoon salt
½ cup cooking sherry

Pour 1 cup boiling water over white raisins and let sit until raisins are plump. In large Dutch oven, cook remaining fruit in 2 cups of water until tender, approximately 5 to 10 minutes. *Do not overcook.* Drain all fruit well. Mix sugar, fruit juices, butter, flour and salt. Cook over medium heat until thick. Mix all of fruit in casserole. Add hot mixture and sherry. Bake for 30 minutes at 350 degrees. Excellent with turkey or ham. Serves 6 to 8.

MRS. MIKE (BETTY) POWERS

HOT FRUIT CASSEROLE

3 oranges, thinly sliced (do not peel)
1 28-ounce can pineapple
1 28-ounce can peaches
1 28-ounce can pears
1 small jar maraschino cherries
½ stick butter
⅔ cup sugar
½ cup sherry
½ cup flour
½ teaspoon salt
Brown sugar

Cover orange slices with water; cook until tender and cool. Drain fruit. Cut into bite-sized pieces, except for cherries. Melt butter; blend in flour, sugar and salt. Mix well with fruit. Add sherry; pour into 3-quart buttered casserole. Sprinkle generously with brown sugar. Heat thoroughly in 350-degree oven. This can be made the day before. Leave off brown sugar until ready to cook. Serves 15.

MRS. JACK (CAROLYN) CUNNINGHAM, MILAN, TN

LAYERED GREEN SALAD I

- 1 small head lettuce, torn in bite-sized pieces
- ½ cup chopped celery
- ½ cup chopped green pepper
- 1 small thinly sliced onion
- 1 10-ounce package frozen sweet peas (raw)
- 1 cup mayonnaise
- 1 cup sour cream
- 1 4-ounce package Hidden Valley Ranch dressing mix
- 2 tablespoons sugar
- 4 to 6 ounces shredded Cheddar cheese
- Crumbled bacon (optional)

Peas should be patted dry with paper towel to remove excess ice crystals. Place above vegetables in layers, in the order listed, in a 9 x 13-inch dish. Combine mayonnaise, sour cream and dressing mix. Spread this over vegetables. Sprinkle sugar and Cheddar cheese on top. Sprinkle with crumbled bacon if desired. Cover tightly with plastic wrap and store in refrigerator at least overnight. Will keep for 2 days. Serves 8 to 10.

MRS. JAMES (PAT) CRAIG

LAYERED GREEN SALAD II

- 2 heads lettuce, torn in bite-sized pieces
- 1 red onion, sliced
- 1 head cauliflower
- 2 cucumbers, sliced
- 2 1-pound cans sweet peas, drained
- 1 green pepper, chopped
- 2 cups mayonnaise
- 2 tablespoons sugar
- 8 ounces Parmesan cheese, grated

Layer above vegetables in order given. Spread mayonnaise over top, sealing edges. Sprinkle with sugar and Parmesan cheese. Cover with plastic wrap. Refrigerate overnight. Toss before serving. Serves 8 to 12.

MRS. WILLIAM (LAURA) BURNETT

LAYERED GREEN SALAD III

8 ounces of fresh spinach
1 head lettuce, torn in bite-sized pieces
1 10-ounce package frozen sweet peas, cooked and drained
½ red onion, sliced in thin rings
1 cup mayonnaise
½ cup sour cream
½ pound Swiss cheese, grated
4 boiled eggs, sliced
8 slices crisp bacon, crumbled
1 teaspoon salt
1 teaspoon pepper
2 teaspoons sugar

Wash and dry spinach and press into a 3-quart bowl or Pyrex baking dish. Sprinkle with salt, pepper and sugar. Spread bacon crumbs on top and add sliced eggs. Press lettuce on top and sprinkle with sweet peas. Layer onion rings on peas. Mix mayonnaise and sour cream and spread smoothly. Sprinkle with grated cheese. Cover with plastic wrap and refrigerate 24 hours before serving. Will keep 4 to 5 days in refrigerator. Serves 6 to 8.

MRS. C. DAVID (PAT) HOLBROOK

CHICKEN SALAD WITH A DIFFERENCE

2 tablespoons lime juice (fresh is best)
2 cups cooked chicken, diced
1 cup celery, diced
1 cup seedless grapes, halved
¾ cup almonds, toasted
⅓ cup mayonnaise
½ teaspoon salt
⅛ teaspoon pepper
Dash nutmeg
Crisp, chilled lettuce

Sprinkle 1½ tablespoons lime juice over chicken and ½ tablespoon over celery; let stand 1 hour (minimum). Lightly mix chicken, celery, grapes, almonds and mayonnaise seasoned with salt, pepper and nutmeg. Serve in lettuce cups or on a bed of lettuce leaves.

MRS. THOMAS (LINDA) HAYES

HOT CHICKEN SALAD I

3 cups chicken or turkey, chopped
2 10½-ounce cans cream of chicken soup
1 cup celery, chopped
4 tablespoons onions, chopped
½ teaspoon salt
Pepper to taste
1 cup mayonnaise
1 cup cracker crumbs
6 hard-cooked eggs, chopped
1 cup slivered almonds
1 teaspoon lemon juice
Chow Mein noodles or grated cheese

Mix all ingredients. Top with noodles or grated cheese. Bake at 350 degrees for 30 minutes or until bubbly hot. Serves 12 to 15.

MRS. LARRY (WANNA) CASEY

HOT CHICKEN SALAD II

2 whole chickens, cooked and boned
1 10½-ounce can cream of chicken soup
1 10½-ounce can cream of mushroom soup
2 cups celery, chopped
2 tablespoons onion, minced
1 teaspoon salt
5 hard-boiled eggs, sliced
1½ cups mayonnaise
Slivered almonds, reserved for topping
Potato chips, reserved for topping

Combine all ingredients and toss well. Place in large casserole and top with slivered almonds and potato chips. Bake at 325 degrees for 30 to 40 minutes. Serves 12 to 14.

MRS. CHARLES (G.G.) BRAY

HOT CHICKEN SALAD III

3 cups chicken, diced (3 large breasts)
2 10½-ounce cans cream of chicken soup
2 cups celery, diced
4 tablespoons onion, minced
1 cup mayonnaise
1 cup saltine crackers, crushed
1 cup or 4-ounce package slivered almonds
½ teaspoon white pepper
2 tablespoons lemon juice
6 hard-boiled eggs, chopped
⅓ cup pimiento, chopped

Mix ingredients in order listed. Place in a 10-inch casserole and bake at 350 degrees for 40 minutes. Serve plain, in patty shells or on toast. Serves 6 plain, or approximately 16 in patty shells or on toast.

MRS. ROBERT (HELEN) SMITH

FANTASTIC FRUIT SALAD

FRUIT:

1 1-pound can fruit cocktail, well-drained
1 1-pound can pineapple chunks, well-drained, reserving liquid
2 11-ounce cans mandarin oranges, well-drained
2 apples, chopped in chunks
4 bananas, chopped
1 4-ounce can coconut
1 cup pecans, chopped or broken

SAUCE:

1 cup fresh or frozen orange juice
3 tablespoons cornstarch
1 egg, beaten
Pineapple juice from reserved liquid
½ cup sugar
18 large marshmallows

Combine sugar and cornstarch until smooth; add beaten egg. Mix until smooth and add the juices. Cook until thickened, stirring constantly. Add marshmallows and stir until melted. Remove from heat. Chill until cool and add to drained fruit mixture. This amount of sauce makes enough for 2 fruit recipes and keeps well in refrigerator. Serves 15.

MRS. WILLIAM (DELORIA) HAYNES

PLUM CONGEALED SALAD

1 10½-ounce can plums (reserve liquid)
1 12-ounce can pineapple chunks in own juice (reserve liquid)
1 3-ounce package black cherry gelatin

Dissolve gelatin in 1 cup heated juice from plums and pineapple chunks. Add second cup of cold reserved juice. Add water to make cupful if needed. Add plums and pineapple chunks. Pour into a 9-inch square Pyrex dish. Congeal in refrigerator. To serve, cut into squares and serve on lettuce leaf. Serves 8.

MRS. GERALD (TERRIE) REED

APRICOT SUNRISE SALAD

2 3-ounce packages apricot gelatin
1 20-ounce can crushed pineapple (drain and save juice)
2 cups miniature marshmallows
2 bananas, sliced
½ cup pineapple juice
¾ cup sugar
2 tablespoons flour
8 ounces cream cheese
1 package Dream Whip
1 3½-ounce can Angel Flake coconut

Mix gelatin according to package directions. Refrigerate and allow to congeal slightly. Add pineapple, marshmallows and bananas. Pour into a 9 x 13-inch pan and allow to congeal. Mix together pineapple juice, sugar and flour and cook until thickened. Watch and stir while cooking to prevent sticking. While the mixture is hot, stir in cream cheese until melted. Let this topping get cold. Mix Dream Whip according to directions. Fold this into cold topping mixture. Spread over chilled gelatin. Sprinkle coconut on top. Place in refrigerator until ready to serve. Serves 8.

MRS. DAVE (MARGE) JORDAN

PEACH BAVARIAN SALAD

1 3-ounce package lemon-flavored gelatin
2 tablespoons sugar
⅛ teaspoon salt
1 cup hot water
1 29-ounce can sliced yellow cling peaches
1 cup heavy cream, whipped

Dissolve gelatin, sugar and salt in hot water. Drain peaches. Add ½ cup peach liquid to gelatin mixture. Pour ¼ cup gelatin mixture in bottom of 1-quart mold. Arrange 8 peach slices in gelatin in petal-like fashion. Chill until almost firm. Chill remaining gelatin mixture until slightly thickened; then fold in whipped cream. Cut remaining peaches in halves and fold into cream mixture. Pour into mold and chill until firm. Unmold onto serving plate. Garnish with mint leaves. Serves 8.

MRS. JAMES (SHARON) MATTHEWS

AVOCADO MOUSSE

2½ to 3 cups avocado, mashed
6 tablespoons lemon juice
2 tablespoons onion, grated
2½ teaspoons salt
Dash of Tabasco
¾ cup mayonnaise

2 envelopes unflavored gelatin
¼ cup cold water
1¼ cups hot water
Optional: cucumber rounds,
    cherry tomatoes, parsley

Mix avocado with lemon juice, onion, salt, dash of Tabasco and mayonnaise. Soften gelatin in cold water. Add hot water to gelatin and blend thoroughly. Oil a 6-cup mold and rinse with cold water. Pour in avocado mixture and chill at least 3 hours. Unmold and serve with suggested vegetables or any fresh vegetables you desire. Serves about 16.

MRS. JIM (BETTY) EMISON, ALAMO, TN

SPICED PEACH SALAD

1 cup hot water
1 3-ounce package
   lemon gelatin

1 30-ounce jar spiced peaches
1 cup spiced peach juice
3 ounces cream cheese

Drain peaches, reserving 1 cup juice. Dissolve gelatin in hot water and add spiced peach juice. In blender purée spiced peaches and cream cheese. Mix all ingredients and chill. Serves 4 to 6.

MRS. BOB (BARBARA) HIGGS

TUNA PATÉ

1 3-ounce can chopped mushrooms
1 package unflavored gelatin
2 6½-ounce cans tuna, drained (preferably tuna packed in spring water)

½ cup Green Goddess dressing
½ cup pitted ripe olives
¼ cup parsley leaves
½ cup boiling water

Drain mushroom liquid into blender. Add gelatin and let soften. Add ½ cup boiling water. Blend 10 seconds on low speed. Add remaining ingredients and blend until thoroughly mixed. Pack into oiled mold. Chill overnight. To serve, unmold and serve with assorted crackers. Serves 6.

MRS. JAMES (CAROL) MANNON, TRENTON, TN

ORIENTAL SALAD

1 16-ounce can English peas, drained
1 16-ounce can French style green beans, drained
1 16-ounce can bean sprouts, drained
1 8½-ounce can bamboo shoots, drained
1 8½-ounce can water chestnuts, drained and sliced
3 medium onions, sliced
1¼ cups celery, chopped
1 cup sugar
¾ cup vinegar

Combine peas, beans, bean sprouts, bamboo shoots, water chestnuts, onions and celery in large bowl. Add sugar and vinegar and stir lightly. Marinate overnight. Serves 12.

MRS. MICHAEL (JUDY) STILES

ASPARAGUS-EGG MOLD

1 tablespoon gelatin
¼ cup cold water
1 cup hot asparagus liquor
½ teaspoon salt
½ teaspoon onion, minced
2 tablespoons lemon juice
2 cups diced, cooked or canned green asparagus
4 hard-cooked eggs, sliced
1 cup celery, chopped
1 cup mayonnaise

Soften gelatin in cold water and dissolve in the hot asparagus liquor. Add salt, pepper, onion and lemon juice; cool. When mixture begins to thicken, fold in asparagus, three of the eggs, chopped celery and mayonnaise. Slice the remaining egg; place in mold. Pour asparagus mixture into mold and chill until firm. Serves 6 to 8.

MRS. CHARLES (CARMEN) BRUER

SPICED BEAN SALAD

2 16-ounce cans whole green beans, drained
¾ cup sugar
¾ cup vinegar
½ cup water
1 clove garlic
3 tablespoons salad oil
1 medium sweet red onion, sliced thinly
Salt and pepper to taste
Dash red pepper

Combine beans and sliced red onions. Combine other ingredients and pour over beans and onions. Cover and refrigerate at least 24 hours. Serve as a side dish on crisp greens or as a vegetable on the dinner plate. Serves 6 to 8.

MRS. EDWARD (GAYLE) CROCKER

MANDARIN ORANGE AND ONION SALAD WITH POPPY SEED DRESSING

SALAD:
- 1 small head of lettuce, rinsed, drained and chilled
- 1 small red onion
- 1 11-ounce can mandarin oranges, drained

DRESSING:
- 2 tablespoons wine vinegar
- 1 teaspoon Dijon mustard
- ½ teaspoon salt
- ⅛ teaspoon cayenne pepper
- 1 tablespoon honey
- 6 tablespoons oil
- 1½ teaspoons poppy seeds

Combine dressing ingredients in jar and shake well. Tear lettuce into bite-sized pieces. Peel and slice onion into very thin rings. Combine lettuce, onion and oranges. Toss with dressing in salad bowl. Serves 4 to 6.

MRS. COLLINS (SUZANNE) BONDS, MILAN, TN

"SECRET" DILLED CUCUMBERS

- 3 medium cucumbers
- ¾ cup white vinegar
- ¾ cup sugar
- 1 teaspoon salt
- ¼ teaspoon white pepper
- ⅓ cup mayonnaise
- ¼ cup heavy cream, whipped
- ⅓ cup sour cream
- 2 tablespoons dill weed
- ¼ teaspoon salt
- ½ teaspoon white pepper

Slice cucumbers *very* thinly; do not peel. Combine vinegar, sugar, 1 teaspoon salt and ¼ teaspoon pepper in a heavy plastic bag. Marinate cucumbers in this for 2 to 3 hours. Remove from bag and press all liquid from cucumbers. Combine mayonnaise, whipped cream, sour cream, dill weed, ¼ teaspoon salt and ½ teaspoon pepper. Add to cucumbers. Chill 3 hours before serving on bed of crisp romaine lettuce. Serves 6 to 8.

MRS. JIM (BETTY) EMISON, ALAMO, TN

TOMATO SOUP ASPIC

2 tablespoons unflavored gelatin
½ cup cold water
1 8-ounce package cream cheese
1 10¾-ounce can tomato soup
1 cup chopped celery
2 tablespoons grated onion
2 tablespoons lemon juice
1 tablespoon Worcestershire
1 teaspoon Tabasco
Salt to taste

Soften gelatin in cold water. Heat soup in double boiler; then add cream cheese. Whip with a rotary egg beater and add gelatin. Stir until completely dissolved. Cool. Add other ingredients. Pour into mold. Chill until firm. Unmold on bed of lettuce. Serves 6 to 8.

MRS. FRED (LINA) BOWYER

GERMAN SAUERKRAUT SALAD

1 1-pound can kraut, drained
1 cup celery, chopped
1 medium onion, chopped
1 bell pepper, chopped
1 2-ounce jar pimiento
⅛ cup sugar

Mix and let stand several hours before serving. Serves 8 to 10.

MRS. JOHN (PEGGY) CAMPBELL, PONTOTOC, MS

OVERNIGHT SLAW

1 large green cabbage, shredded
1 large Spanish onion, sliced thinly
1 large bell pepper, diced
¾ cup sugar
1 cup oil
1 cup vinegar
1 teaspoon celery seed
1 teaspoon prepared mustard
1 tablespoon salt

Prepare the vegetables and sprinkle with sugar. Combine remaining ingredients except the oil. Bring to a hard boil. Remove from heat and add oil. Pour over vegetables. Refrigerate at least 12 hours. Will keep for 1 week in refrigerator. Serves 8.

MRS. LARRY (MANDY) WILLIAMS

BEST-KEPT SECRETS

FROZEN FRUIT CUPS

16 ounces sour cream
2 tablespoons lemon juice
¾ cup sugar
⅛ teaspoon salt
¼ cup chopped maraschino cherries

8¼-ounce can crushed pineapple, undrained
3 bananas, cubed
¼ cup chopped pecans

Combine all ingredients and pour into muffin tins lined with paper baking cups. Freeze. When ready to serve dip muffin tin in water to loosen paper baking cups. Serves 18.

MRS. LARRY (BARBARA) DOOLEY, EAST GREENWICH, CT

CHERRY FREEZE SALAD

1 21-ounce jar cherry pie filling
1 14-ounce can sweetened condensed milk

1 9-ounce container Cool Whip
1 15¼-ounce can crushed pineapple, well-drained

Mix all ingredients. Pour into a 7½ x 11½-inch Pyrex dish and freeze. Serves 8.

MRS. MIKE (BETTY) POWERS

CAULIFLOWER SOUP

1 large cauliflower
2½ cups chicken broth
1 cup onion, chopped
2 tablespoons butter
2 tablespoons flour
¾ cup milk

½ cup heavy cream
1 teaspoon salt
Few drops Tabasco
⅛ teaspoon ground nutmeg
1 egg yolk, beaten
½ teaspoon lemon juice

Separate cauliflower into small flowerets. Coarsely chop all but a few. Boil whole flowerets in chicken broth about 10 minutes or until just barely tender. Remove and reserve for garnish. Boil chopped cauliflower in same broth until very tender. Cool to room temperature. In a large pan sauté chopped onion in butter until soft. Stir in flour and cook about ½ minute. Remove from heat and add cooled cauliflower and broth. Heat, stirring until thickened. Purée in blender or food processor. Add milk, cream, salt, Tabasco and nutmeg. Thoroughly blend a little of mixture with beaten egg yolk. Add egg yolk mixture back to soup. Add lemon juice. Heat, but do not boil. Serve garnished with whole cauliflowerets. Serves 4 to 6.

MR. DON LAYCOOK

CREAM OF WATERCRESS SOUP

1½ quarts milk
½ cup celery leaves
¼ cup onion slices
⅙ cup flour
⅙ cup butter

1 tablespoon salt
⅛ teaspoon white pepper
3 bunches watercress, chopped
Optionals: chives, garlic salt, onion salt

Heat celery leaves and onion slices with milk and strain. Blend flour, butter, salt and pepper and add to hot milk. Stir and cook for 10 minutes. Add watercress and heat thoroughly. Serve immediately with sprinkled chives. Season to taste with garlic salt and onion salt. Serves 12.

LINDA HAWS

CREAM OF CORN SOUP

2 strips bacon, chopped finely
2 tablespoons onions, chopped
2 cups frozen or fresh corn
2 tablespoons butter
2 tablespoons flour
2 cups milk
1 teaspoon salt
½ teaspoon pepper
2 cups light cream

Fry bacon until crisp; add onions and sauté until soft. Put corn through a food chopper; add to onions and bacon and cook until mixture begins to brown. Add butter and then flour. Cook slowly for 3 minutes. Add milk, salt and pepper and cook until thickened. Add cream and heat until smooth. Serve with crackers. Serves 6.

MRS. ROBERT (JAN) KILBURN

OYSTER ARTICHOKE SOUP

½ pint (8 to 12) oysters (drained)
1 14-ounce can artichoke hearts (drained)
2 tablespoons butter
3 cups milk or half and half
¼ cup oyster water (optional)
⅛ teaspoon white pepper
1 teaspoon butter-flavored salt
1 dash paprika

Melt butter in saucepan. Add oysters and cook on low heat until edges of oysters begin to curl. In a blender, place drained artichoke hearts and milk, and blend on medium speed for 2 to 3 minutes. Pour into cooked oysters and add pepper, salt and paprika. If you are a real oyster lover, add ¼ cup oyster water to mixture to enhance flavor. Simmer for 30 minutes. This is a nice way to begin a candlelight dinner for 4. Remember, a good hostess will check oysters for pearls as she drains them. Yields approximately four 8-ounce servings.

MRS. JERRY (RUTH ANN) SMITH

CHICKEN AND AVOCADO SOUP

6 cups chicken broth
1 whole chicken breast
2 onions, sliced
½ teaspoon ground coriander
½ teaspoon oregano
½ teaspoon salt
¼ teaspoon black pepper, freshly ground
1 ripe avocado

Pour the chicken broth into a large saucepan. Add chicken breast, onions and seasonings. Bring to a boil; reduce heat; cover and poach in the simmering broth for 20 minutes. Remove the chicken breast and let it cool. Strain the stock into a saucepan and set it aside. Discard cooked onions. When chicken is cold and firm to the touch, peel off the skin; then, using the sharpest knife you own, cut it into small julienne strips. Just before serving, stir the strips into the soup and heat. Peel the avocado; cut it into slices and add to the soup. The slices will float on top. Serves 6.

MRS. WILLIAM (SUSIE) OLD

ALASKAN CLAM-CORN CHOWDER

2 cans (7 ounces each) minced clams
1 cup clam liquor and water
3 slices bacon, chopped
2 cups raw potatoes, diced
1½ cups whole kernel corn, drained
2 cups milk
2 tablespoons flour
2 tablespoons butter
1 teaspoon celery salt
1 teaspoon salt
Dash pepper
½ cup coarse cracker crumbs

Drain clams; pour clam liquor into measuring cup and add water to 1 cup level. Fry bacon; add onions and cook until tender. Add potatoes, clam liquor and water. Cover; simmer until potatoes are tender. Add corn and milk. Blend flour and butter and stir into soup. Cook slowly until mixture thickens slightly, stirring constantly. Add seasonings and clams; simmer another 5 minutes. Top with cracker crumbs. Perfect with a green salad. Serves 4 to 6.

MRS. JAMES (SHARON) MATTHEWS

SPRING TONIC SOUP

3 1-pound cans tomatoes
2 stalks celery and leaves
2 carrots, scraped
1 green pepper, seeded
1 large onion
3 peppercorns
2 whole cloves
1 teaspoon salt
½ teaspoon basil
½ teaspoon sugar
¼ cup port wine
1 tablespoon fresh lemon juice

Put tomatoes in a pot and break them up with a fork. Cut celery, carrots, green pepper and onions in chunks and add them to the pot. Stir in peppercorns, cloves, salt, basil and sugar. Cover pot tightly and bring to a boil. Lower heat and simmer 1 hour, stirring occasionally. Cool; then strain soup through a fine sieve, squeezing juices out of vegetables. Return juice to pot. Add more salt and pepper if desired. Add port and lemon juice. Bring to boil and serve, adding a few croutons to each serving. Especially good for calorie watchers. Serves 6 to 8.

MRS. THOMAS (NANCY) CRENSHAW, HUMBOLDT, TN

CREAM OF WILD RICE SOUP

1 package long grain and wild rice mix
1½ tablespoons butter
1 cup onion, chopped
1½ tablespoons flour
1 teaspoon salt
Few twists black pepper
3 10-ounce cans chicken broth
1 pint half and half
¼ cup dry white wine
Sour cream or chopped parsley as garnish

Cook rice mix as package directs. Melt butter in Dutch oven; add onion and saute′, stirring until tender, about 8 minutes. Stir in flour, salt and pepper until smooth. Add cooked rice, chicken broth, half and half and wine. Heat, stirring until mixture just comes to boiling point. Remove from heat. Ladle about 1½ cups into blender and blend until smooth. Pour into large bowl. Repeat until all soup is blended. Return to Dutch oven and heat, stirring occasionally until heated through. Garnish and serve. Makes 2½ quarts.

MRS. GEORGE (JANIE) THOMAS

FRENCH ONION SOUP

STOCK:
4-pound beef brisket
2 onions
3 carrots
3 garlic cloves

Garni of parsley, bay leaf, celery tops (may be tied in bag or not)
½ teaspoon thyme
5 quarts water

SOUP:
3 tablespoons butter
1 tablespoon olive oil (may use vegetable oil)
1½ pounds (5 to 6) yellow onions, thinly sliced
1 teaspoon salt
½ teaspoon sugar
3 tablespoons flour

1 cup hot stock
2 quarts plus 1 cup remaining stock
1 cup red wine (do not omit) use good Burgundy or Cabernet
1 bay leaf
½ teaspoon sage

CROUTONS:
French bread sliced ½ inch thick

Oil or butter

CHEESE MIXTURE: (Grated in equal amounts)
Swiss cheese

Parmesan cheese (fresh)

Brown meat and vegetables in pan in oven. Put these in a large stock pot and add 5 quarts cold water. Simmer until lessened by about half. Cool uncovered; then refrigerate overnight. Next day, skim off excess fat and reheat and then strain, discarding vegetables. At this point you may season the brisket with salt and pepper and wrap it in foil and bake at 200 degrees for about 1 hour per pound until it is tender. This can be sliced across the grain and served as sandwiches with the soup. Sauté thinly sliced onions in butter and oil covered until translucent, stirring occasionally. Uncover pan and add salt and sugar. Cook for 30 minutes until evenly cooked. Reduce heat and stir in flour and brown lightly. Pour in 1 cup hot stock; mix; then add remaining stock, wine, bay leaf and sage. Simmer 30 to 40 minutes. Season to taste with salt and pepper. To serve, pour soup into heated bowls. Sprinkle lightly with cheeses; place browned croutons on top and add more cheeses liberally. Brown in oven at 350 degrees until cheeses melt and are bubbly. Can serve with extra croutons at table. Very good served as a meal with roast beef sandwiches with horseradish sauce. Served as a first course, it will probably serve 30 to 50 people. To prepare croutons, dip slices of bread in oil or butter; then toast in oven until dry.

MRS. RUFFIN (JENNY) CRAIG

MID-AMERICA GUMBO

2½ cups okra, cut up
3 tablespoons fat
1 large onion, chopped
1 green pepper, diced
1 8-ounce can tomato sauce
2 7-ounce cans crabmeat
2 6-ounce cans shrimp, rinsed (may use more crabmeat or shrimp)
3 tablespoons ham, chopped
3 cups water
2 tablespoons flour
1 teaspoon thyme
2 bay leaves
1 teaspoon parsley, chopped
1 teaspoon salt
1 teaspoon pepper
½ teaspoon cayenne

Brown okra in fat and add all the above ingredients. Cook in pressure cooker 15 minutes at 15 pounds and let pressure drop slowly, or simmer for 1½ hours. Serve over rice. Quick and easy. Keep ingredients in pantry for unexpected company. Serves 6.

MRS. JAMES (ANNE) BARKER

BRUNSWICK STEW
(An Old Virginia Recipe)

1 large hen (baked or stewed)
1 pint baked ham, scraps and juices
3 or 4 pounds roast beef
½ gallon butter beans
1 quart carrots, diced
1 quart potatoes, diced
2 or 3 bunches of celery, chopped (stems and leaves)
½ dozen peppers (sweet, green, or red)
1 bunch parsley, chopped
6 onions, chopped
1 small head of cabbage, chopped
½ gallon sweet corn
½ gallon ripe tomatoes
1 cup sugar
1 stick margarine
Salt to taste
Pepper to taste

Cook meats ahead and cut into bite-sized pieces. Prepare and boil in a large kettle for 1 hour in enough water to cover the following vegetables: beans, carrots and potatoes. Add cut up meats and their juices and simmer for ½ hour. Add the following chopped vegetables: celery, peppers, parsley, onions and cabbage. Simmer. Then add corn, tomatoes, sugar, salt and pepper and margarine. Cook for 10 to 15 minutes. Stir often to prevent sticking. If too thick, add more hot water. Cool and store in plastic refrigerator-freezer boxes. Makes about 6 quarts.

MRS. WILLIAM (LAURA) BURNETT

MARINADE FOR PORK CHOPS

1 cup oil
½ cup soy sauce
2 green onions, chopped
Cavender's Greek seasoning

Shake Cavender's on chops to coat. Combine remaining ingredients and pour over chops. Refrigerate overnight, turning occasionally. Grill over hot coals.

MRS. LARRY (MANDY) WILLIAMS

MARINADE FOR SHISH KABOBS

1½ cups vegetable oil
1 tablespoon ground pepper
½ cup wine vinegar
¾ cup soy sauce
¼ cup Worcestershire
2 tablespoons dry mustard
¼ teaspoon garlic powder
1½ teaspoons parsley
⅓ cup lemon juice

Mix all ingredients together. Cut meat into 2-inch cubes and place in large plastic container. Pour marinade over cubes of meat. Marinate for at least 24 hours, shaking occasionally to coat meat on top. Serves 6 to 8.

MRS. JACK (BETTYE) SMITH

LIME MARINADE FOR BAKED CHICKEN

½ cup lime juice
⅓ cup peanut oil
2 tablespoons dark brown sugar
2 tablespoons onion, minced
2 garlic cloves, minced
Salt and pepper to taste

Combine all of the above ingredients. Stir until sugar dissolves. Chill and marinate chicken for 6 to 8 hours before baking. Yields 1 cup.

MR. JIM (DONNA) RAMSEY, GREEN BAY, WI

BÉARNAISE SAUCE

½ cup white wine
1 tablespoon vinegar
1 pinch dried tarragon leaves

3 egg yolks
1 stick butter, not margarine
Freshly grated black pepper

Combine wine, vinegar and tarragon and cook, reducing by half. Put 3 egg yolks in blender. Slowly add 1 stick of melted butter with blender running. Add wine mixture with blender running. Add freshly grated black pepper. Yields 1½ cups.

MRS. RUSSELL (PEGGY) ROBBINS

HENRY BAIN SAUCE

1 17-ounce jar chutney
1 12-ounce bottle chili sauce
1 14-ounce bottle catsup

1 11-ounce bottle A-1 Steak Sauce
1 10-ounce bottle Worcestershire

Combine chutney, chili sauce, and catsup in blender. Pour into a large bowl and stir in steak sauce and Worcestershire. Store in tight container in refrigerator. Delicious on beef, pork and chicken. We even like it on some vegetables.

MRS. B. C. (MARY VIRGINIA) COX, UNION CITY, TN

HORSERADISH CREAM

1 cup horseradish
1 cup sour cream

¼ cup mayonnaise
½ teaspoon curry powder

Mix all ingredients and blend well. Serve with roast beef as a sauce or spread. Yields 2¾ cups.

BARBECUE SAUCE

3 tablespoons catsup
2 tablespoons vinegar
3 tablespoons Worcestershire sauce
4 tablespoons water
2 tablespoons brown sugar
1 tablespoon lemon juice
2 tablespoons butter
½ teaspoon red pepper
1 teaspoon salt
1 teaspoon chili powder
1 teaspoon paprika
1 teaspoon dry mustard

Heat all ingredients together. Makes approximately 1 cup.

MRS. AB (ELIZABETH) TAYLOR

BEST-KEPT SECRETS

MARGUERITE'S SUKIYAKI

2 to 3 pounds sirloin, cut on the diagonal into thin strips
1 bunch green onions, including tops, chopped diagonally
4 medium potatoes, cut like French fries
1 small head cabbage, shredded in strips
1 14-ounce can bean sprouts
1 package celery hearts, sliced diagonally
1 small package fresh mushrooms, sliced
1 8-ounce can water chestnuts, sliced
1 8-ounce can bamboo shoots
¼ cup cooking sherry
½ cup bourbon whiskey
½ cup peanut oil
1 10-ounce can beef broth
1 cup water
1 5-ounce bottle soy sauce
¼ cup sugar (optional)

Sauté sirloin strips in oil until browned. Drain. Stir in all other ingredients in electric skillet or wok and cook covered over low heat, or simmer for approximately 1 hour, stirring occasionally. Serve with rice. Dish is done when potatoes are tender. Serves 8 to 10.

MRS. TOM (FAITH) HADLEY, HUMBOLDT, TN

SPEARCARRIER

SPEARCARRIER:
4 asparagus spears
2 thin slices ham
½ lightly toasted English muffin

Roll 2 asparagus spears in each ham slice. Place both on English muffin. Top with cream cheese sauce. Yields 1 spearcarrier.

SAUCE:
8 ounces cream cheese
½ cup milk
1 tablespoon dry sherry
½ teaspoon onion salt
Dash nutmeg

Heat cream cheese and milk in small, heavy saucepan over low heat, stirring often until smooth. Blend in sherry, onion salt and nutmeg; keep warm. Yields 3 servings.

This was served as a main dish at the 1979 Antique Show Tea Room.

SAUERBRATEN

3 to 3½ pounds beef round or rump (boneless chuck roast)
1 teaspoon salt
½ teaspoon pepper
4 bay leaves
½ teaspoon peppercorns
8 whole cloves

2 medium onions, sliced
1 small carrot, minced
1 stalk celery, chopped
1½ cups red wine vinegar
2½ cups water
¼ cup butter

Rub meat with salt and pepper; place in deep earthenware crock or ovenware glass bowl; add bay leaves, peppercorns, cloves, onions, carrot and celery. Heat vinegar and water to boiling; pour hot over meat. Let cool. Cover bowl; refrigerate. Let marinate at least 48 hours, turning meat twice a day. When ready to cook, remove meat from marinade and dry with paper towels. Melt butter in Dutch oven and brown meat all over. Strain marinade and pour over meat. Cover tightly; simmer slowly 2½ to 3 hours or until fork tender. Remove to warmed platter; slice and keep warm. Serves 6.

GINGERSNAP GRAVY:

2 tablespoons sugar
1½ cups hot marinade
½ cup water

8 gingersnaps, crumbled
½ cup sour cream
¼ teaspoon salt

Melt sugar in skillet, stirring until brown. Gradually stir in hot marinade and water. Add gingersnap crumbs; cook and stir until mixture thickens. Add sour cream and salt to gravy; ladle some over sauerbraten and pass remainder. Yields 2 cups gravy.

MRS. RICHARD (SUSAN) DAVIDSON
MRS. BILL (BECKY) BAIN

FLANK STEAK SANDWICHES

1½ to 2 pounds flank steak
2 teaspoons salt
1 teaspoon pepper
½ teaspoon rosemary
1 teaspoon onion juice
½ teaspoon basil
½ teaspoon garlic salt
2 tablespoons wine vinegar
4 tablespoons oil
1 package (6 rolls) Pepperidge Farm club rolls cut in half lengthwise
2 ounces margarine, softened
2 ounces bleu cheese, softened

Mix salt, pepper, rosemary, onion juice, basil, garlic salt, wine vinegar and oil together. Marinate flank steak in mixture not less than 8 hours. Cook meat over charcoal about 10 minutes per side (medium) 5 inches from coals. Slice in strips and serve open-face style on club rolls. Whip margarine and bleu cheese to blend well. Spread mixture on cut club rolls. Bake club rolls according to package directions, but checking frequently. Makes 12 open-face sandwiches. For children's portions, you might want to spread club rolls with margarine only.

MRS. PHIL (PAT) BAKER

STIFADO

3 pounds lean beef stew meat, cut in 1½-inch cubes
1½ teaspoons salt
½ teaspoon freshly ground black pepper
½ cup butter
8 small potatoes
6 small onions
1 6-ounce can tomato paste
⅓ cup red table wine
2 tablespoons red wine vinegar
1 tablespoon brown sugar
1 clove garlic, minced
1 bay leaf
1 small cinnamon stick
½ teaspoon whole cloves
¼ teaspoon ground cumin
2 tablespoons currants

Season meat with salt and pepper. Melt butter in heavy kettle with cover. Add meat and coat with butter, but do not brown. Arrange onions and potatoes over meat. Mix tomato paste, wine, vinegar, brown sugar and garlic. Pour over meat, potatoes and onions. Add bay leaf, cinnamon, cloves, cumin and currants. Cover potatoes and onions with a plate to hold them intact. Cover kettle and simmer 3 hours. Serves 8 to 10.

MRS. DAVID (CATHY) FARMER

SIRLOIN AND ROQUEFORT

3 to 4 pounds sirloin steak
1 package Good Seasons Blue Cheese Salad Dressing Mix
⅔ cup salad oil
¼ cup red wine vinegar
Additional oil and vinegar
¼ cup crumbled Roquefort cheese

In a large 2 or 3-quart flat Pyrex dish combine salad dressing mix with ⅔ cup salad oil and ¼ cup vinegar. Place steak in marinade, turning to coat both sides. Mix enough additional oil and vinegar in equal parts to cover steak completely. Marinate 4 to 6 hours. Drain. Cook on grill at high setting for 8 minutes. Turn carefully with tongs; lower heat. Sprinkle with Roquefort cheese and grill 8 minutes more for medium rare. Yields 6 to 8 servings.

SALLY MITCHELL

CREAMED SHRIMP IN SOUR CREAM

1 pound cooked shrimp
1 can sliced mushrooms, drained (or ½ pound fresh mushrooms)
2 tablespoons chopped green onion
2 tablespoons butter, melted
1 tablespoon flour
1 10-ounce can cream of shrimp soup
½ pint sour cream
White pepper
Garlic salt

Prepare shrimp; cut large ones in half. Sauté mushrooms and onion in butter until tender. Blend in flour; then add soup, stirring constantly until thickened. Add sour cream, shrimp, pepper and salt. Heat until bubbly, stirring occasionally. Serve over rice. Serves 4.

MRS. WILLIAM (COLIE) JEFFERS, MEMPHIS, TN

SHRIMP SPAGHETTI

3 ounces cooked thin spaghetti, drained
½ cup butter
4 ounces fresh mushrooms, sliced
10 ounces cooked shrimp, chopped
½ teaspoon garlic salt
3 tablespoons grated Romano cheese
½ teaspoon salt
½ teaspoon monosodium glutamate

Early on day of serving, cook spaghetti; drain and set aside. Cook and chop shrimp; grate cheese; slice mushrooms and set all aside. About 15 minutes before serving melt butter in large skillet; add mushrooms, garlic salt and shrimp. Cook slowly for 5 minutes. Add spaghetti to the skillet. Sprinkle with cheese, salt and monosodium glutamate. Cook until hot, being careful not to overcook. When serving, sprinkle with more grated Romano cheese. Serves 2 people. This may be doubled; however, for large servings, make 2 or 3 skillets full. This is very similar to Elfo's special from Grisanti's in Memphis.

MRS. ROBERT (JAN) KILBURN

SHRIMP JAMBALAYA

- 3 tablespoons butter or margarine
- ½ cup chopped green pepper
- ½ cup chopped celery
- 2 cloves garlic, crushed or minced
- ½ cup chopped onion
- ½ cup chopped green onion
- ¼ pound diced cooked ham
- 2 cups chicken broth
- ¼ cup chopped parsley
- ⅛ teaspoon black pepper
- ⅛ teaspoon cayenne pepper
- 3 large tomatoes, chopped (about 5 cups)
- ½ teaspoon salt
- ¼ teaspoon thyme
- 1 cup uncooked rice
- 3 4½-ounce cans shrimp or 1 pound cooked shrimp
- 1 bay leaf
- ¼ cup chopped green pepper

Heat butter in large iron skillet over low heat. Stir in green pepper, celery, garlic, onions and ham. Cook over medium heat 5 minutes until onion is tender. Add chicken broth, parsley, black pepper, cayenne pepper, tomatoes, salt and thyme. Cover and bring to a boil. Add rice; stir with fork and simmer covered 20 minutes until rice is tender. Add shrimp, bay leaf and green pepper. Simmer uncovered 5 minutes. Makes 6 to 8 servings. Preparation time, 25 minutes; cooking time, 30 minutes.

MRS. RUFFIN (JENNY) CRAIG

SHRIMP CASSEROLE

- 1½ to 2 pounds cooked shrimp, shelled
- 2 10¾-ounce cans cream of shrimp soup, undiluted
- 1 large onion, diced
- 4 stalks celery, diced
- ¼ cup margarine
- 4 tablespoons sherry
- 4 hard-boiled eggs, chopped
- 2 cups cooked rice
- 8 ounces sharp cheese, grated
- ¾ cup buttered bread crumbs

Sauté onion and celery in margarine. Add shrimp, soup, sherry, eggs and rice. Pour into a 13 x 9 x 2-inch buttered casserole. Sprinkle top with cheese and bread crumbs. Bake at 300 degrees for 1 hour. Serves 8. For company, serve with steamed zucchini and a green salad. Homemade rolls add the perfect touch.

MRS. GAYE JOHNSON, LITTLE ROCK, AR

BEST-KEPT SECRETS

HOT TANGY SHRIMP

2 pounds headless shrimp in shells (approximately 50 to 60 average-sized shrimp)
½ pint (8 fluid ounces) Italian salad dressing
Juice of 2 lemons
3 tablespoons freshly ground black pepper
¼ cup butter
¼ cup margarine

Place uncooked shrimp in oven-proof casserole. Melt butter and margarine in saucepan over low heat. Add salad dressing, lemon juice and pepper. Mix well and pour mixture over shrimp. Bake uncovered at 350 degrees, stirring frequently, for 45 minutes. Serves 4. This highly seasoned and spicy dish tastes especially good with a green salad and chilled wine.

MRS. LARRY (MANDY) WILLIAMS

COQUILLES ST. JACQUES

1½ pounds scallops
1½ cups dry white wine
1 teaspoon salt
¼ teaspoon whole peppercorns
½ teaspoon parsley flakes
1 bay leaf
¼ teaspoon thyme
½ cup water
4 tablespoons chopped green onion
½ pound fresh mushrooms
8 tablespoons butter
3 tablespoons flour
1 cup milk

Combine scallops, wine, salt, pepper, parsley, bay leaf, thyme and water; poach for 6 minutes. Remove scallops and reduce pan liquid to 1 cup. Cut scallops into bite-sized pieces; set aside. Sauté green onions and mushrooms in 4 tablespoons butter. In a separate skillet melt 4 tablespoons butter; add flour and lightly brown. Mix well and add milk, cooking on low heat and stirring constantly to make a white sauce. Stir original wine liquid into white sauce. Add mushroom and onion mixture and scallops. Mix well. Place in individual shells or ramekins. Sprinkle with grated cheese and broil 5 minutes. Serves 6 to 8.

MRS. DON (PATTY) LEWIS

SEAFOOD CASSEROLE

2 10½-ounce cans cream of shrimp soup
½ cup mayonnaise
1 small onion, grated
¾ cup milk
Salt, white pepper, seasoned salt, nutmeg and cayenne pepper to taste
3 pounds shrimp, cooked and shelled
1 7½-ounce can crabmeat, drained
1 5-ounce can water chestnuts, drained and sliced
1½ cups celery, diced
3 tablespoons fresh parsley, minced
1⅓ cups uncooked white long-grain rice, cooked until dry and fluffy
Dash paprika
Slivered almonds

Blend soup into mayonnaise in a large bowl. Stir until smooth. Add onion; then add milk. Use a heavy hand in adding seasonings because rice and seafood are bland. Add shrimp, crabmeat, water chestnuts, celery, parsley and rice. Add a few tablespoons of milk if mixture seems dry. Taste to check for seasoning! Put in large, buttered casserole (the long, flat type). Sprinkle with paprika and scatter almonds over top. Bake at 350 degrees for 30 minutes. Serves 10. Freezes well and may be prepared ahead.

MRS. RUFFIN (JENNY) CRAIG

COLD RED SNAPPER

1 3-pound red snapper
1 large onion, chopped
1 stalk celery, chopped
1 tablespoon salt
1 tablespoon red pepper
1 teaspoon black pepper
1½ cups homemade mayonnaise
1 teaspoon salt
½ teaspoon red pepper
1 teaspoon onion juice
Capers (optional)
1 teaspoon Worcestershire sauce

Wrap red snapper in cheese cloth and drop into boiling water seasoned with onion, celery, salt, red pepper and black pepper. When very tender, almost falling off bone, remove from water and cool. Remove cheese cloth and bone, trying to leave in a whole piece if possible. Refrigerate several hours and serve cold on a platter. Top with mayonnaise seasoned with salt, red pepper, onion juice, capers and Worcestershire sauce. Serves 4 to 6. NOTE: Fresh snapper is best. Commercial mayonnaise may be substituted for homemade but is not as good.

MRS. AUGUSTUS (ANN) MIDDLETON

CRABMEAT CASSEROLE

2 cups white crabmeat
6 hard-boiled eggs, finely chopped
2 cups half and half
1 cup mayonnaise
2 tablespoons grated onion
2 tablespoons parsley
1 can water chestnuts, finely chopped
3 cups bread crumbs
1¼ sticks butter
Salt and pepper to taste

Melt butter and sauté crumbs and parsley; set aside enough to top casserole. To remaining crumbs add crabmeat, eggs, half and half, mayonnaise, onion, water chestnuts, salt and pepper. Pour into a greased 1-quart casserole dish. Top with crumbs. Bake at 350 degrees until bubbly. For luncheon, consider making individual servings in shells or ramekins. Serves 4 to 6.

MRS. GEORGE (JANIE) THOMAS

JIFFY HAMBURGER STEW

2 pounds ground chuck
1 1-pound can tomatoes
1 8-ounce can tomato sauce
1 small bell pepper, chopped
1 small onion, chopped
4 potatoes, diced
1 1-pound can kidney beans
1 to 2 teaspoons garlic salt
½ teaspoon pepper

Brown meat, pepper and onions. Add remaining ingredients and cook until potatoes are tender. Serves 10.

MRS. GERALD (TERRIE) REED

PIZZA CASSEROLE

- 1 4-ounce package pepperoni
- 1 chopped medium onion
- ⅓ cup melted margarine
- 1 6-ounce package thin spaghetti
- 1 cup (½ pound) grated Mozzarella cheese
- ½ pound sliced Mozzarella cheese
- 2 8-ounce cans tomato sauce
- 1 4-ounce can drained mushrooms
- ½ teaspoon oregano
- ½ teaspoon basil
- Worcestershire sauce
- Parmesan cheese

Boil pepperoni slices 5 minutes. Drain on paper towels. Sauté chopped onion in small amount of margarine; add tomato sauce, mushrooms, oregano, basil and Worcestershire sauce and Parmesan cheese to taste. Cover and simmer 15 to 20 minutes. Toss cooked spaghetti with the ⅓ cup melted margarine and a generous sprinkling of Parmesan cheese. Place seasoned spaghetti in a dish and cover with grated cheese, pepperoni slices and tomato sauce. Top with slices of Mozzarella. Bake at 350 degrees for 20 minutes uncovered. Serves 6. Children love it, and it fills growing boys! It is great to keep in the freezer for a last-minute emergency.

MRS. ROBERT (HELEN) SMITH

SPANISH DELIGHT

- 1½ pounds ground beef
- 2 tablespoons oil
- 1 green pepper, chopped
- 1 large onion, chopped
- 1 17-ounce can cream-style corn
- 2 small cans tomato paste (12 ounces total)
- 1 3-ounce can mushrooms
- 2½ tablespoons chili powder
- 1 7-ounce package egg noodles, cooked
- 1 teaspoon salt
- 1 cup grated cheese

Brown ground beef and drain excess fat. Sauté green pepper and onion in oil. Combine beef, peppers and onion with corn, tomato paste, mushrooms, chili powder, noodles and salt. Place in two 1½-quart casseroles. Top with grated cheese. Bake 30 minutes at 350 degrees. Serves 8. When preparing this recipe, you may use 1 casserole and freeze the other!

MRS. LINDA RICE FORBES

PARMESAN BAKE

- ⅓ cup chopped onion
- ¼ cup margarine
- ⅓ cup flour
- 1 teaspoon salt
- ⅛ teaspoon pepper
- 2 cups milk
- ¼ cup Miracle Whip salad dressing
- 4 cups chopped turkey, ham or chicken
- 2 10-ounce packages broccoli spears (split) or flowerets, partially thawed
- 1 3-ounce can Parmesan cheese
- 1 8-ounce can crescent dinner rolls

Sauté onion in margarine. Blend in flour, salt and pepper. Gradually add milk. Cook and stir until thickened. Stir in salad dressing. Combine white sauce, chopped meat, broccoli and ½ cup cheese. Mix well. Pour into an 11¾ x 7½-inch baking dish. Separate dinner roll dough into 1 large and 2 small rectangles. Cut large rectangle lengthwise into fourths forming 4 12-inch strips. Cut remaining rectangles into thirds, forming 6 8-inch strips. Place dough strips over casserole mixture in a lattice design. Brush dough lightly with margarine; sprinkle with remaining cheese. Bake at 350 degrees for 40 to 45 minutes or until crust is golden brown. Serves 8 to 10.

MRS. W. R. (GENEVIEVE) TABER

LASAGNA

- 1 package lasagna noodles
- ½ pound sausage
- ½ pound ground beef
- 1 clove garlic, minced
- 1 tablespoon parsley flakes
- 1 tablespoon basil
- 1½ teaspoon salt
- ¼ teaspoon oregano
- 1 16-ounce can tomatoes
- 2 6-ounce cans tomato paste

In a large skillet mix all of above ingredients except noodles and simmer 45 minutes to 1 hour, spooning off excess fat. Cook noodles.

Combine the following ingredients, except sliced cheese:

- 3 cups cottage cheese
- 2 beaten eggs
- 2 teaspoons salt
- ½ teaspoon pepper
- 2 tablespoons parsley flakes
- ½ cup Parmesan cheese
- 1 pound sliced Mozzarella cheese

In a large casserole dish, alternate layers of noodles, meat sauce and cottage cheese mixture. Top with sliced cheese. Bake at 375 degrees for 30 minutes. Serves 4 to 6. This will freeze.

MRS. AB (ELIZABETH) TAYLOR

JO'S ROAST DUCK AND WILD RICE

2 whole ducks
1 or 2 sections each of peeled apple, onion and potato
1 stalk celery
1 10¾-ounce can consommé
1 10¾-ounce can water
Bacon grease
Bacon strips
1 package Uncle Ben's long grain and wild rice

Stuff each duck with as much of the apples, onions, potatoes and celery as possible. Place ducks in roasting pan, arranging remaining apples, onions, potatoes and celery around ducks. Rub bacon grease all over top and sides of ducks. Lay bacon strips across ducks. Pour consommé and 1 can water over ducks. Cover and bake at 275 degrees for 4 hours, basting once or twice every hour. 30 minutes before serving, prepare rice according to package directions. While rice cooks, pull meat off ducks. Discard vegetables. To serve, place cooked rice on plate; put meat on rice and spoon consommé over both like gravy. Serves 4.

MRS. JONATHAN (JO) BUTLER

CHICKEN TETRAZZINI

1 large hen, boiled, boned and cut in shreds
1 pint chicken stock, reserved from boiling chicken
½ pound vermicelli
½ pound sharp cheese, grated
1 medium onion, chopped
1 10½-ounce can cream of mushroom soup
1 cup broken pecans
1 5-ounce can mushrooms, chopped
2 cups celery, chopped
3 tablespoons butter or margarine
1 tablespoon Worcestershire sauce
Salt and pepper to taste

In a large electric fry pan or Dutch oven cook celery and onion in butter until tender. Add chicken stock, salt, pepper and Worcestershire sauce and simmer for 15 minutes. Slowly add soup, then cheese. Boil vermicelli in stock and add to mixture. Let stand 1 hour. Add chicken and mushrooms. Put in long, flat casserole; sprinkle with pecans and heat at 350 degrees for 30 to 40 minutes. Serves 8.

MRS. WILLIAM (LAURA) BURNETT

SAVORY CHICKEN CASSEROLE

1½ cups mayonnaise
1 cup chopped celery
1 10¾-ounce can cream of mushroom soup
1 10¾-ounce can cream of chicken soup
3 cups cooked chicken cut into bite-sized chunks
6 chopped hard-boiled eggs
1 cup chicken broth
½ cup milk
1 3-ounce can Chow Mein (crunchy) Chinese noodles
3 cups cooked rice
½ pound Velveeta cheese, cubed
1 cup crushed potato chips

In a 4-quart mixing bowl combine all ingredients except potato chips. Pour mixture into 2 2-quart baking dishes and cover with foil. Bake 1 hour at 350 degrees. Uncover last 15 minutes; cover with crushed potato chips and continue baking. Serves 14 to 16. This is good to make when taking a dish to someone. There will be enough for your family dinner, too. It also freezes well for up to 3 months.

MRS. JAMES (ANNE) BARKER

MILKY-WAY CHICKEN

3 tablespoons oil
1 quart milk
3 pounds chicken, cut in serving pieces (preferably breasts)
Salt and pepper
2 teaspoons sugar
1 teaspoon ground coriander
1 tablespoon gin
3 cloves garlic, pierced on toothpicks
Aluminum foil
1½ cups raw rice
1 teaspoon salt

Smear the oil in the bottom of a large heavy casserole, preferably enameled cast iron. Pour in 1 cup of milk. Salt and pepper the chicken and add to the pot. Pour in the rest of the milk (should almost cover the chicken). Add sugar, coriander, gin and garlic. Gently bring milk to simmer over low heat. Fit a piece of foil directly over chicken; then put top on pot. Reduce heat and simmer for 30 minutes. Remove foil and discard. Add the rice and 1 teaspoon salt, stirring into the milk gently so as not to tear chicken. Cover and simmer for 20 minutes more. Remove garlic and serve. To reheat leftover chicken, more rice and milk may be added if needed. Amounts of gin and garlic may be increased, but do not decrease. Serves 6.

MRS. WILLIAM (MARCIA) MOSS

CHICKEN MONTERREY

- 1½ cups instant rice
- 1 10½-ounce can chicken broth
- 1 10¾-ounce can cream of chicken soup
- ½ cup milk
- ½ tablespoon Worcestershire
- 1 tablespoon sherry
- 6 ounces mushroom pieces
- 1 8-ounce can sliced water chestnuts
- 2 pounds cooked chicken, chopped
- 2 cups sharp Cheddar cheese, grated

Combine all ingredients except Cheddar cheese. Pour into a 9 x 13-inch pan. Top with cheese. Bake for 45 minutes at 350 degrees. This dish can be frozen after being cooked. Serves 8 to 10.

CHICKEN SPECTACULAR

- 2 cups diced cooked chicken breasts (about 6 average size)
- 1 15½-ounce can drained French style green beans
- 1 box Uncle Ben's long grain and wild rice, cooked according to package directions, using chicken broth in place of water
- 1 10¾-ounce can Campbell's cream of celery soup
- ½ cup Hellmann's mayonnaise
- 1 small onion (about ⅔ cup)
- 1 2-ounce jar diced pimiento
- 1 8½-ounce can sliced water chestnuts

Mix together and bake in 2-quart casserole at 350 degrees for 25 minutes. Serve with salad and bread. Makes a complete meal. Freezes well! Great company dish. Serves 10 to 12.

MRS. JACK (CAROLYN) CUNNINGHAM, MILAN, TN
MRS. ROLLIE (GAYLE) OLSON, PROVIDENCE, RI

CHICKEN CASSEROLE (With Rice)

2 cups cooked, diced chicken
¼ cup mayonnaise
1 cup cooked rice
½ teaspoon salt
4 ounces canned mushrooms, drained
1 cup diced celery
1 tablespoon lemon juice
1 tablespoon finely chopped onion
½ cup almond slivers
1 10½-ounce can cream of chicken soup
1 cup corn flake crumbs
2 tablespoons soft butter

Combine all ingredients except corn flake crumbs and butter. Put in an 8-inch square baking dish. Mix corn flake crumbs with butter and place on top of casserole. Bake 30 to 40 minutes in 350-degree oven. Serves 6.

MRS. AUGUSTUS (ANN) MIDDLETON

WILLIAMSBURG CHICKEN

2 medium-sized chickens
1 chopped onion
2 or 3 stalks celery
2 tablespoons butter
1 tablespoon flour
1 pint thin cream
Chicken stock saved from boiling chickens
Salt and pepper to taste
Cracker crumbs to cover chickens (about ½ cup)

Cook chickens in boiling water with celery and onion until tender (about 30 to 40 minutes). Remove skin and bones. Place in buttered casserole. Melt butter. Add flour and cream and stir until slightly thickened. Pour over chicken. Add some stock and salt and pepper to taste. Bake for 1 hour at 350 degrees. Serves 10 to 12.

MRS. AUGUSTUS (ANN) MIDDLETON

PRESSED CHICKEN

2 cups chicken, diced
1 cup almonds or pecans, well-chopped
2 hard-boiled eggs, chopped
1 package plain gelatin
½ cup green olives, sliced
½ cup celery, diced
1 cup mayonnaise
2 cups chicken broth (reserved from cooking chicken)

Boil chicken until tender (about a 3-pound hen). Drain all fat from broth. Soak gelatin 5 minutes in ¼ cup cold broth. Pour 1¾ cups hot broth over gelatin. Stir well and let cool. Mix chicken, nuts, eggs, olives, celery and mayonnaise. Pour gelatin over this and mix well. Salt to taste. Pour into a 2-quart Pyrex bowl to mold. Keep refrigerated. Serves 8 to 10.

MRS. ROBERT (HELEN) SMITH

BARBECUED CHICKEN

1 2 to 2½-pound chicken, fried
3 tablespoons brown sugar
6 ounces beer
1 cup prepared barbecue sauce
3 tablespoons white cooking wine

Place fried chicken in skillet or saucepan. Pour sauce over chicken and simmer for 1 hour. Serves 4.

MRS. ALLEN (BEVERLY) FAIL

CHICKEN AND DRESSING

1 large stewing hen or turkey
12 cups bread crumbs
1 cup chopped onions
1 tablespoon sage
1 tablespoon black pepper
1 tablespoon celery seed
½ cup sugar
4 eggs
Salt to taste

To make bread crumbs, bake a 10-inch pan of corn bread. Add enough cracker and light bread crumbs to equal 12 cups. Boil bird; cool; and remove from bone, reserving broth. Mix bread crumbs, onion, sage, pepper, celery seed, sugar, eggs and salt. Add enough broth for proper consistency, making thinner than desired. (It thickens as it bakes.) Bake until heated through and brown on top. Meat may be mixed with dressing or placed on top. If preferred, bird may be stuffed. Serves 12 to 15.

MRS. BESS COX, MEDINA, TN

CHICKEN BREASTS IN WINE SAUCE

4 large chicken breasts, halved and boned
Salt
Pepper
¼ stick butter
4 tablespoons green pepper, chopped
2 carrots, finely chopped
1 cup mushrooms, finely chopped
2 small onions, minced
2 cups chicken broth
1 tablespoon flour
¾ cup white wine

Clean chicken breasts and rub with salt and pepper. Brown lightly in melted butter. Remove and place in buttered casserole or baking pan. Set aside. To the skillet in which breasts were prepared add green pepper, carrots, mushrooms and onions, sautéing approximately 5 minutes. Stir flour into chicken stock and add to browned vegetables. Continue to stir until sauce thickens. Season to taste and simmer 10 minutes. While sauce is simmering, pour wine over breasts and place casserole in a 350-degree oven for 10 minutes. Remove from oven; pour vegetable sauce over chicken breasts; cover and return to oven. Bake 1 hour or until tender. Serve with wild rice or saffron rice. NOTE: Consider adding an extra chicken breast per man for heartier serving. Serves 6 to 8.

MRS. GEORGE (JANIE) THOMAS

CHICKEN IN CHEESE SHELL

PASTRY SHELL:
1½ cups sifted all-purpose flour
½ teaspoon salt
½ cup shortening
⅓ cup shredded sharp Cheddar cheese
4 to 5 tablespoons cold water

Set aside 3 tablespoons flour. Cut shortening into remaining flour to which salt and cheese have been added. Add 4 tablespoons of the water to the flour which was set aside. Mix well. Add to flour and cheese mixture and work well. If too dry, add the additional tablespoon of water. Roll out and place in an 8½-inch or a shallow 9-inch pie plate. Bake at 400 degrees for 12 to 14 minutes. Cool.

FILLING:
1½ cups diced cooked chicken
1 9-ounce can drained pineapple tidbits
1 cup chopped California walnuts
1 cup sour cream
⅔ cup mayonnaise
¼ cup grated cheese
Ripe olives for trim

Combine chicken, pineapple and nuts. Blend sour cream and mayonnaise. Add ⅔ cup dressing mixture to chicken mixture, mixing well. Spoon into cooled pastry shell. Top with remaining dressing. Sprinkle grated cheese on topping. Chill. Trim with ripe olives. Serves 6 to 8.

MRS. JAMES (CAROL) MANNON, TRENTON, TN

CHICKEN AND BEEF CACCIATORE

1 large round steak
7 chicken breast halves
3 tablespoons salad oil
2 tablespoons margarine
1 cup onions, sliced
1 8-ounce can tomato sauce
1 34-ounce can whole tomatoes, undrained
1 cup dry white wine
1½ teaspoons dried basil leaves
1 teaspoon dried oregano
1 clove garlic, chopped
2 tablespoons chopped parsley
1 teaspoon salt
¼ teaspoon pepper
3 tablespoons flour
1 6-ounce can whole mushrooms, drained (or 1 pound fresh)
Chopped parsley

Boil chicken until tender and bone. Wipe beef with damp paper towels; cut into 1-inch cubes. Heat oil and margarine together in 6-quart Dutch oven. Over high heat, brown beef cubes on all sides, one half at a time and sauté onion. Remove beef as it browns until all beef is browned (about 20 minutes). Return beef to Dutch oven and add tomato sauce, tomatoes, wine, basil, oregano, garlic, 2 tablespoons parsley, salt and pepper. Bring to boiling; then reduce heat and simmer covered for 60 minutes. Add chicken and continue simmering for 1 hour more, or until beef and chicken are tender. Combine flour with 3 tablespoons water; mix well. Stir into sauce in Dutch oven. Add mushrooms and cook 10 to 30 minutes longer or until sauce is thickened and mushrooms have cooked. Sprinkle with chopped parsley. This may be served as is or over pasta. Yields 10 to 12 generous portions and is good with broccoli in white sauce and rolls. Well received by adults.

MRS. SIMPSON (CONNIE) RUSSELL

CHICKEN BIENVILLE

6 chicken breast halves, boned
½ stick butter
¾ cup orange juice
1 10¾-ounce can golden mushroom soup
1 large onion, chopped
3 dashes cayenne
Salt and pepper to taste
½ teaspoon garlic powder
1 teaspoon oregano
3 tablespoons parsley
1½ cups grated Cheddar cheese
½ cup Parmesan cheese

Cube raw chicken and sauté in butter until lightly browned. Add orange juice and simmer 10 minutes. Combine mushroom soup, onion, cayenne, garlic powder, oregano and parsley in saucepan and bring to boil. Immediately lower heat to simmer and add chicken mixture and both cheeses. Simmer 10 minutes, stirring frequently. Serve over hot cooked rice. Serves 4 to 6.

MR. JEFF McNINCH, NASHVILLE, TN

CHICKEN LAS VEGAS

6 or 8 chicken breasts (skinned and boned)
1 10¾-ounce can condensed cream of mushroom soup (undiluted)
1 cup dry sherry or sauterne (optional)
1 2.5-ounce jar Armour dried beef
1 8-ounce carton sour cream
Bacon slices

Cut chicken breasts in half if they are large. Roll a slice of dried beef around chicken; then wrap with ½ slice of bacon. Place in a baking dish. Mix soup, sour cream and wine. Pour over chicken. (Use no salt.) Bake at 300 degrees for 2 to 3 hours covered with foil. Uncover and bake at 350 degrees for 20 to 30 minutes. Baste. May broil to brown bacon. Serve over Uncle Ben's wild rice. Serves 6 to 8. This makes a lot of sauce. I usually cook 12 to 15 chicken breasts when I have a crowd and this is plenty of sauce. Delicious!

MRS. JACK (CAROLYN) CUNNINGHAM, MILAN, TN
MRS. COLLINS (SUZANNE) BONDS, MILAN, TN

QUICHE

1 unbaked pie crust
½ pound bacon or any cooked meat or vegetable (especially ham, chicken, ground beef, mushrooms)
6 to 8 slices Swiss cheese, grated
3 heaping tablespoons flour
Dash cayenne pepper
3 eggs plus enough milk to fill 2-cup measuring cup

Dredge cheese in flour and cayenne. Mix eggs and milk. In a casserole dish layer meat, cheese mixture and egg mixture. Repeat. Bake at 375 degrees for 45 minutes. Serves 6 to 8.

MRS. WILLIAM (BRENDA) STONE

SPECIAL MACARONI CHEESE

4 cups (1 pound) elbow macaroni (twists are also good)
2 tablespoons salt
4 to 6 quarts boiling water
2 cups onion, chopped
¼ cup margarine
2 cups sour cream
1 cup creamed cottage cheese
¼ cup chopped parsley
1 teaspoon salt
½ pound sharp Cheddar cheese, grated

Gradually add macaroni and salt to rapidly boiling water so that water continues to boil. Cook, uncovered, stirring occasionally, until tender. Drain. Sauté onion in margarine until tender. Combine macaroni, sour cream, cottage cheese, onion, parsley and 1 teaspoon salt; mix well. Turn into greased 3 to 4-quart casserole and sprinkle with grated cheese. Bake 30 minutes at 350 degrees. Serves 8.

MRS. LOU (BOBBIE) BOUDREAU, CINCINNATI, OH

CREOLE EGG CASSEROLE

8 eggs, hard-boiled
1 medium onion
1 small bell pepper
5 celery stalks
1 stick butter
1 10¾-ounce can tomato soup
1 10½-ounce can mushroom soup
1 4-ounce can sliced mushrooms
1 teaspoon chili powder
Dash salt, pepper, Tabasco and Worcestershire sauce
Cracker crumbs
Grated sharp cheese

Chop onion, bell pepper and celery and sauté in butter. Add tomato soup and simmer for 20 minutes. Add mushrooms, mushroom soup, chili powder, salt, pepper, Tabasco and Worcestershire sauce and simmer for 5 minutes. Slice eggs and place in a 1 to 1½-quart casserole; then cover with sauce, cracker crumbs and grated cheese. Bake in hot oven at 450 degrees for 15 minutes. Serves 6. This is excellent with ham. It may be made a day in advance and heated when ready to serve. It may also be frozen until ready to cook.

MRS. DAVE (MARGE) JORDAN

CHEESE SANDWICHES

8 slices American cheese
16 slices bread, crusts removed
Butter
1 teaspoon dry mustard
1 teaspoon salt
8 eggs, lightly beaten
4 cups milk
1 cup Rice Krispies cereal

Butter bread on both sides. Make 8 sandwiches with bread and cheese and place in rectangular baking dish. Sprinkle sandwiches with mustard and salt. Mix beaten eggs and milk and pour over sandwiches. Sprinkle crushed Rice Krispies on top. Refrigerate overnight. Bake at 350 degrees for 1 hour. Serves 8.

MRS. LARRY (BARBARA) DOOLEY, EAST GREENWICH, CT

SWEET AND SOUR BEANS I

1 20½-ounce can green beans, drained
3 slices bacon
½ cup vinegar
⅓ to ½ cup sugar

Fry bacon until crisp; crumble and set aside. Drain off bacon fat, reserving 1 tablespoon. Stir sugar and vinegar into grease and stir until dissolved. Add beans and simmer for 25 minutes. To serve, top with bacon. Serves 4.

MRS. BRUCE (MARY) FISCHER, SACRAMENTO, CA

SWEET AND SOUR GREEN BEANS II

2 1-pound cans green beans
4 strips bacon
2 tablespoons pimiento
2 tablespoons red vinegar
¼ teaspoon sugar
1 tablespoon Worcestershire sauce
¼ teaspoon dry mustard
Dash Tabasco

Drain beans and steam in saucepan. Fry bacon in skillet and remove. In bacon drippings, bring pimiento, red vinegar, sugar, Worcestershire sauce, dry mustard and Tabasco to a boil and simmer 10 minutes. Pour sauce over beans and crumble bacon on top. Serves 6.

MRS. DON (PATTY) LEWIS

ELLEN SMITH'S BEAN CASSEROLE

8 bacon slices
4 onions, sliced and ringed
1 cup brown sugar
½ cup vinegar
1 teaspoon dry mustard
½ teaspoon salt
½ teaspoon garlic powder
1 15-ounce can butter beans
1 15-ounce can lima beans
1 15-ounce can dark red kidney beans
1 11-ounce can Morton's baked beans
1 15-ounce can cut green beans

Fry bacon until crisp and drain. Cook onions in bacon drippings until clear. Add brown sugar, vinegar, mustard, salt, garlic powder and simmer for 20 minutes. Drain cans of beans well and combine with onions and spices. Pour mixture in 3-quart casserole dish and bake in 350-degree oven until hot. Do not overcook or beans will be mushy. Crumble bacon on top before serving. Serves 8 to 10.

MRS. DON (PATTY) LEWIS

CURRIED TOMATOES

6 fresh tomatoes, cut in half
¾ cup mayonnaise
¾ cup sour cream
¾ teaspoon curry
Lawry's salt

Combine mayonnaise, sour cream and curry. Spread over tomatoes. Sprinkle with Lawry's salt. Place on greased cookie sheet. Bake in 350-degree oven for 30 to 40 minutes. Serves 6 to 8.

MRS. LOU (BOBBIE) BOUDREAU, CINCINNATI, OH

ITALIAN ZUCCHINI CASSEROLE

2½ pounds (about 8 cups) zucchini squash
½ cup chopped onion
½ cup chopped green pepper
4 tablespoons butter
1 3-ounce can sliced mushrooms, drained
1 1½-ounce package spaghetti sauce mix (McCormick if possible)
1 cup water
1 6-ounce can tomato paste
1 4-ounce package shredded Mozzarella cheese
2 tablespoons grated Parmesan cheese

Peel zucchini squash and cut into ⅜-inch slices. In a large covered saucepan, cook zucchini squash in boiling salted water until crisp and tender, about 4 to 5 minutes. Drain well and set aside. In same saucepan, cook onion and green pepper in butter until tender but not brown. Remove from heat and stir in mushrooms, dry spaghetti sauce mix, water and tomato paste. Mix well. Gently stir in zucchini and Mozzarella cheese. Pour mixture into a 10 x 6 x 2-inch baking dish or a 1½-quart shallow casserole dish. Sprinkle with Parmesan cheese. Bake in 350-degree oven for 30 to 35 minutes. Serves 8 to 10.

MRS. JAMES (HALINA) WARMBROD

CAROL'S BAKED BEANS

1 28-ounce can pork and beans
1 8-ounce can chili without beans
1½ cups onion, chopped
1 cup celery, chopped
1 bell pepper, chopped
1 cup catsup
⅔ cup brown sugar
¼ cup Worcestershire sauce
3 tablespoons prepared mustard
Dash Tabasco

Combine beans, chili, onion, celery, pepper, catsup, sugar, Worcestershire sauce, mustard and Tabasco and pour in a 2-quart Pyrex dish. Bake in 325-degree oven for 1½ hours. Serves 10.

MRS. DWIGHT (CAROL) HAWKS, HUMBOLDT, TN

RICE CASSEROLE

- 2 cups uncooked rice
- 1 bunch green onions, chopped
- ½ stick butter
- 1 3-ounce can mushrooms
- 1 8-ounce can water chestnuts, thinly sliced
- 1 garlic bud, mashed
- 4 ounces soy sauce
- 1 cup slivered almonds, toasted in butter

Cook rice as directed on package. Saute' onins in butter. Add mushrooms, including liquid. Add water chestnuts, garlic and soy sauce. Pour mixture in greased 1½ to 2-quart casserole dish and sprinkle almonds on top. Bake in 350-degree oven about 20 to 25 minutes or just long enough to heat thoroughly. Serves 6 to 8. (If this dish is frozen, add almonds just before placing in oven.)

MRS. THOMAS (NANCY) CRENSHAW, HUMBOLDT, TN

LIMA BEAN AND ONION CASSEROLE

- 1 16-ounce package frozen lima beans
- 1 16-ounce can small onions, drained
- 1 4-ounce can mushrooms, drained
- 1 5-ounce jar American cheese spread
- Celery salt to taste

Cook lima beans as directed on package and drain. Add onions, mushrooms, cheese spread and celery salt. Pour into 1½-quart baking dish. Bake in 350-degree oven for 20 minutes or until bubbly. Serves 8.

MRS. LARRY (WANNA) CASEY

BEST-KEPT SECRETS

SUPER-DUPER POTATOES

9 medium-sized red potatoes
1 stick butter
2 cups half and half
1 scant tablespoon Lawry's seasoned salt

½ pound medium Cheddar cheese, grated

Boil potatoes (do not peel) until done (not mushy). Refrigerate overnight. Peel and grate potatoes on medium-sized grater. Set aside. Grate cheese and add to grated potatoes. Melt butter in pan; add half and half and salt. Mix all ingredients and pour into a 2-quart casserole dish. Bake covered in 350-degree oven for 1 hour and 15 minutes. Serves 8 to 10.

MRS. T. O. (CAROL) LASHLEE, HUMBOLDT, TN

THREE VEGETABLE CASSEROLE

3 10-ounce packages frozen vegetables (cauliflower, spinach and broccoli)
1 6-ounce roll Kraft garlic cheese
4 ounces Velveeta cheese

½ 10¾-ounce can cream of mushroom soup
⅓ cup evaporated milk
¼ cup Pepperidge Farm fine stuffing

Cook vegetables as directed on packages and drain well. Melt cheeses, soup and milk. Mix stuffing with vegetables and add cheese mixture, tossing well. Pour in buttered 9 x 12-inch casserole dish. Bake in 350-degree oven for 30 minutes. Serves 12.

MRS. LOU (BOBBIE) BOUDREAU, CINCINNATI, OH

VEGETABLE BOUQUET

6 15½ or 16-ounce cans green beans
4 15½ or 16-ounce cans artichoke hearts
4 4-ounce cans mushroom buttons
3 4-ounce cans ripe pitted olives
4 cups celery, sliced diagonally
1 Bermuda onion, thinly sliced
1 cup tarragon vinegar
4 teaspoons Accent
4½ teaspoons salt
4 teaspoons sugar
2 teaspoons each crushed thyme, oregano and rosemary
1 teaspoon Tabasco
2½ cups Crisco or Wesson oil

Drain all canned vegetables and add celery and onion. Marinate overnight in sauce made of vinegar, Accent, salt, sugar, thyme, oregano, rosemary, Tabasco and oil. Drain before serving. Will keep several days. May be used as a salad, serving 12, or as an appetizer with toothpicks, serving 15 to 20.

MRS. JAMES (PAT) CRAIG

GREEN VEGETABLE CASSEROLE

1 16-ounce can asparagus
1 16-ounce can lima beans
1 16-ounce can English peas
1 cup grated Cheddar cheese

Drain vegetables. Place in a 2-quart casserole, spooning white sauce over them. Sprinkle cheese on top, and bake in a 350-degree oven for 1 hour.

WHITE SAUCE:
4 tablespoons butter or margarine
3 tablespoons flour
¼ teaspoon butter-flavored salt
1⅓ cups milk
Dash white pepper

Melt butter in saucepan; add salt, pepper and flour; blend. Add milk, stirring constantly until thick.

MRS. ROGER (MARY HELEN) BARKER, TRENTON, TN

SWISS VEGETABLE CUSTARD

¼ cup butter, melted
1½ cups yellow squash, sliced
1½ cups broccoli, sliced in
   1-inch pieces
1 egg
¼ cup milk
1 teaspoon salt
¼ teaspoon dry mustard
½ cup Swiss cheese
¼ cup grated Parmesan cheese

Sauté vegetables in butter until they can be pierced with a fork. In a large mixing bowl, beat egg; stir in milk, salt, mustard and Swiss cheese. Place vegetables in a 1-quart casserole dish. Pour egg mixture over vegetables and sprinkle grated Parmesan cheese on top. Bake in 375-degree oven for 15 to 20 minutes or until cheese is lightly browned and the custard is firm. Serves 4 to 6.

MRS. JAMES (ANNE) BARKER

STIR FRY VEGETABLES

2 tablespoons butter
2 tablespoons oil
1 bunch carrots, peeled and
   thinly sliced
¾ to 1 pound mushrooms, thinly sliced
5 medium green onions with
   tops, thinly sliced
1 tablespoon lemon juice
¼ teaspoon salt
¼ teaspoon pepper

Heat butter and oil in wok or frypan until bubbly. Add carrots, mushrooms and onions. Stir and fry until crisp and tender, about 7 to 8 minutes. Stir in lemon juice, salt and pepper. Serves 8 to 10.

MRS. PHIL (PAT) BAKER

ARTICHOKE VELVET

- 2 9-ounce packages frozen artichoke hearts (or 2 1-pound cans)
- 1 pint fresh mushrooms, sliced
- 2 tablespoons butter or margarine
- 1 envelope chicken gravy mix
- Dash dried thyme
- Dash dried marjoram
- 4 ounces Swiss cheese, diced (1 cup)
- 1 tablespoon dry white wine

Cook artichokes according to package directions. Drain. Cook mushrooms in butter until tender. Combine artichokes and mushrooms in 1-quart casserole dish. Prepare gravy according to package directions. Remove from heat and add thyme, marjoram and cheese. Stir until melted and add wine. Pour over artichokes and mushrooms. Bake covered in 350-degree oven for 30 minutes. Serves 6 to 8.

MRS. WILLIAM (SUSIE) OLD

ORIENTAL CABBAGE

- ½ cup melted margarine
- 1 medium head cabbage, chopped
- 1 green pepper, cut into strips
- 2 stalks celery, chopped
- 2 carrots, thinly sliced
- 1 large onion, sliced into rings
- Salt and pepper to taste

Combine margarine, cabbage, pepper, celery, carrots and onions in a large skillet. Cover and cook over medium heat for 10 minutes. Add salt and pepper to taste. Serves 6 to 8.

MRS. THOMAS (NANCY) CRENSHAW, HUMBOLDT, TN

DEVILED ENGLISH PEA CASSEROLE

1 17-ounce can English peas, drained
1 8-ounce can water chestnuts, chopped
4 eggs, hard-boiled and chopped
½ can pimiento, chopped (or 1 2-ounce jar, drained)
1 cup grated cheese
1 10¾-ounce can mushroom soup
1 3-ounce can onion rings

Combine peas, water chestnuts, eggs, pimiento, cheese, soup and ½ can onion rings. Pour in a 1½-quart casserole dish. Bake in 350-degree oven for 15 minutes. Sprinkle remaining onion rings on top and bake until brown. Serves 4.

MRS. TOM (FAITH) HADLEY, HUMBOLDT, TN

BRAISED CELERY

1 small bunch celery
3 tablespoons butter
1 tablespoon onion, chopped
Beef consommé
Salt and pepper to taste

Trim leaves and coarse outer stalks from celery. Wash celery and cut stalks into 1-inch lengths. In a saucepan, melt 2 tablespoons of the butter and add onion and sauté until golden. Add beef consommé and celery pieces. Simmer covered for about 20 minutes or until tender. Remove from heat and add 1 tablespoon butter. Pour into a 1-quart casserole dish and bake uncovered in a moderate oven (350 degrees), basting frequently until most of the liquid is absorbed. Season to taste with salt and pepper. Serves 4.

MRS. RUFFIN (JENNY) CRAIG

FAR EAST CELERY

4 cups 1-inch celery slices
1 5-ounce can water chestnuts
1 10¾-ounce can cream of chicken soup
¼ cup diced pimiento
½ cup soft bread crumbs
¼ cup toasted almond slices
2 tablespoons melted butter

Cook celery slices in small amount salted water for 12 minutes, leaving them still crisp. Drain. Add water chestnuts, soup and pimiento. Pour into 1½-quart casserole dish. Combine bread crumbs and butter and sprinkle over mixture. Top with almonds. Bake 1 hour at 350 degrees. Serves 8.

MRS. BRUCE (MARY) FISCHER, SACRAMENTO, CA

"SIMPLY DELICIOUS" SQUASH CASSEROLE

2 cups cooked, mashed squash (1 pound)
1 cup sour cream
1 10¾-ounce can cream of chicken soup
1 small onion, grated
2 carrots, grated
1 stick butter or margarine
1 8-ounce package Herb Seasoned Pepperidge Farm Stuffing

Cook squash; mash and drain. (Frozen squash may be used.) Combine squash, sour cream, soup, onion and carrots. Melt butter and combine with stuffing. Line the bottom of a 2-quart casserole dish with ½ of the stuffing mixture. Pour in squash mixture and put remaining stuffing mixture on top. Bake in 350-degree oven for 30 minutes. Serves 6 to 8.

MRS. DAVID (ARLENE) JOSLIN

SQUASH CASSEROLE

¾ cup green pepper, chopped
¾ cup onion, chopped
2 tablespoons butter
1 15-ounce can stewed tomatoes
1 10-ounce package frozen yellow squash
1 tablespoon Worcestershire sauce
1 cup grated sharp Cheddar cheese

Cook squash in salted water until tender and drain. Brown onion and green pepper in butter in a 10-inch skillet. Add tomatoes and Worcestershire sauce and simmer until thick. In a 1-quart casserole dish, put a layer of squash, then a layer of tomatoes and top with the grated cheese. Bake at 350 degrees for 45 minutes. Serves 6. (Parmesan cheese may be substituted for Cheddar cheese if desired.)

MRS. JAMES (PAT) CRAIG

BROCCOLI CASSEROLE

1 10-ounce package chopped broccoli
1 onion, chopped
¾ stick margarine
2 tablespoons flour
⅛ teaspoon salt
1 cup milk
¾ small can Parmesan cheese
1 beaten egg
Cracker crumbs for topping

Boil broccoli according to package directions and drain. Brown onion in margarine in skillet. Stir in flour, milk, salt, Parmesan cheese and egg. Add broccoli and pour into a 1-quart casserole dish. Top with buttered cracker crumbs. Bake in 325-degree oven for 30 minutes. Serves 4. This recipe can be made the day before serving.

MRS. A. U. (GRANNY) TAYLOR

COLD BROCCOLI SPEARS

2 10-ounce packages frozen broccoli spears
1 cup mayonnaise
2 teaspoons grated onion
Juice of 1 lemon
Dash Tabasco

Cook broccoli according to package directions and drain. Refrigerate. Combine mayonnaise, onion, lemon juice and Tabasco. When ready to serve, arrange spears on serving plate and top with mayonnaise dressing. Serves 6.

MRS. BRUCE (MARY) FISCHER, SACRAMENTO, CA

PANCAKES

2 cups flour
3 teaspoons baking powder
½ teaspoon salt
¼ cup sugar

2 eggs
2 cups milk
¼ cup Crisco oil

Sift flour, baking powder, salt and sugar together. Beat eggs and milk. Beat this into dry ingredients. Add salad oil. If too thick, add more milk. Bake on hot griddle. Yields 8 servings.

MRS. FRED (LINA) BOWYER

ENGLISH MUFFIN BREAD

1 package dry yeast
1 tablespoon granulated sugar
½ cup warm water
2½ cups all-purpose flour
2 teaspoons salt

⅞ cup warm milk
¼ teaspoon baking soda
dissolved in 1 tablespoon warm water

Combine yeast, sugar, and warm water in large bowl. Stir until yeast and sugar are dissolved and let mixture stand until it bubbles. Add flour mixed with salt and warm milk in alternate portions while stirring vigorously with a wooden spoon. Holding bowl tightly, beat dough very hard until it shows some elasticity and looks almost ready to leave sides of bowl. When it has almost gummy quality, cover and let rise in a warm place for about 1½ hours until doubled in bulk. Stir down with a wooden spoon; add dissolved soda and carefully distribute soda thoroughly or bread will be streaked. Then butter one 10-inch or two 8 x 4 x 2-inch tins and fill with dough, using a rubber spatula to scrape it from the bowl. Let rise again in a warm place for about 1 hour. Bake at 375 degrees until golden on top and shrinks slightly from sides of pan. Cool in pans for 5 minutes; then turn out onto a rack. This bread is good for toasting only.

MRS. CARL (ALICE) KIRKLAND

BRAN FLAKES MUFFINS

1 cup biscuit mix
2 tablespoons sugar
¾ cup milk
1 egg, beaten
1¼ cups 40% Bran Flakes

Mix together biscuit mix and sugar. Combine milk and egg. Add this mixture to dry ingredients. Mix only enough to dampen. Fold in bran flakes. Fill greased muffin pans about ⅔ full. Bake at 400 degrees for 20 minutes. Makes 8.

MRS. THOMPSON (SALLY) DABNEY

BASIC MUFFINS

1¾ cups flour
½ cup sugar (or honey)
2½ teaspoons baking powder
½ teaspoon salt
1 egg
¾ cup milk
⅓ cup melted butter or margarine

Sift flour, baking powder, sugar and salt into mixing bowl. Add egg, milk and melted butter. (If using honey, add here.) Blend at medium speed until moistened. Do not over mix. Grease 12 muffin cups or line with baking cups. Fill ⅔ full and bake about 25 minutes at 400 degrees. Variations may include adding 1 cup fresh blueberries, ¾ cup chopped dates, ½ cup raisins or ¾ cup walnuts to batter.

MRS. THOMAS (LINDA) HAYES

SIX WEEKS BRAN MUFFINS

1 15-ounce box Kellogg's Bran Flakes or All Bran
3 cups sugar
5 cups flour
5 teaspoons soda
1 teaspoon salt
4 eggs, beaten
1 cup oil
1 quart buttermilk

Mix cereal with sugar, flour, soda and salt. Then add eggs, oil and buttermilk. Mix all ingredients well and bake at 400 degrees for 15 minutes in muffin tins. This will keep in the refrigerator for 6 to 8 weeks and is an especially good breakfast muffin.

SISSY FRANKLAND

BEST-KEPT SECRETS

BUCKET BREAD

1 cup raisins
1 cup chopped dates
2 cups boiling water
2 teaspoons soda
1 cup pecans
3 tablespoons shortening

1½ cups sugar
2 eggs
4 cups plain flour
2 teaspoons vanilla
1 teaspoon salt

Mix raisins, dates, boiling water and soda and let cool. Cream sugar with shortening and eggs. Combine with raisin and date mixture. Add vanilla, flour and salt. Blend and add pecans. Bake in 3 greased coffee cans for 1 hour in a 350-degree oven. Yields 3 loaves. This bread can be eaten plain, toasted or spread with cream cheese.

MRS. E. L. (CAROLYN) ROBINSON

SOURDOUGH BREAD

BASIC SOURDOUGH STARTER:

2 cups unsifted all purpose flour
1 teaspoon salt
3 tablespoons sugar
1 envelope active dry yeast
2 cups warm water

Combine flour, salt, sugar and yeast in a large mixing bowl. Gradually stir in warm water until mixture resembles smooth paste. Cover with a clean towel or several layers of cheese cloth and let stand in a warm place to sour and bubble for 2 or 3 days. Then keep refrigerated for 2 or 3 weeks.

SOURDOUGH BREAD:

2½ cups water
1 cup sugar
7 or 8 cups sifted all-purpose flour
1 tablespoon salt
½ cup cooking oil

After dinner take starter mixture from refrigerator and empty into large bowl. Then add 1 cup water, ½ cup sugar and 2 cups sifted all-purpose flour. Cover and let stand until morning. Put *half* the starter back in refrigerator. To the other half add 1½ cups water, ½ cup sugar, 1 tablespoon salt, ½ cup cooking oil and 5 or 6 cups sifted flour. Empty onto floured board and knead until it can easily be handled. Put into large bowl and cover with damp cloth. Let rise until doubled. Then empty onto lightly floured board and pat out air bubbles. Divide into 2 parts. Grease loaf pans and place dough in pans. Let rise in warm place until doubled. Keep covered with damp cloth during rising. Place in cold oven and set oven at 350 degrees. Bake until golden brown (about 1 hour). Remove from oven and butter while hot. Turn onto board and let cool. Place back in oven in foil to warm.

MRS. LEON (DORIS) MULLEN

LOAF BREAD

1 cup hot milk
1 cup warm water
2 eggs
¾ cup oleo

1 cup sugar
1½ teaspoons salt
2 packages dry yeast
6 to 7 cups flour

Place oleo, sugar, salt in a bowl. Pour 1 cup hot milk over this mixture. Beat well. Beat in eggs. Add 3 cups of flour. Beat well. Dissolve yeast in 1 cup warm water and add 3 more cups flour. Place on board and work until not sticky. Add more flour if necessary. Let rise until doubled and punch down. Knead enough to handle. Divide into 3 parts and let rise again in loaf pans. Bake 30 minutes in 350-degree oven. Brush with melted butter. Makes 3 loaves.

MRS. W. R. (GENEVIEVE) TABER

BUTTERMILK WHITE BREAD

2 packages dry yeast
1 tablespoon granulated sugar
½ cup warm water
4 cups unbleached hard-wheat flour

1 tablespoon salt
3 tablespoons melted butter
1 to 1½ cups buttermilk

Combine yeast, sugar and water. Mix the flour, salt, melted butter and buttermilk together. Work flour mixture into a smooth dough. Then add yeast mixture. Beat well for 2 minutes; then remove to a well-floured board and knead for 10 minutes until dough is smooth. Place dough in a buttered bowl and turn to coat the dough with butter. Cover and set in a warm spot to rise until more than doubled in bulk. Punch down dough, remove to a floured board, and knead for 2 minutes. Form into a loaf. Put into a buttered 9 x 5 x 3-inch pan; cover and let rise again until more than doubled in bulk. Bake in 375-degree oven for 40 to 50 minutes. Remove from pan and bake for another 5 to 8 minutes on its side to give crisp brown crust. Yields 1 loaf.

MRS. CARL (ALICE) KIRKLAND

CHEESE BREAD

2 packages dry yeast
1½ cups lukewarm water
2 tablespoons sugar
2¼ teaspoons salt
6½ cups flour

2 eggs, beaten
2 cups sharp cheese
¼ cup caraway seed
½ stick butter, melted

Add yeast to water. Stir in sugar and salt until dissolved. Add 2 cups flour and beat well. Then add eggs, cheese, and caraway seed and beat well. Add 4 more cups flour to make soft dough. Turn dough onto lightly floured board. Cover with bowl and let rest 10 minutes. Then knead remaining flour into the dough and work 8 to 10 minutes. Place dough in greased bowl and let rise 1½ hours. Punch down and let rise again. Turn out and cover for 10 minutes. With a sharp knife, divide dough into 4 parts. Roll out each with hands and twist. Seal ends by turning under. Let loaves rise until doubled in size, which takes about 1 hour. Brush with melted butter and bake at 300 degrees for 1 hour.

SISSY FRANKLAND

OATMEAL BREAD

2 cups Quaker oats
1 cup brown sugar
2 tablespoons salt
6 ounces vegetable oil
⅓ cup sorghum molasses

3 packages yeast
3 cups whole wheat flour
½ cup wheat germ
5 to 8 cups white flour

Mix oats, brown sugar, salt, vegetable oil, and molasses with 2 cups boiling water. Stir well. Add 2 cups cold water and set aside until just warm. Dissolve yeast in ½ cup of warm water. Add yeast, whole wheat flour and wheat germ to the first mixture. Mix thoroughly. Add white flour and knead until smooth. Place in large greased bowl, turning to grease sides of dough. Let rise for 1½ hours. Punch down and divide in 4 greased loaf pans. Let rise again until doubled in bulk. Bake at 350 degrees for 40 to 45 minutes. Makes 4 loaves.

SALLY MITCHELL

FILLED BREAD

1½ cups lukewarm milk
2 packages dry yeast
1 tablespoon vanilla
1 teaspoon salt
3 eggs, beaten

1 cup sour cream
1 cup oleo
⅔ cup sugar
6 cups flour

NUT-RAISIN FILLING:

3 egg whites
2 tablespoons oleo
1 tablespoon vanilla
1½ cups sugar

2 cups chopped pecans
1 cup raisins
½ cup lukewarm milk

Dissolve yeast in warm milk. Add vanilla, salt, eggs and sour cream. Beat with egg beater. Mix flour, oleo and sugar separately. Add to milk mixture. Mix well. Dough will be sticky; so add a little flour and shape into a ball. Let rise in a large covered bowl in a warm place until it doubles. Punch down and let rise again. Punch down and divide into desired amounts for loaves. On lightly floured surface, roll out part of dough into a rectangle. Spread filling over rectangle. Roll lengthwise. Seal edges. Let rest 20 minutes on greased baking sheet. Brush top with beaten egg yolk. Bake in 350-degree oven for 30 minutes. This makes several rolls, depending on size. May be frozen for several months. To prepare filling, beat egg whites until stiff peaks form. Add vanilla and butter. Gradually add sugar. Beat well and add enough milk to make it spreadable.

MRS. GARY (CATHY) DUNAWAY, RALEIGH, NC

NAVAJO FRY BREAD

6 cups unsifted flour
1 tablespoon salt
  (only for non-Indians!)
2 tablespoons baking powder
½ cup instant nonfat dry milk
2¾ cups lukewarm water
Shortening

In a bowl combine flour, salt, baking powder and dry milk. Add enough water to form a soft dough. Knead thoroughly. Pinch off a ball of dough about the size of a large egg. Shape round and flat by working back and forth from one hand to the other, making it thinner and thinner, and about 8 inches in diameter. (You may roll like pie crust to save time.) In a frying pan, preferably cast iron, have ready about 1-inch deep hot shortening. Drop the thin, round dough into hot oil and fry to light brown on each side. As it fries, the bread puffs up and becomes light and crisp. Drain each piece on paper towels. It is best served as quickly as possible. Serves 8. This versatile recipe may be used from breakfast dish to dinner dessert. For breakfast it may be served hot with powdered sugar, syrup or jams and jellies. It is an excellent base for dishes such as chicken ala king, or similar dishes, and makes a marvelous dessert served with butter and honey, or for strawberry shortcake. The recipe was given to me by a Navajo girl from Monument Valley, Utah.

MRS. ROBERT (TONI) CONOVER, BRADFORD, TN

CREAM CHEESE BRAIDS

1 cup sour cream
½ cup sugar
1 teaspoon salt
½ cup melted butter

2 packages dry yeast
½ cup warm water
2 eggs, beaten
4 cups all-purpose flour

Heat sour cream over low heat; stir in sugar, salt and butter; cool to lukewarm. Sprinkle yeast over warm water in a large bowl, stirring until yeast dissolves. Add sour cream mixture, eggs and flour; mix well. Cover tightly and refrigerate overnight. The next day, divide dough into 4 equal parts. Roll out each part on a well-floured board into a 12 x 8-inch rectangle. Spread ¼ of cream cheese filling on each rectangle. Roll up jelly roll fashion, beginning at long sides. Pinch edges under. Place each roll seam side down on greased baking sheets. Slit each roll at 2-inch intervals about ⅔ of the way through dough to resemble a braid. Cover and let rise in a warm place until doubled. Bake at 375 degrees for 12 to 15 minutes. Spread with glaze while warm. Yields 4 loaves.

CREAM CHEESE FILLING:

2 8-ounce packages cream
    cheese
¾ cup sugar

1 egg, beaten
⅛ teaspoon salt
2 teaspoons vanilla

Combine cream cheese, sugar and salt in a small mixing bowl. Add egg and vanilla and mix well.

GLAZE:

2 cups powdered sugar
4 tablespoons milk

2 teaspoons vanilla

Combine all ingredients in a small bowl and mix well.

MRS. CARL (ALICE) KIRKLAND

SHUGFETER LIGHT BREAD

½ cup sugar
2 teaspoons salt
½ cup shortening
1 cup hot milk

2 eggs, beaten
2 packages dry yeast
1 cup warm water
6 to 6½ cups all-purpose flour

Place sugar, shortening and salt in large mixing bowl. Add hot milk and stir. Cool before beating in eggs. Dissolve yeast in warm water. Stir into shortening mixture. Add 4 cups flour and beat until smooth. Add enough of the remaining flour to make a dough. Turn dough out onto floured surface. Knead until smooth, about 10 minutes. Place in a large greased bowl, turning once to grease surface. Cover and let rise in a warm place until doubled. Punch down and let rise 10 minutes. Divide dough into halves or thirds. Shape into loaves. Place in 2 greased 9 x 5 x 3-inch or 3 greased 8½ x 4½ x 2½-inch loaf pans. Let rise until doubled. Bake at 400 degrees for 25 minutes.

FOR BRAID:
After first rising, divide dough into 6 parts. Roll each into a 15-inch long rope. Shape into 2 braids, using 3 ropes for each braid. Let rise until doubled on baking sheet. Brush with unbeaten egg white. Sprinkle with sesame seeds or poppy seeds. Bake at 375 degrees for 20 to 25 minutes. Makes 2 braids.

FOR PAN ROLLS:
After first rising, shape dough into 36 rolls. Place into 2 greased 13 x 9 x 2-inch baking pans. Let rise until doubled.

FOR WREATH:
Form wreath with 2 braids. Bake as for braids.

MRS. RICHARD (PAT) BRADLEY

FIESTA BREAD

1 short loaf French bread, split lengthwise
¼ cup margarine, softened
1 cup Cheddar cheese, grated
⅓ cup onions, chopped
⅓ cup ripe olives, chopped
⅓ cup green pepper, chopped
⅓ cup catsup

Mix margarine, grated cheese, onions, olives, green pepper and catsup together. Spread on split French bread. Broil open-faced until bubbling. Good for Sunday supper. Cooked ground beef may be added for a heavier meal. Serves 6 to 8.

MRS. CHARLES (CARMEN) BRUER

WHOLE WHEAT BREAD

1 package dry yeast
¼ cup warm water
1½ cups hot water
⅓ cup honey or brown sugar
2 teaspoons salt
3 tablespoons shortening
2 cups whole wheat flour
3 to 3¼ cups all-purpose flour

Dissolve dry yeast in ¼ cup warm water. Combine hot water, honey, salt and shortening. Cool to lukewarm. Stir in whole wheat flour and 1 cup white flour. Beat well. Stir in yeast. Add enough of remaining flour to make a moderately stiff dough. Turn out onto lightly floured surface. Knead until smooth (about 10 minutes). Shape dough into ball. Place in lightly greased bowl, turning to grease surface of dough. Cover and let rise until doubled. Punch down. Cut into 2 portions. Shape each into smooth ball and let rest 10 minutes. Shape into loaves. Place in greased 8½ x 4½ x 2½-inch pans. Let rise until doubled. Bake at 375 degrees for 45 minutes. Cover with foil last 20 minutes. Makes 2 loaves.

MRS. CARL (ALICE) KIRKLAND

CORN LIGHT BREAD

2 cups self-rising corn meal
1 cup self-rising flour
½ cup sugar
2 cups buttermilk
½ cup Wesson or Crisco oil

Mix all ingredients by hand until very smooth. Slightly grease Bundt pan with oil and sprinkle ½ teaspoon sugar in bottom of pan. Add mixture and bake for 50 to 55 minutes in 350-degree oven.

MRS. ROBERT (HELEN) SMITH

CORN MEAL LIGHT BREAD

2 cups white corn meal
1 cup sugar
1 cup flour
½ teaspoon salt
1 teaspoon soda
3 tablespoons vegetable oil
2 cups buttermilk

Combine all ingredients and bake in a greased loaf pan for 1 hour at 300 degrees.

SISSY FRANKLAND

BACON CORN BREAD

1½ cups corn meal
¾ cup flour
4 teaspoons baking powder
½ teaspoon soda
½ tablespoon sugar
1½ cups buttermilk
2 eggs
2 tablespoons chopped bacon
2 tablespoons bacon grease

Sift flour; measure and sift again with corn meal, baking powder, soda and sugar. Combine with buttermilk, eggs, bacon and bacon grease. Bake on a waffle iron. This is an unusual bread that is especially good with vegetables. Serves 6.

MRS. LARRY (BARBARA) DOOLEY, EAST GREENWICH, CT

SOUR CREAM CORN BREAD

1 cup Hot Rize corn meal mix
½ cup Crisco
2 eggs
1 8-ounce carton sour cream
1 8½-ounce can cream-style corn

Mix all ingredients. Bake in a greased 8 x 8 x 2-inch Pyrex pan at 400 degrees for 20 to 30 minutes. Serves 6 to 8.

MRS. BOBBY (POLLY) CARTER

HUSH PUPPIES

1 cup corn meal
1 teaspoon baking powder
1 teaspoon salt
1 medium onion, finely chopped
2 teaspoons sugar
½ cup milk

Mix dry ingredients and onion. Gradually add milk so batter holds together but is not thin. Drop by spoonfuls in hot oil. Cook in fryer on medium-hot temperature until brown. Serves 8.

MRS. LARRY (BARBARA) DOOLEY, EAST GREENWICH, CT

CORN MEAL CAKES
(With Fried Fish)

1 cup corn meal
½ cup flour
1 teaspoon sugar
Sweet milk
½ teaspoon salt
1 egg
2 teaspoons baking powder
3 tablespoons shortening
Red pepper to taste

Sift dry ingredients. Add egg and stir in well. Melt shortening and add. Use enough sweet milk to make a soft batter. Pour off most of the fat in which the fish was fried; then fry cakes in same pan. Serve with plenty of butter. Serves 4. (This can also be fried in bacon grease.)

MRS. AUGUSTUS (ANN) MIDDLETON

PUMPKIN BREAD

3½ cups flour
2 teaspoons soda
1½ teaspoons salt
1 teaspoon each cloves, cinnamon, allspice, ginger and nutmeg
3 cups sugar
1 cup cooking oil
4 eggs
1 16-ounce can pumpkin
⅔ cup water
1 cup raisins or dates, chopped
1 cup nuts, chopped

Sift dry ingredients together. Cream sugar and oil; then add eggs and beat. To this, add dry ingredients, water and pumpkin, then nuts and fruit. May be baked in 2 greased loaf pans for 1½ hours at 350 degrees or in 4 one-pound greased and floured coffee cans for 50 to 60 minutes at 350 degrees. Freezes well.

MRS. EDWARD (GAYLE) CROCKER
LINDA COX

TIMBALES

1 cup plain flour
1 cup milk
½ teaspoon salt
2 teaspoons sugar
1 egg
1½ pounds shortening

Mix egg, milk, sugar, salt and flour until it is a smooth batter. Heat shortening to 365 degrees. Heat timbale iron in shortening. When temperature is right, dip timbale iron in batter and return to fat, frying until golden brown. Drain timbales on paper towels. Serve with creamed turkey. For dessert timbales, sprinkle them with powdered sugar while they are hot. Can be frozen as long as 6 months. Yields 5 dozen shells.

MRS. LEONARD (DELL) HERRINGTON, SR., NEW ALBANY, MS

EASY YEAST ROLLS

2 packages dry yeast
1¼ cups lukewarm water
⅓ cup sugar plus 1 tablespoon
½ cup shortening
1 egg
4 cups sifted flour
1 teaspoon salt

Dissolve yeast in water in a large mixing bowl. Add all other ingredients and beat well. Allow to rise in a warm place until doubled in bulk. Beat down and roll dough out. Cut rolls, dipping each roll in melted butter. Place on baking sheet, allowing rolls to touch. Let them rise again until doubled in bulk. Bake at 400 degrees for 10 to 12 minutes on top rack. Serves 15 to 20 people. To freeze rolls, bake in oven on top rack for only 7 minutes. Rolls should look done, but not brown. Cover with foil and freeze up to 4 months.

MRS. LEONARD (MARY KATHRYN) HERRINGTON, JR.
ACKERMAN, MS

LIGHT ROLLS

1 quart sweet milk
1 cup sugar
1 cup shortening
1 package dry yeast
¼ cup warm water

6 to 7 cups all-purpose flour
1 scant teaspoon soda
1 heaping teaspoon baking powder
1 tablespoon salt

Scald sweet milk and add sugar, stirring until dissolved. Then add shortening, stirring until melted in milk mixture. Let stand until lukewarm. Mix 1 package of yeast with the warm water. Add this to the cool milk mixture. Then add about 3 to 3½ cups of flour to make a sticky paste. Stir to blend mixture. Set aside in warm place, covered, to rise for 1 hour. Stir mixture down and add soda, baking powder, and salt. Then add remaining 3 to 4 cups of flour to make a soft dough. Refrigerate for at least 3 hours before using. This will keep refrigerated for 1 week. To bake, take out as much dough as needed and roll out on floured board to ¼-inch thickness. Cut with small round cutter and dip into melted butter. Then fold over in half in pan. Let rise until doubled in bulk. Bake at 400 degrees for 10 to 15 minutes. These can be cut out and placed on cookie sheet, frozen and bagged for later use. They will keep frozen about 1 month.

To make cinnamon rolls, roll dough out in rectangle. Sprinkle liberally with melted butter, brown sugar, cinnamon, chopped nuts and raisins. Roll up jelly roll fashion. Then slice 1 inch thick. Place in pan which has been buttered and let rise until doubled in bulk. Bake at 400 degrees for 10 to 15 minutes.

MRS. WALTER (DIXIE) HARDIN, LEXINGTON, TN

BRAN BUDS REFRIGERATOR ROLLS

1 cup Crisco
¾ cup sugar
1 cup Kellogg's Bran Buds
½ teaspoon salt

2 eggs
1 cup warm water
2 packages yeast
6 cups plain flour

Combine Crisco, sugar, Bran Buds, salt and eggs in a large bowl. Dissolve 2 packages yeast in warm water, adding to bran mixture when cooled. Add unsifted plain flour to bran-yeast mixture. At this point, dough may be refrigerated. When ready to use dough, roll out and cut rolls. Place in a pan with sides touching. Allow to rise 2 hours. Bake at 350 degrees 12 to 20 minutes. May be frozen after baking. Yields 3 dozen rolls.

MRS. STEPHEN (SUSAN) GANNAWAY

BUTTER BRAID COFFEE CAKE

¼ cup warm water
1 package dry yeast
1 cup milk
½ cup Wesson oil or melted butter

⅓ cup sugar
½ teaspoon salt
1 egg, beaten
4 to 5 cups flour

Dissolve yeast in warm water. To milk, add oil, sugar and salt. Stir in egg and dissolved yeast. Add 2 cups flour to mixture and beat until smooth. Gradually add enough of remaining flour to make a soft dough. Turn onto a floured board and knead until dough is smooth and does not stick to board, adding more flour if necessary. Place dough in buttered bowl and brush with melted butter. Let rise 1½ to 2 hours. Dough is then ready to be shaped into coffee cake.

FILLING:
1½ sticks butter
1½ cups confectioners sugar

1 teaspoon vanilla
¼ cup finely chopped pecans

During last few minutes while dough is rising, prepare filling by creaming butter and gradually adding confectioners sugar, beating until light and fluffy. Blend in vanilla and pecans.

Divide dough in half. Roll each part into 9 x 18-inch rectangle. Cut each into 3 strips and spread with butter filling. Make a lengthwise roll of each strip, sealing edges well. Braid 3 strips together and shape into wreath to form coffee cake. Repeat with other 3 strips. Place on 2 buttered 12 x 15-inch baking sheets and let rise 30 minutes. Bake in 350-degree oven for 20 to 25 minutes. Remove from oven and cool slightly.

ORANGE SNOW ICING:
1 cup confectioners sugar
2 tablespoons orange juice

2 teaspoons vanilla
¼ cup finely chopped pecans

Mix confectioners sugar, orange juice, vanilla and pecans and drizzle on coffee cake. Candied fruit may also be used to decorate the 2 braids.

MRS. S. M. (LEILA) LAWRENCE

BEST-KEPT SECRETS

TRULY DIFFERENT CUPCAKES

4 squares semi-sweet chocolate
2 sticks margarine
¼ teaspoon butter flavoring
1½ cups chopped pecans, optional

4 large eggs
1¾ cups sugar
1 cup unsifted, plain flour
1 teaspoon vanilla

Melt chocolate and margarine. Add butter flavoring and nuts. Stir until nuts are well-coated. Combine sugar, flour, eggs and vanilla. Stir only until well-blended. *Do not beat*. Very carefully fold in chocolate and nut mixture until well-blended. Bake at 325 degrees for 35 minutes. Yields 18 to 20 cupcakes.

MRS. JOHN (LINDA) WOMACK

MOTHER'S ORANGE SLICE CAKE

1 cup margarine
2 cups sugar
4 eggs
½ cup buttermilk
1 teaspoon soda
3½ cups flour

2 cups nuts, chopped
1 pound candy orange slices, chopped
1 8-ounce box dates, chopped
1 cup flaked coconut

GLAZE:

1 cup orange juice

2 cups powdered sugar

Cream margarine and sugar until smooth. Add eggs, 1 at a time and mix well after each. Dissolve soda in buttermilk and add to creamed mixture. Place flour in large bowl. Add dates, orange slices and nuts. Stir to coat each piece. Add flour mixture and coconut to creamed mixture. (This makes a stiff dough and should now be stirred by hand.) Put into a greased and floured 13 x 9-inch cake pan. Bake at 250 degrees for 2½ to 3 hours. Combine orange juice and powdered sugar and pour over cake. Let stand in pan overnight. Cut in squares and serve. May be topped with sweetened whipped cream. Serves 14 to 16.

MRS. WILLIAM (MARCIA) MOSS

BUTTER PECAN TORTE

1 box butter pecan cake mix
1 box butter pecan dry icing mix
1 pint whipping cream

1 can Betty Crocker chocolate icing
3 to 4 Heath bars, refrigerated and crushed

Bake cake by directions on box. Cool and slice each layer in half horizontally. Beat whipping cream and dry icing mix until it stands in peaks. Layer cake with this mixture; then frost sides with chocolate icing. Sprinkle crushed heath bars on top. Refrigerate until serving time. Best when made a day ahead. Serves 12 to 15. This cake was a welcome gift to me when we moved to town, and my whole family liked it.

MRS. ROBERT (HELEN) SMITH

WHIPPING CREAM POUND CAKE

3 cups sugar
1 cup Crisco
1 stick oleo
½ pint whipping cream
3 cups flour

6 eggs
1 teaspoon vanilla extract
1 teaspoon lemon extract
1 teaspoon almond extract
 (optional)

Cream together the sugar, Crisco and oleo. Add the cream and 2 eggs at a time with 1 cup of the flour each time until all the flour and eggs have been incorporated into the batter. Add the extracts and mix. Pour into greased and floured tube pan. Bake at 275 degrees for 1 hour then 15 minutes at 300 degrees. Serves 15 to 20.

MRS. LLOYD (ARVA) RAY, RED BAY, AL

PINEAPPLE SUPREME CAKE

CAKE:

2 cups sugar
2 sticks soft margarine
3 eggs

1 cup milk
3 cups self-rising flour
1 teaspoon vanilla

Cream margarine and sugar; add eggs 1 at a time. Add flour, alternating with milk. Add vanilla and beat well. Turn into 3 lightly greased and floured 8-inch cake pans. Bake at 350 degrees 35 minutes.

CAKE FILLING:

1 20-ounce can crushed pineapple

⅓ cup sugar

Combine pineapple and sugar and boil for 7½ minutes.

FROSTING:

⅓ cup margarine, melted
1 8-ounce package cream cheese

1 box confectioners sugar

Cream cheese with margarine; blend in sugar. Stack cake, spreading each layer with filling, then frosting. Frost top and sides also. Serves 12. Very good and moist.

MRS. HAROLD (SHELBY) BROYLES

PAT'S PUMPKIN CAKE

4 eggs, beaten separately
2 cups sugar
1 cup salad oil
2 cups sifted flour
2 teaspoons baking soda
2 teaspoons cinnamon
½ teaspoon salt
2 cups canned pumpkin

Mix beaten eggs with sugar. Slowly add oil. Mix sifted flour, baking soda, cinnamon and salt. Add to liquid mixture. Add pumpkin. Pour into a greased tube or Bundt pan. Bake at 350 degrees for approximately 60 minutes or until done. Cool at least 3 hours before frosting.

ICING:

1 8-ounce package cream cheese
1 stick butter
1 box confectioners sugar
2 teaspoons vanilla

Blend all ingredients until smooth. Chopped or whole nuts may be added for flair. Very rich and moist. Serves 14 to 18.

MRS. JAMES (PAT) CRAIG

FRESH APPLE CAKE

2 cups sugar
3 eggs
2 cups self-rising flour
1 cup cooking oil
1 teaspoon vanilla extract
1 teaspoon cinnamon
1 teaspoon nutmeg
3 cups diced fresh apples
1 cup chopped nuts

Combine sugar, eggs, flour, oil, vanilla extract, cinnamon and nutmeg; then stir in apples and nuts. Pour into a well-greased Bundt pan. Bake at 350 degrees for 40 to 45 minutes.

MRS. AB (ELIZABETH) TAYLOR

PERFECT PRUNE CAKE

CAKE:

2 cups sugar
1 cup corn oil
3 whole eggs
2 cups flour
½ teaspoon salt
1 teaspoon soda
1 teaspoon cinnamon
1 teaspoon allspice
1 cup buttermilk
1 cup chopped pecans
1 cup cooked prunes

Cream sugar, oil and eggs. Mix flour, salt, soda and spices. Gradually add flour mix alternately with buttermilk to creamed mixture. Add nuts and prunes. Pour into greased Bundt pan. Bake 1 hour and 10 minutes at 350 degrees.

GLAZE:

1 cup sugar
½ cup buttermilk
1 tablespoon corn syrup
Pat of butter
¼ teaspoon soda
¼ teaspoon salt
1 teaspoon vanilla flavoring
1 teaspoon rum flavoring

Combine all ingredients except flavorings in saucepan. Heat over low heat, stirring constantly. Boil for 4 or 5 minutes; add both flavorings. Pour onto hot cake while still in pan. Cool cake in pan. Loosen edges with spatula to be sure sugar has not stuck to pan.

(My bridge club loves this cake. At least, they haven't had the nerve to complain!)

MRS. DAVID (CATHY) FARMER

MAW'S JAM CAKE

1½ cups sugar
¾ cup butter or margarine
4 eggs
2½ cups flour
1 teaspoon soda

1 cup buttermilk
1 cup jam (strawberry is best)
1 teaspoon each cinnamon, cloves and nutmeg

Cream sugar and butter. Add eggs 1 at a time, beating after each addition. Dissolve soda in buttermilk and add alternately with flour. Add jam, cinnamon, cloves and nutmeg. Pour into four 8-inch or three 9-inch cake pans which have been greased and floured. Bake 25 or 30 minutes at 350 degrees or until cake springs back when pressed in center. Cool on racks.

BUTTER CREAM FROSTING:
2 cups sugar
1 cup butter or margarine

½ cup milk

Boil all ingredients for 5 minutes. Beat until cool. Quickly spread onto cooled cake. NOTE: Although margarine may be substituted in both cake and frosting, much flavor is sacrificed.

MRS. J. FRANK (DOROTHY) HAYES

BROWN SUGAR FLUFF

1 cup brown sugar
⅓ cup sifted flour
½ teaspoon soda
1 egg, beaten

1 cup broken pecans
1½ teaspoons vanilla
½ pint whipping cream
Sugar to taste

Mix sugar, flour, soda, egg, pecans and vanilla. Cook in aluminum pie pan at 325 degrees for 25 minutes. Remove from pan while hot and crumble into small pieces. Cool in refrigerator. A few hours before serving (about 2 or 3 hours) fold in 1 cup sweetened, whipped cream. Serve in sherbets with dollop of whipped cream and cherry on top. Serves 4 to 6.

MRS. STAN (JEANNE) LITTLE, HUMBOLDT, TN

MY SINFULLY EASY CHOCOLATE MOUSSE

8 ounces semi-sweet chocolate
Finely grated zest of 1 orange (Zest is the orange part of the rind, none of the white pulp)
Juice of 1 orange
4 eggs, separated
2 tablespoons of orange liqueur or dark rum (optional)

Slowly melt chocolate in the top of a double boiler over simmering water. Into the melted chocolate beat the orange juice, zest and egg yolks, 1 at a time, beating well after each addition. Add the liqueur if desired. Beat egg whites until stiff and carefully fold into chocolate mixture. Pour into champagne glasses and chill. Garnish with sweetened whipped cream and a slice of orange. Serves 6 to 8.

MRS. JIM (BETTY) EMISON, ALAMO, TN

CHOCOLATE CHIP PIE

1 cup sugar
½ cup plain flour
1 stick oleo, melted
2 eggs, beaten
1 cup chocolate chips
1 cup chopped pecans
1 teaspoon vanilla
1 unbaked pie shell

Mix sugar and flour. Add eggs and melted butter. Mix well. Add nuts, chocolate chips and vanilla. Pour into pie shell and bake at 350 degrees for 30 to 40 minutes. Serves 6 to 8.

MRS. JOHN (BETH) HALE, HUMBOLDT, TN
MRS. VERNON (DEBBIE) WOOD, MILLEDGEVILLE, GA

EASY FRUIT COBBLER

1 stick butter
1 cup self-rising flour
1 cup sugar
1 cup milk
1 quart fruit

In oven melt butter in 2-quart dish. In a bowl mix flour and sugar. Add melted butter and milk. Stir until smooth. Pour fruit into dish in which butter was melted. Pour batter over fruit. Bake at 350 degrees for 40 minutes. Serves 6.

MRS. WILLIAM (DELORIA) HAYNES

PINEAPPLE PIE

1 baked pie shell
1 20-ounce can crushed pineapple
3 tablespoons cornstarch
⅔ cup sugar
½ teaspoon salt
3 eggs, separated
1 tablespoon butter

Mix cornstarch, sugar and salt. Add pineapple. Cook until clear and thickened. Add butter and pour half of mixture over beaten egg yolks. Mix well; then add remaining mixture and cook over low heat 1 minute longer. Cool. Pour into baked shell. Top with meringue made by folding ½ cup sugar into 2 stiffly beaten egg whites. Brown in 325-degree oven. Can use Cool Whip, whipped cream or any prepared topping mix in place of meringue. Makes one 9-inch pie or 8 tarts.

MRS. CHARLES (CARMEN) BRUER

BLUM'S COFFEE-TOFFEE PIE
(Requires 2 Days' Preparation)

DAY 1:

PASTRY SHELL:

½ package 11-ounce pie crust mix, not sticks
¼ cup light brown sugar
1 teaspoon vanilla
¾ cup finely chopped pecans
1 square unsweetened chocolate, grated

FILLING:

½ cup soft butter, not melted
¾ cup sugar
1 square unsweetened chocolate, melted and cooled
2 teaspoons instant coffee
2 eggs

Preheat oven 300 to 325 degrees. Mix dry ingredients; add vanilla and 1 tablespoon water. Blend well. Press into 9-inch pie plate. Bake 10 to 15 minutes or until lightly browned. Cool. Cream butter and sugar until light. Blend in melted chocolate and coffee. Add 1 egg and beat for 5 minutes. Add second egg and beat 5 minutes. Turn into pie shell and chill overnight.

DAY 2:

TOPPING:

1 cup heavy cream
1 tablespoon instant coffee
¼ cup confectioners sugar

Combine coffee and cream and refrigerate for 1 hour. Beat until stiff, gradually adding sugar, and top pie. Garnish with grated chocolate and refrigerate *at least* 2 hours before serving. Serves 8. The time this requires is well worth the effort. The result is excellent.

MRS. RUFFIN (JENNY) CRAIG
MRS. JO-ANN ADAMS, NEW ORLEANS, LA

BROWN SUGAR PECAN PIE

1½ cups brown sugar
2 tablespoons melted butter
2 eggs
2 teaspoons vanilla
1 cup pecans

CRUST:
1 cup flour
1 stick butter
1 3-ounce package cream cheese

Cream flour and butter; then add cream cheese. Press into 9-inch pie dish. Pour pie mixture of brown sugar, butter, eggs, vanilla and pecans into crust. Bake at 350 degrees for 45 or 50 minutes. Serves 6 to 8.

MRS. WILLIAM (BRENDA) STONE

CHRISTMAS PIE

1 16-ounce can red sour cherries, pitted
1 15¼-ounce can crushed pineapple
2 cups sugar
6 tablespoons cornstarch
1 tablespoon red food coloring
Pinch salt
6 bananas, sliced
1 cup chopped pecans
1 container whipped topping
2 pie shells, baked

Drain cherries, pineapple, saving juice. Add water to make 2 cups. Add sugar, salt, cornstarch and food coloring. Mix well; then add cherries and pineapple. Cook over medium heat until thick. Remove from heat and add bananas and nuts. Pour into pie shells. Chill and top with whipped topping before serving. Serves 12 or 16.

MRS. TOBY (DORA JANE) ROSS

LEMON RIBBON PIE

6 tablespoons butter
Grated peel of 1 lemon
⅓ cup lemon juice
1 cup sugar
⅛ teaspoon salt
2 eggs

2 egg yolks
1 quart vanilla ice cream
1 baked 9-inch pie shell
3 egg whites
6 tablespoons sugar

To make a lemon butter sauce, melt butter; add lemon peel and juice, salt and 1 cup sugar. Slightly beat whole eggs with egg yolks. Add to lemon mixture. Mix and cook over boiling water, beating constantly with a whisk until thick and smooth. Cool. Smooth half the ice cream into pie shell. Freeze. Cover with half the lemon sauce. Freeze. Cover with remaining ice cream. Freeze. Top with remaining lemon sauce. Freeze. Beat 3 egg whites until stiff. Gradually add 6 tablespoons sugar. Spread meringue onto pie. Place on wooden board. Lightly brown in 475-degree oven. Serve at once or freeze. Serves 6 to 8.

MRS. CLAIBORNE THOMPSON, HOLLY SPRINGS, MS

JAPANESE FRUIT PIE

1 unbaked pie shell
1 stick oleo, melted
2 eggs, beaten
1 cup sugar

1 tablespoon vinegar
½ cup pecans
½ cup raisins
½ cup coconut

Mix the oleo, eggs, sugar and vinegar well. Add nuts, raisins and coconut. Pour into pie shell and bake at 325 degrees for 40 minutes. Serves 6.

MRS. HOBERT (ANN) BANKS

VERSATILE CHOCOLATE PIE

1 baked pie shell
½ stick butter or margarine
1 cup sugar
3 egg yolks

1 teaspoon vanilla
½ cup milk
2 tablespoons Hershey's unsweetened powdered chocolate

MERINGUE:
3 egg whites
½ cup sugar

Combine margarine, sugar, egg yolks, vanilla, milk and Hershey's chocolate in saucepan and cook over medium heat until thickened. Pour into pie shell. Top with meringue made by beating egg whites until stiff and gradually beating in sugar. Place pie in 450-degree oven until brown. Cool before serving. Serves 6 to 8. NOTE: For a coconut pie, substitute ¾ cup coconut for the chocolate.

MRS. MIKE (PAULA) BUTLER

AMAZING PIE

2 cups milk
4 eggs
1½ teaspoons vanilla
¾ cup sugar

¼ cup butter
½ cup Bisquick
Pinch of salt
1 3½-ounce can coconut

Put all ingredients except coconut into blender for 3 minutes. Pour into buttered pie pan (deep dish) and let stand 5 minutes. Cover with coconut. Bake at 350 degrees for 40 minutes. Serves 6 to 8. Just like old-fashioned egg custard!

MRS. JASPER (GUINN) PYEATT, SEARCY, AR

TOFFEE ICE CREAM PIE AND SAUCE

17 to 18 vanilla or brown edge wafers
½ gallon vanilla ice cream
1 cup chopped Heath English toffee candy bars (about 5 bars)
1½ cups sugar
1 cup evaporated milk, undiluted
¼ cup butter
¼ cup light corn syrup
Dash of salt

Line bottom and sides of buttered pie pan with wafers. Spoon ice cream into wafer shell, sprinkling ½ cup of the toffee between layers of ice cream. Store pie in freezer until serving time. Prepare toffee sundae sauce by combining sugar, milk, butter, syrup and salt. Boil 1 minute. Remove from heat. Stir in remaining toffee. Cool by stirring occasionally. Serve sauce over pie wedges. Yields one 9-inch pie (6 to 8 servings) and 2½ cups sauce.

MRS. WILLIAM (SUSIE) OLD

BROWN SUGAR CRUST

1 cup flour, sifted
¼ cup brown sugar
½ cup oleo
½ cup chopped nuts

Mix flour and sugar. Add to softened oleo and nuts. Press on bottom and sides of pie pan. Bake at 400 degrees for 10 minutes. This is a good crust for apple or pumpkin pies.

MRS. BEN (BERTHA) JACKSON

CHERRY SURPRISE

2 cups plain flour
2 sticks melted butter
1 cup chopped nuts
1 8-ounce package cream cheese
1 box confectioners sugar
2 packages Dream Whip
1 cup cold milk
1 teaspoon vanilla
1 can cherry pie filling

Blend together flour, butter and nuts. Pat into a 9 x 13-inch pan. Bake at 350 degrees until light brown; then let cool. Blend the cream cheese and confectioners sugar. Set aside. Whip two packages of Dream Whip with 1 cup cold milk until it stands in peaks. Add 1 teaspoon vanilla. Mix with cheese mixture and spread on cooled crust. Spread 1 can of cherry pie filling on top. Other fruits, fresh or canned, may be used. Refrigerate. Use a heavy sharp knife to cut. Serves 12 or more.

MRS. DWIGHT (CAROL) HAWKS, HUMBOLDT, TN

SUGAR PLUM PUDDING

2 cups plain flour
1½ cups sugar
3 whole eggs
1¼ teaspoons soda
1 cup buttermilk
¾ cup salad oil
1 cup chopped nuts
1 teaspoon nutmeg
1 teaspoon cinnamon
1 teaspoon allspice
1 cup cooked prunes, chopped

GLAZE:
1½ cups sugar
1 stick butter
1 teaspoon vanilla
1 small (5.33-ounce) can Pet milk

Have 9 x 13 x 2-inch pan greased and floured. Put salad oil and sugar into a bowl and mix well. In another bowl beat 3 whole eggs. Add these to sugar and oil mixture. Then add flour to mixture. Dissolve soda in buttermilk and add to salad oil and flour mixture. Add prunes, nutmeg, cinnamon and allspice and mix well. Finally, add chopped nuts. Mix well and pour into prepared pan. Bake at 325 degrees for 40 minutes. While pudding-cake is baking, make glaze. In saucepan melt butter; add sugar, Pet milk and vanilla. Cook for 3 minutes and pour over hot pudding-cake. Punch holes in cake with fork. Glaze will soak in. This cake freezes well. Make ahead; the longer it sits, the better it gets. Serves 10 to 12.

MRS. JACK (CAROLYN) CUNNINGHAM, MILAN, TN

LEMON BISQUE

1 13-ounce can Pet milk
1 3-ounce box lemon gelatin
1 8-ounce can crushed pineapple
1 cup sugar
3 tablespoons lemon juice
1 10-ounce sack vanilla wafers

Prepare gelatin with 1 cup of boiling water. Drain juice from the can of pineapple into a 1-cup measure. Add enough water to equal 1 cup. Stir this into gelatin. Place in refrigerator to chill until syrupy. Pour Pet milk into a large mixing bowl. Place in freezer and chill well. While gelatin and milk are chilling, crush vanilla wafers into fine crumbs. Butter the bottom of a 9 x 13-inch pan. Press all but 1 cup of crumbs on the bottom of the pan. Reserve 1 cup of crumbs for topping. Beat chilled milk on high speed of mixer until it peaks. Beat gelatin until frothy. Beat gelatin into whipped milk. Then beat in sugar, lemon juice and crushed pineapple. Pour over crumb crust and sprinkle with reserved crumbs. Freeze. Serves 12.

MRS. THOMAS (NANCY) CRENSHAW, HUMBOLDT, TN

CHRISTMAS PUDDING

2 cups white sugar
2 sticks butter
4 eggs, separated
1 cup golden raisins (or ¾ cup dark raisins)
1 box crushed vanilla wafers (12 ounces)
2 cups broken pecans
½ cup bourbon (less, if desired)

Melt butter and sugar together and cool. Add this to 4 egg yolks beaten with bourbon. Add these ingredients to crushed vanilla wafer crumbs. Fold in 4 stiffly beaten egg whites. Refrigerate overnight. Cook next day at 400 degrees for 20 minutes in a 3-quart Pyrex dish. Cut into squares and garnish with a dollop of sweetened whipped cream. Delicious served warm or cool. This dessert freezes well. Serves 10 to 12.

MRS. WALTER (SYLVIA) HILLS
MRS. ALLEN (BEVERLY) FAIL
MRS. T. O. (CAROL) LASHLEE, HUMBOLDT, TN

RASPBERRY PECAN TORTE

1¼ cups flour
⅓ cup powdered sugar
½ cup soft butter or margarine
1 10-ounce package frozen raspberries*
¾ cup chopped pecans

2 eggs
1 cup sugar
½ teaspoon salt
½ teaspoon baking powder
1 teaspoon vanilla extract
Whipped cream

SAUCE:
½ cup water
½ cup sugar

2 tablespoons cornstarch
1 tablespoon lemon juice

*If using berries in plastic bag, add sugar and let stand a while. Berries packaged in boxes are already sweetened. Preheat oven to 350 degrees. Combine 1 cup of the flour, powdered sugar and margarine and mix as for pastry. Press mixture into a 9 x 13-inch pan. Bake at 350 degrees for 15 minutes. Cool. Drain raspberries, reserving liquid. Spoon berries over cooled pastry and sprinkle with nuts. Beat eggs with sugar until fluffy; add salt, ¼ cup flour, baking powder and vanilla. Blend well. Pour over berries and nuts. Bake at 350 degrees for 30 to 35 minutes until golden brown. Cool. Cut into squares and serve with whipped cream and raspberry sauce. Serves 9 to 12. To prepare sauce, combine water, reserved liquid from raspberries, sugar and cornstarch in pan. Cook, stirring constantly, until thickened and clear. Stir in lemon juice and cool.

MRS. RUFFIN (JENNY) CRAIG

UGLY DUCKLING CAKE

1 package yellow cake mix (2 layer size)
1 16-ounce can fruit cocktail
2⅓ cups Angel Flake coconut
2 eggs

½ cup firmly packed brown sugar
½ cup butter or margarine
½ cup sugar
½ cup evaporated milk

Combine cake mix, fruit cocktail (undrained), 1 cup of coconut and eggs in a large bowl. Blend; then beat at medium speed for 2 minutes. Pour into a greased 13 x 9-inch pan. Sprinkle with brown sugar and bake at 325 degrees for 45 minutes. Bring butter, sugar and milk to boiling in small pan for 2 minutes. Remove from heat and stir in remaining coconut. Spoon over hot cake in the pan. This is a very moist cake and stays very fresh for days. Serves 12.

MRS. W. E. HAYNES, SR., DUNNELLON, FL

ANGEL DELIGHT

1 large angel food cake, broken into pieces
6 Butterfinger candy bars, refrigerated and crushed
1 pint whipping cream
¼ cup butter
4 egg yolks
2 teaspoons vanilla
2 cups powdered sugar

Whip together butter, egg yolks and vanilla. Add powdered sugar and blend well. Whip cream. Fold butter mixture into whipped cream. In a 9 x 13-inch Pyrex dish, layer cake pieces, cream mixture and candy; repeat. Refrigerate overnight. Serves 10 to 12.

MRS. JAMES (HALINA) WARMBROD

SHERRY CAKE

4 egg yolks
½ cup sugar
½ cup cooking sherry
1 tablespoon Knox gelatin
½ cup milk
4 egg whites
½ cup sugar
½ pint whipping cream
1 angel food cake (use large bought cake or 1 mix)

Mix egg yolks and sugar in top of double boiler and cook. Add sherry and continue cooking until thickened. Remove from heat. Mix gelatin and milk and add to cooked custard. Cool. Whip egg whites until stiff; then add sugar. Whip cream until thick; then add to egg whites. Fold this into cooled custard. Break large angel food cake into small pieces. Line the bottom of an 8 x 10-inch Pyrex dish with broken cake. Pour half the custard over this. Repeat, using remaining cake and custard. Refrigerate for several hours before serving. To serve, cut into squares and put whipped cream and a cherry on top. Serves 12 to 15.

MRS. MIKE (BETTY) POWERS

ORANGE SLICE COOKIES

1½ cups light brown sugar
½ cup butter or shortening
2 eggs
½ teaspoon salt
2½ cups plain flour
1 teaspoon soda
1 pound orange slices (cut in small pieces and dropped into ½ cup of the flour)
½ cup coconut
1 cup pecans, chopped
½ teaspoon vanilla

Cream butter and sugar; add eggs and beat until very light. Sift 2 cups flour, salt and soda. Add alternately with the coconut and nuts. Then add orange slices mixed with ½ cup flour to creamed mixture. Add vanilla. Drop by small teaspoonfuls on greased cookie sheet. Bake 10 minutes or until light brown at 350 degrees. Makes approximately 5 dozen cookies.

MRS. ROBERT (SYLVIA) JELKS

MARVELOUS MERINGUE COOKIES

2 egg whites
1 cup dates
1 cup powdered sugar
1 cup nuts (optional)

Beat egg whites until stiff; then add sugar, dates and nuts. Drop by ½ teaspoon on pan. Bake at 325 degrees until set and brown. This recipe is as good with nuts as without them.

MRS. ROBERT (BRENDA) HILL

BEST-KEPT SECRETS

SOUR CREAM CASHEW DROPS

2 cups flour
1 teaspoon baking powder
¾ teaspoon baking soda
¼ teaspoon salt
1 egg

½ cup soft butter
½ cup sour cream
6¾ ounces cashews
1 cup brown sugar
1 teaspoon vanilla

Preheat oven to 375 degrees. Grease cookie sheet. Mix flour, baking powder, soda and salt. In blender put egg, butter, brown sugar, vanilla and sour cream. Blend until smooth; then add nuts; chop coarsely. Add this mixture to the dry ingredients, mixing well. Drop by teaspoonfuls onto cookie sheet. Bake for 10 minutes. Cool. Makes approximately 5 dozen cookies.

FROSTING:

4 ounces cream cheese
2 tablespoons butter
3 tablespoons cream

1 teaspoon vanilla
3 cups powdered sugar
½ teaspoon salt

Mix all ingredients and spread on cookies.

MRS. BRUCE (MARY) FISCHER, SACRAMENTO, CA

OLD-FASHIONED TEA CAKES

3 eggs
2 cups sugar
4 tablespoons buttermilk
1 cup shortening or lard
1 teaspoon vanilla

4 cups flour
1 teaspoon baking powder
1 teaspoon soda
½ teaspoon salt

Beat sugar and eggs; add buttermilk, shortening and vanilla. Sift the flour, baking powder, soda and salt together and add to sugar mixture. Blend. Refrigerate for about 30 minutes for easier handling. Roll on floured board; cut and space far apart on greased cookie sheet. Sprinkle with white sugar (optional). Bake at 400 degrees until lightly browned, about 10 to 12 minutes. Lard gives the texture of old-fashioned cookies. Makes 5 dozen.

MRS. LARRY (WANNA) CASEY

PECAN TASSIES

DOUGH:

1 stick butter
1 3-ounce package cream cheese
1 cup flour

Mix butter, cream cheese and flour. Chill thoroughly. Roll into 24 balls. Press into miniature tart pans. Fill shells with 1 teaspoon filling and bake at 350 degrees for about 30 minutes. (If you have a very hot oven, try 325 degrees.) Makes 24 tassies. Store in airtight container.

FILLING:

1 tablespoon butter (soft)
¾ cup brown sugar
1 whole egg
1 teaspoon vanilla
⅛ teaspoon salt
1 cup chopped pecans

Combine all ingredients and fill shells.

MRS. JACK (CAROLYN) CUNNINGHAM, MILAN, TN

PRINGLE COOKIES

1 pound butter (not oleo)
1 cup sugar
2 teaspoons vanilla extract
3½ cups flour
1 cup Pringles (original) potato chips, crushed (do *not* substitute brands)

Combine all ingredients. Roll into balls; press flat with fingers on cookie sheet. Bake 10 to 15 minutes at 325 degrees. Makes 3 to 4 dozen cookies.

MRS. LOWELL (MARY ANN) STONECIPHER

CHOCOLATE TRUFFLES

4 ounces bitter-sweet chocolate (cut into chunks)
5 tablespoons unsalted butter
1 egg
1 teaspoon vanilla
1 tablespoon dark rum
1 pound box confectioners sugar
1 cup finely chopped pecans
½ cup unsweetened cocoa

Melt chocolate and butter over hot (not boiling) water. Remove from heat and cool. Beat egg lightly and add vanilla and rum. Add sifted confectioners sugar and mix well. Blend in the chocolate until none of the white sugar is visable. Add the nuts and knead by hand until thoroughly blended. Roll into walnut sized balls. Roll the balls in the cocoa until well coated. Truffles may be stored in an airtight container, with layers separated by waxed paper, for about a week. Yields 35-40 truffles.

CHINESE ALMOND COOKIES

4 cups flour
2½ cups sugar
2½ cups shortening
½ cup peanut butter
1 egg
1 tablespoon almond extract
1½ tablespoons water
1 teaspoon baking powder
½ teaspoon baking soda

Mix shortening, peanut butter, and sugar. Add flour. Make 3 wells in the flour. Add egg to first well; water, baking powder and baking soda to second well (making sure it bubbles); and almond extract to the third well. Mix thoroughly. Knead several minutes. Roll into ¾ inch balls. Cook in 325-degree oven for 15 minutes. Yields 100 cookies.

FUDGE FOR MEMORIES

3 cups sugar
3 tablespoons cocoa
1 cup pecan pieces
½ stick butter
1½ cups half and half
1 teaspoon vanilla
⅛ teaspoon salt

Combine sugar and cocoa; then add half and half and stir. Place lid on saucepan and heat to boiling. Allow to boil 1 minute. Remove the lid and lower heat and cook to a medium soft-ball stage when dropped by a teaspoon into cold water. Remove candy from heat. Add butter, salt and nut pieces. Place saucepan in cold water and stir as it cools. Do not beat the candy. When mixture begins to be creamy, pour into a buttered platter. Candy has to be made with feeling or it just won't do. I grew up eating "Miss Marjorie's" fudge as a child. I've never found a fudge recipe to compare to it. It's definitely the old-fashioned kind.

MRS. MARJORIE HOUSTON, NEW ALBANY, MS

GRANNY TAYLOR'S CARAMEL CANDY

½ cup milk
4 cups sugar
1 13-ounce can Pet milk
1⅔ cups (scant) caramelized sugar
⅛ teaspoon salt
⅛ teaspoon baking soda
1 stick butter (not oleo)
1 teaspoon vanilla
1 cup pecans (optional)

Grease your cooking pot with margarine; then combine in it ½ cup milk, 4 cups sugar and 1 13-ounce can Pet milk. Cook to a rolling boil. To caramelize sugar, put a scant 1⅔ cups sugar in an iron skillet. Turn burner on next to high to caramelize. Sugar will melt. When it is melted, remove from heat and add to Pet milk mixture in a small stream, stirring constantly. Turn heat from high to medium. Boil this mixture to hard-ball stage. Add salt, soda, butter and vanilla, also nuts if desired. Place pan in cool water and stir occasionally until it begins to thicken. Drop by spoonfuls on waxed paper. Yields 3 dozen pieces.

MRS. A. U. (GRANNY) TAYLOR

CHOCOLATE MILLIONAIRES

1 package Kraft caramels
2 cups chopped pecans
¼ block paraffin

2 tablespoons Pet milk
1 large Hershey bar

Melt in double boiler the caramels and Pet milk. Add chopped pecans. Drop on greased cookie sheet by teaspoonfuls. While these are cooling, melt Hershey and paraffin together. Dip cooled balls in the chocolate mixture. Drop on waxed paper to harden. Makes about 3 dozen balls. These taste like turtles or the $100,000 candy bar.

MRS. JACK (CAROLYN) CUNNINGHAM, MILAN, TN

MARZIPAN

1 small boiled potato (peeled and mashed)
2 pounds powdered sugar

½ teaspoon almond flavoring
⅓ cup cookie crumbs (vanilla wafer or other "white" cookie)

Add sugar to potato to make a paste. Mix well. Add cookie crumbs and flavoring to paste. Divide dough into parts and color with food coloring appropriate for bananas, strawberries, etc. Take lump of dough the size of Ping-pong ball and shape into miniature fruit. Store in tightly covered containers.

FOURTH GRADE CLASS OF THE EPISCOPAL DAY SCHOOL

MAGNIFICENT PRALINES

2 cups light brown sugar
2 cups granulated sugar
1 cup whipping cream

½ cup milk
2 tablespoons butter
1 cup chopped pecans

Mix sugars, cream and milk. Stir well and cook to a soft ball with candy thermometer. Add butter. Place hot candy pan in pan of cold water and beat with wooden spoon until creamy. Put in nuts; mix and drop quickly from teaspoon onto waxed paper. Be careful not to over beat. Allow candy to cool and harden. Store in airtight containers. Makes about 4 dozen.

MRS. ROBERT (JAN) KILBURN

CHOCOLATE BARK

1 package (12 ounces) semi-sweet or milk chocolate chips
1 cup sliced almonds

Place chocolate in 1-quart saucepan; cover and cook 5 minutes on medium setting. Stir well. Add nuts and mix well. Spread onto waxed paper in thin layer. Chill until firm. Break into pieces.

MRS. TOM (FAITH) HADLEY, HUMBOLDT, TN

BEST-KEPT SECRETS

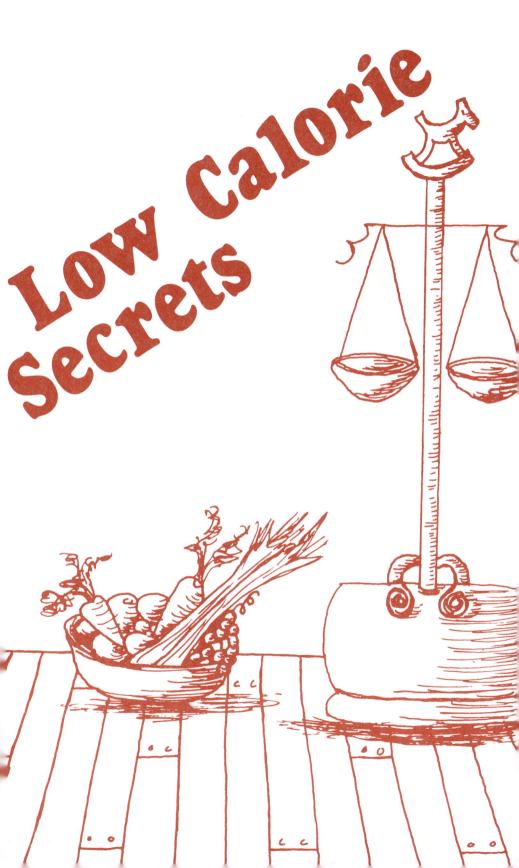

LOW CALORIE IDEAS

Note: *The number of calories per person for the entire meal appears in parentheses after the word MENU in each of the following menus. The number of calories per serving for each item on the menu appears in parentheses under each dish in the following menus.*

Dieting Ideas that have helped others:

1. Keep low calorie snack food prepared and in refrigerator at all times.
2. Add 2 packages Sweet 'n Low to low calorie gelatin to improve flavor.
3. Keep fresh vegetables cut up and clean in jar with ice cubes at all times.
4. Eat 2 or 3 dates to satisfy craving for sugar. Although they have 20 calories each, they are high in natural sugar.
5. Chill canned salmon; serve on lettuce with cracked black pepper and fresh lemon juice.
6. Add caraway seeds and small amount of diet margarine to cooked cabbage.
7. Add sliced water chestnuts and soy sauce instead of fat to cooked French beans.
8. Dijon mustard has no sugar.
9. Substitute nonfat dry or skim milk for whole.
10. Use chicken bouillon to replace fat when cooking vegetables.
11. Keep fresh lemon in the kitchen as a stock item.
12. Make menus for 1 week in advance and have ingredients available to make preparation easier.
13. Eat meals from a salad plate instead of a dinner plate.
14. Hunger is a good feeling; learn to live with it.
15. When recipe calls for browned ground beef, brown patties under broiler; then crumble up patties.
16. Try some of our menu suggestions.

LOW CALORIE SECRETS

DELICIOUS LOW CALORIE SNACK

1 12-ounce carton Light 'n Lively cottage cheese
1 0.56-ounce package green onion dip mix
1 teaspoon dill weed

Mix all ingredients well. Refrigerate 6 to 8 hours before using. Serve as a dip with fresh, crisp vegetables. Makes 12 ounces dip. 90 calories per 4-ounce serving.

MRS. LINDA RICE FORBES

LOW CALORIE SALAD

1 12-ounce carton cottage cheese
1 4½-ounce carton Cool Whip
1 8-ounce can diet pineapple, drained
1 3-ounce package low calorie gelatin, sprinkled in dry

Combine all ingredients and refrigerate. Serves 6. 103 calories per serving.

MRS. NEIL (TONI) SMITH

HORSERADISH CHEESE MOUSSE

1 cup 1% milkfat cottage cheese
¼ cup skim milk
2 tablespoons horseradish
2 tablespoons vinegar
1 teaspoon gelatin (plain)
¼ cup cold water

Put cottage cheese, milk, horseradish and vinegar into blender and whip to consistency of whipped cream. Mix gelatin with water; melt and add to other mixture. Pour into a mold and refrigerate. Serves 6. 35 calories per serving.

MRS. EDMOND (SUSAN) ARNETT, PARIS, TN

FAMILY-STYLE BARBECUE SAUCE

1 cup water
½ cup catsup
1 chopped large dill pickle, if desired
½ teaspoon salt
½ teaspoon dry mustard
Artificial sweetener to taste

Blend all ingredients well and refrigerate. Use to baste chicken, spareribs or hamburgers. Yields 1⅔ cups sauce. 26 calories per ¼ cup.

MRS. NATHAN (CAROLYN) McKEE, GREENWOOD, MS

FRUIT WHIZZ

½ cup fresh fruit (banana, strawberries, peaches)
¾ cup skim milk
1 fresh egg
2 individual packages Sweet 'n Low
1 tablespoon frozen orange juice concentrate
1 teaspoon vanilla
3 ice cubes, crushed

Combine the above ingredients in a blender; blend and serve immediately. Makes 12 fluid ounces. 225 calories per recipe. NOTE: Use Whizz as a meal substitute for 1, 2 or 3 meals a day.

MRS. ROBERT (JAN) KILBURN

LOW CALORIE SECRETS

HOT SPICED COCOA MIX

2¼ cups nonfat dry milk powder
⅓ cup unsweetened cocoa powder
¼ cup granulated sugar replacement
½ teaspoon ground cinnamon
¼ teaspoon ground nutmeg

In a quart jar combine nonfat milk, cocoa powder, sugar replacement and spices. Shake well to combine thoroughly. Store in covered glass jar. Makes 2½ cups mix or 13 servings. To prepare 1 serving, spoon 2 heaping teaspoons (more if desired) of mix into coffee mug; blend in ¾ cup boiling water. 30 calories per serving. (For a better blended drink, stir cold water into dry mix and heat.)

MRS. COLLINS (SUZANNE) BONDS, MILAN, TN

TUNA APPLE MOLD
(A Meal in Itself)

1 package regular lemon gelatin (regular tastes better than low calorie; calories here are for regular)
1 cup boiling water
¼ teaspoon salt
1 cup cold water
2 tablespoons fresh lemon juice
1 6½-ounce can water packed tuna, drained
½ cup chopped celery
1 cup diced, unpeeled red apple
½ cup seedless white grapes

Dissolve gelatin in boiling water. Add salt, cold water and lemon juice. Chill until slightly thickened. Fold in tuna, celery, apples and grapes. Mix well and turn into 5-cup mold. Chill until firm. Unmold and serve on bed of lettuce. Serves 4. 210 calories per serving.

MRS. JAKE (JOAN) McINNIS

MENU (282)

PUFFS FILLED WITH SHRIMP SALAD
(220 per 2 medium)

FRESH, STEAMED ASPARAGUS WITH LEMON
(8 ounces 35)

QUICK AND EASY FRUIT
(27)

LOW CALORIE SECRETS

PUFFS WITH SHRIMP SALAD

PUFFS:
- 1 cup water
- ½ cup diet margarine
- 1 cup enriched flour
- ⅛ teaspoon salt
- 4 eggs

Bring water and margarine to boil. Add flour and salt all at once. Reduce heat and cook, stirring vigorously until mixture is smooth and forms a ball (1 to 2 minutes). Remove from heat and cool. Add eggs 1 at a time, beating well after each. Drop by rounded teaspoons for cocktail puffs or rounded tablespoons for medium puffs onto greased baking sheet. Bake in preheated 400-degree oven for 30 to 40 minutes or until golden brown. Yields 18 medium puffs or 36 cocktail puffs. Fill with shrimp salad.

SALAD:
- 2 4½-ounce cans shrimp
- ¼ cup low fat yogurt
- 2 tablespoons low calorie thousand island dressing
- 2 tablespoons lemon juice
- ½ cup chopped celery
- 2 tablespoons chopped green pepper
- 1 tablespoon minced onion
- 1 teaspoon capers
- 2 tablespoons chopped pimiento
- 1 teaspoon seafood seasoning
- ½ teaspoon salt

Drain and rinse shrimp. Add remaining ingredients. Mix well and fill puffs. Two medium puffs filled with shrimp salad yield 220 calories per serving.

MRS. WILLIAM (DELORIA) HAYNES

QUICK AND EASY FRUIT

1 16-ounce can diet fruit
1 tablespoon unflavored gelatin
1 package Sweet 'n Low
1 drop food coloring
4 tablespoons Cool Whip

Keeping fruit in the can, drain liquid from fruit into saucepan. Add gelatin and food coloring. Heat liquid mixture to dissolve gelatin. When dissolved, pour back into can over fruit. Congeal in can. To serve, open bottom of can and remove to a dish. Slice and serve. Garnish with Cool Whip. Serves 4. 27 calories per serving.

MRS. BOB (NELDA) WHITSON, TRIMBLE, TN

MENU (634)

**SHISH KABOBS WITH
PEPPERS, ONIONS, AND MUSHROOMS
(333)**

**SPINACH STUFFED TOMATO
(85)**

**BAKED POTATO
(100)
WITH MOCK SOUR CREAM
(14 per tablespoon)**

**BOSTON LETTUCE SALAD WITH DIET RUSSIAN DRESSING
(22)**

**PINEAPPLE MINT DESSERT
(80)**

LOW CALORIE SECRETS

SHISH KABOBS WITH PEPPERS, ONIONS AND MUSHROOMS

12 ounces lamb	1 green pepper
10 tablespoons low calorie Italian dressing	1 onion
	12 mushrooms

Cut lamb into 4 equal pieces. Divide each of these pieces into 6 equal pieces or cubes. Marinate lamb in low calorie dressing at least 6 hours. Boil peppers and onions 1 minute before placing on skewer. Alternate pieces of green pepper, onion, mushrooms and lamb. Broil on grill 7 minutes per side. Yields 4 servings with 333 calories per skewer.

LOW CALORIE SECRETS

SPINACH STUFFED TOMATOES

6 medium, ripe tomatoes
1 10-ounce package frozen spinach, cooked according to package directions
1 tablespoon green onion, chopped
1 tablespoon diet margarine
1 teaspoon Cavender's Greek seasoning
1 tablespoon horseradish
Salt and pepper to taste
½ cup dry bread crumbs
¼ inch water in baking dish

Sauté onion in margarine. Add salt, pepper, horseradish and cooked spinach which has been drained well. Core tomatoes and sprinkle insides with Cavender's seasoning. Stuff tomatoes with equal amounts of spinach mixture and sprinkle bread crumbs on top. Place in a greased baking dish with ¼ inch of water. Bake at 350 degrees for 30 minutes. Serves 6 with 85 calories per serving.

MRS. TYLER (KATHRYN) SWINDLE

MOCK SOUR CREAM

1 12-ounce carton lowfat cottage cheese
⅓ cup water
1 tablespoon lemon juice

Blend cottage cheese, water and lemon juice in blender until creamy and smooth. Add desired seasoning and refrigerate. Can be substituted for regular sour cream. Yields 2¼ cups with 14 calories per tablespoon.

SUSAN B. CAMPBELL, JACKSON, MS

PINEAPPLE MINT DESSERT

4 cups diced fresh pineapple
2 tablespoons green crème de menthe
18 small after dinner mint candies

Toss pineapple with crème de menthe. Marinate at least 2 hours or overnight, stirring occasionally. Spoon into 6 dessert bowls or wine glasses. Top each with 3 crushed mints and serve immediately. Yields 6 servings with approximately 80 calories per serving.

MRS. JAMES (SALLY) WALLACE

MENU (329)

BACON AND EGG BAKE
(249)

CREAMED MUSHROOMS ON TOAST
(50)

FRESH CANTALOUPE SLICE
(30)

BACON AND EGG BAKE

4 ounces cooked Canadian bacon, cubed
½ cup (2 ounces) finely chopped Muenster or Cheddar cheese

4 large eggs
1½ cups skim milk
⅛ teaspoon pepper

Preheat oven to 450 degrees. Spray a 9-inch pie pan with Pam. Spread meat in bottom of pan and sprinkle with cheese. Beat eggs with milk and pepper. Pour over meat and cheese. Bake 15 minutes. Reduce heat to 350 degrees and bake 10 to 15 minutes longer until browned and puffed and firm in center. Place pie plate on a wire rack to cool for 10 minutes before cutting into 4 wedges. 249 calories per wedge.

MRS. DAVID (ARLENE) JOSLIN

CREAMED MUSHROOMS ON TOAST

1 3½-ounce can whole mushrooms
1 teaspoon oil
⅛ teaspoon dried thyme
⅓ teaspoon Italian seasoning
⅛ teaspoon garlic powder
⅛ teaspoon cracked black pepper
1 teaspoon flour
1 teaspoon sour cream
Salt to taste
1 teaspoon minced fresh parsley (optional)
½ slice thin toasted bread per serving

Drain mushrooms, reserving the liquid. Heat oil in a small, heavy skillet. Add seasonings and mushrooms. Cook over high heat until almost all liquid from mushrooms has evaporated. Measure reserved liquid and add water, if necessary, to make ½ cup. Mix flour with sour cream and add the mushroom liquid gradually. Pour over the mushrooms and cook, stirring constantly until sauce is thickened. Add salt if needed. Pour over toast; sprinkle with fresh parsley and serve. Will serve 2 with approximately 50 calories per serving.

MRS. JAKE (JOAN) McINNIS

MENU (282)

SLICED TURKEY
(115)
ON LOW CALORIE WHOLE WHEAT BREAD
(110)

WITH
YOGURT GARLIC DRESSING
(12)

SLICED ORANGE SECTIONS
(4 ounces 45)

YOGURT GARLIC DRESSING

1 cup plain lowfat yogurt
1 teaspoon lemon juice
½ teaspoon lemon zest, grated
1 clove garlic, minced
2 tablespoons parsley, minced
1 tablespoon chives, minced
½ teaspoon salt
½ teaspoon pepper

Put all ingredients in a bowl and blend with wire whisk. 12 calories per 2 tablespoons. NOTE: Good as a substitute for mayonnaise on roast beef sandwiches. Also tasty over a green salad.

MRS. JAKE (JOAN) McINNIS

LOW CALORIE SECRETS

LOW CALORIE SECRETS

MENU (487)

SKINNY CLAM CHOWDER
(130)

CHICKEN KABOBS
(231)

SLICED TOMATOES
(17)
WITH DIET POPPY SEED DRESSING
(1 ounce 44)

FRESH GREEN GRAPES
(6 ounces 65)

SKINNY CLAM CHOWDER

2 cups water
1 teaspoon salt
2 medium potatoes
2 carrots, diced
1 rib celery, chopped

1 medium onion, minced
1 6½ to 8-ounce can chopped clams, undrained
1 cup skim milk

In large saucepan boil water; add salt, potatoes, carrots, celery and onion. Cook 20 minutes or until potatoes and carrots are tender. Add clams and milk; bring to boil. Reduce heat and simmer 5 minutes. Serves 4. 130 calories per serving.

MRS. WILLIAM (DELORIA) HAYNES

CHICKEN KABOBS

3 boned chicken breasts, cut in 1-inch chunks
1 8-ounce can diet pack pineapple chunks
3 medium apples, cubed
½ cup soy sauce
¼ teaspoon oil
½ cup water (or juice from pineapple and water)
1 clove garlic, minced
1 package Sweet 'n Low
¼ cup wine vinegar
¼ cup sherry

Combine soy sauce, oil, water (or pineapple juice and water), garlic, Sweet 'n Low, wine vinegar and sherry. Add chicken, pineapple and apple. Marinate for 15 minutes. Alternate chicken, pineapple and apple on skewers. Broil approximately 15 minutes, basting occasionally with marinade. Serve with marinade for dipping. Serves 4. 281 calories per serving.

MRS. DAVID (JANIS) FITE

DIET POPPY SEED DRESSING

1 cup lowfat yogurt
1 cup lowfat cottage cheese
½ tablespoon sour cream
½ tablespoon oil
½ teaspoon salt
½ cup cucumbers, peeled and chopped
½ cup radishes, chopped
2 tablespoons chives, chopped (or 1 tablespoon dried)
½ teaspoon poppy seeds
½ teaspoon oil

Put all ingredients in a bowl and blend well with wire whisk until smooth. Refrigerate. Makes 2¼ cups. 44 calories per ounce.

MRS. WILLIAM (MARCIA) MOSS

LOW CALORIE SECRETS

LOW CALORIE SECRETS

MENU (333)

FISH FANTASTIC
(158)

SUPREME WATER CHESTNUTS AND CELERY
(35)

BAKED TOMATO
(61)

FRESH STRAWBERRIES
(55)

WITH LOW CALORIE WHIPPED TOPPING
(24)

FISH FANTASTIC

4 fish filets (any sort of good quality fish, the fresher, the better)
½ onion, chopped
2 tablespoons fresh parsley or 1 tablespoon parsley flakes
Seasoned salt and pepper to taste
1 teaspoon dill weed
½ cup white wine
¼ cup grated Parmesan cheese
2 teaspoons diet margarine, optional

On large piece of heavy-duty foil, sprinkle chopped onion and arrange fish filets on top. Sprinkle fish with salt, pepper, parsley and dill; dot with diet margarine. Pour wine over all and seal tightly in foil. Bake at 375 degrees for 20 minutes. Pour off liquid into cup. Cover fish with Parmesan cheese and run under broiler until brown. If your diet allows, make cream sauce, using fish liquid as ingredient. Serves 4. 158 calories per serving.

MRS. LINDA RICE FORBES

SUPREME WATER CHESTNUTS AND CELERY

1 celery heart, sliced
2 tablespoons thinly sliced scallions (include some of tops)
1 8-ounce can water chestnuts, drained and sliced
1 tablespoon vegetable oil
1 tablespoon soy sauce
1 tablespoon cornstarch

Sauté celery, scallions and water chestnuts in vegetable oil until translucent. Stir in soy sauce and cornstarch. Simmer until thickened. Serve hot. Serves 6. 35 calories per serving.

BAKED TOMATOES

4 firm medium-sized tomatoes
Small amount of Jane's Krazy Mixed-Up salt or Lawry's seasoned salt
Small amount of seasoned pepper
Small amount of garlic salt
Dried chives
Seasoned croutons
1 ounce grated cheese (Swiss or diet Cheddar)

With sharp knife cut out cone-shaped opening at stem of tomato, large enough to hold small amount of ingredients. Sprinkle into each tomato liberal amounts of salt, pepper, garlic salt and chives. Top with grated cheese and 3 or 4 croutons. (If diet permits, a teaspoon of diet margarine may be added.) Place in shallow casserole with small amount of water in bottom. Cook about 15 minutes at 350 degrees or until tomato skins are crinkly. Serves 4. 61 calories each.

MRS. LINDA RICE FORBES

LOW CALORIE WHIPPED TOPPING

½ cup cold water
1 tablespoon lemon juice
1 teaspoon unflavored gelatin
½ cup lowfat dry milk powder
2 tablespoons sugar
¼ teaspoon vanilla

In small chilled mixer bowl, with chilled beaters, beat water, lemon juice and gelatin until mixed. Gradually blend in dry milk until moistened. Whip at high speed until light and fluffy and soft peaks form. Gradually add sugar and vanilla. Serve at once or chill. NOTE: If topping loses volume after chilling, rewhip. Serves 8 to 10. 24 calories per 3 tablespoonfuls. Makes 2½ to 3 cups.

MRS. WILLIAM (MARCIA) MOSS

LOW CALORIE SECRETS

MENU (391)

FILET OF SOLE, NORMANDY
(175)

SPINACH SALAD
(146)

STRING BEANS IN FOIL
(3 ounces 45)

FRESH PLUM
(25)

FILET OF SOLE, NORMANDY

4 filets of sole, (4 ounces each)
4 thin slices white onion
Salt
¼ cup white wine (Chablis is nice)
½ cup bottled clam juice

1 egg yolk with 2 tablespoons water
Juice of ½ lemon
4 canned artichoke bottoms, optional
4 cooked shrimp, optional

Place filets in a baking dish which has been sprayed with Pam. Place onion slice on top of each filet. Sprinkle lightly with salt. Add wine and clam juice. Cover with foil. Bake 12 minutes at 375 degrees. Remove to a warm serving dish and keep warm. Add egg yolk to liquid and let come to a boil. Add juice of ½ lemon and mix well. Pour sauce over fish. Place in 350-degree oven until hot. NOTE: If using artichokes and shrimp, place both on top of onion; then pour sauce over all. Serves 4. 175 calories per serving.

MRS. ROBERT (JAN) KILBURN

SPINACH SALAD

3 tablespoons wine vinegar
6 tablespoons polyunsaturated oil
½ teaspoon salt
⅛ teaspoon pepper
¼ teaspoon dry mustard
2 tablespoons parsley, chopped
1 clove garlic, cut in half
½ pound spinach leaves
½ cauliflower, cut into flowerets
½ red onion, sliced and separated into rings
½ cup radishes, sliced

Mix together wine vinegar, oil, salt, pepper, mustard, parsley and garlic; let stand for 30 minutes. Remove garlic. While dressing is standing, wash the spinach and remove stems. Dry well and combine with cauliflower, onion and radishes in a salad bowl. Add dressing and toss lightly to mix well. Serves 6. 146 calories per serving.

MRS. JAMES (SHARON) MATTHEWS

STRING BEANS IN FOIL

1 10-ounce package frozen string beans (thawed)
½ teaspoon salt
½ teaspoon pepper
1 teaspoon Accent
2 tablespoons water
1 tablespoon diet margarine
½ teaspoon oregano

Place beans in center of a square of aluminum foil. Sprinkle with remaining ingredients. Fold foil over beans and seal edges to make an airtight package. Place in a shallow pan and bake at 375 degrees for 55 minutes. Yields 3 servings. 45 calories per serving.

MRS. BOBBY (WANDA) McWHERTER

LOW CALORIE SECRETS

MENU (329)

CHICKEN TO LOSE WEIGHT BY
(148)

MIXED DIET VEGETABLE SALAD
(105)

ZUCCHINI CREOLE
(76)

CHICKEN TO LOSE WEIGHT BY

4 chicken breast halves, skin removed
¼ cup soy sauce
1 3-ounce can sliced mushrooms
Seasoned salt
Seasoned pepper
Dried chives
1 8-ounce can sliced carrots
1 8-ounce can green beans, optional

Place each piece of chicken on a square of heavy-duty foil. Sprinkle both sides of chicken with seasoned salt, pepper and dried chives. Also brush both sides with soy sauce. Top with a few sliced mushrooms, green beans and carrots. Wrap tightly in foil. Cook at 350 degrees for 1 hour. Serves 4. 148 calories per serving.

MRS. LINDA RICE FORBES

MIXED DIET VEGETABLE SALAD

1 16-ounce can seasoned sliced green beans (Del Monte)
1 6-ounce can bean sprouts
6 green onions, chopped
1 16-ounce can carrots

SAUCE:
10 individual packages Sweet 'n Low
⅔ cup vinegar
⅓ cup oil
2 teaspoons Jane's Krazy Mixed-Up Salt
½ teaspoon seasoned pepper

Combine vegetables gently in a large plastic bowl with tight-fitting cover. Combine ingredients for sauce and pour over vegetables. Refrigerate overnight. Serve cold on bed of lettuce. Will keep a week or more in refrigerator. Serves 8 to 10. 105 calories per serving.

MRS. LINDA RICE FORBES

ZUCCHINI CREOLE

2 onions, chopped
4 ribs celery, chopped
1 small green pepper, chopped
1 bay leaf
1 16-ounce can tomatoes
3 to 4 medium zucchini
4 tablespoons diet margarine
Salt and pepper to taste

Brown onions, celery and pepper in margarine. Add tomatoes and bay leaf; simmer covered 1 hour. Thinly slice squash. Stir into tomato mixture. Remove bay leaf. Add salt and pepper. Simmer 1 hour. Remove cover and simmer longer if it is too juicy. Serves 6 to 8. 76 calories per serving. NOTE: Can be turned into a greased casserole and topped with 1 ounce grated Cheddar cheese for 105 extra calories.

MRS. JAMES (PAT) CRAIG

LOW CALORIE SECRETS

MENU (470)

BONELESS CHICKEN CACCIATORE
(248)

LOW CALORIE SPINACH CASSEROLE
(75)

ACORN SQUASH
(47)

ROMAINE AND ENDIVE SALAD
(10)

LOW CALORIE DRESSING
(90)

BONELESS CHICKEN CACCIATORE

2 fryers (1½ pounds each)
2 cups water
2 8-ounce cans tomato sauce
1 tablespoon leaf oregano, crushed
½ cup dry white wine
½ cup chopped onion
1 large green pepper, seeded and sliced
1 clove garlic, minced
½ teaspoon salt
¼ teaspoon pepper

Simmer chicken in water in large covered saucepan for 30 minutes. Remove chicken from liquid and allow to cool slightly. Pour chicken stock into a 2-cup measuring cup and refrigerate it. Remove all bone and skin from chicken. Skim off fat from refrigerated stock. Put chicken and 2 cups of stock and *all* other ingredients in a covered saucepan. Simmer for 20 minutes. Uncover; allow to simmer, stirring occasionally for about 10 minutes or until sauce thickens. Remove from saucepan and place in an attractive serving dish. Serves 6. 248 calories per serving.

MRS. TYLER (KATHRYN) SWINDLE

LOW CALORIE SPINACH CASSEROLE

- 1 10-ounce package frozen spinach, cooked
- 3 eggs, separated
- ½ teaspoon salt substitute
- ½ teaspoon pepper
- ⅛ teaspoon garlic powder
- ¼ cup buttermilk
- 1 ounce Colby cheese, grated

Beat yolks; add salt substitute, pepper, garlic, buttermilk and cheese. Drain liquid from cooked spinach and mix with yolk mixture. Beat whites until stiff. Fold into mixture. Bake at 375 degrees for 30 minutes. Serves 6. 75 calories per serving.

MRS. JAMES (ANNE) BARKER

ACORN SQUASH

- 1 acorn squash
- 1 12-ounce bottle Shasta diet creme soda
- 1 tablespoon brown Sugar Twin
- 1 tablespoon imitation butter flavoring

Slice acorn squash and put brown Sugar Twin and butter flavoring over it. Pour creme soda over entire squash. Bake for 1 hour at 350 degrees. Serves 4. 47 calories per serving.

MRS. WILLIAM (LAURA) BURNETT

LOW CALORIE SECRETS

MENU (383)

DIET QUICHE
(245)

BROILED TOMATO
(63)

FRESH PINEAPPLE CHUNKS
(8 ounces 75)

DIET QUICHE

3 cups shredded zucchini squash (salt and set aside)
Mix together the following:
4 eggs, beaten
2 6½-ounce cans drained tuna (water pack)
1½ cups skim milk
1 heaping cup Mozzarella cheese, grated
1 small onion, chopped
Juice from 1 lemon
½ teaspoon salt
½ teaspoon pepper
½ teaspoon dill weed

Drain and pat zucchini dry. Add zucchini to liquid mixture. Pour into 2 Teflon pie tins. For more calories, pour into 2 pastry shells. Bake at 350 degrees for 40 minutes. Serves 8. 245 calories per serving.

MRS. EVANS (GYNEL) WILSON

BROILED TOMATOES

4 medium tomatoes
8 teaspoons diet margarine
8 teaspoons Parmesan cheese

Cut tomatoes in half and core, if needed. Spread a teaspoon of diet margarine over each half. Sprinkle a teaspoon of Parmesan cheese over each half. Broil tomatoes until cheese looks hot but not burned (about 5 minutes). Yields 8 servings. 63 calories per serving.

MRS. ROGER (MARY HELEN) BARKER, TRENTON, TN

MENU (330)

CHICKEN PINEAPPLE MOLD
(80)

CHEESE CUSTARD
(110)

TINY BRAN MUFFIN
(140)

CHICKEN PINEAPPLE MOLD

1 envelope unflavored gelatin
2 cups chicken stock
1 teaspoon salt
1 teaspoon sugar
½ cup canned, diced, unsweetened pineapple
1¼ cups cooked, diced chicken
1 pimiento, diced

Sprinkle gelatin on ½ cup cold chicken stock to soften it. Heat remaining stock to boiling. Remove from heat and add salt. Stir in softened gelatin until entirely dissolved. Add sugar. Chill until it just begins to thicken. Fold in pineapple, chicken, and pimiento. Turn into a mold and chill until firm. Serves 6. 80 calories per serving.

CHEESE CUSTARD

4 egg yolks
1½ cups skim milk
1½ cups grated Swiss cheese
⅛ teaspoon nutmeg
¼ teaspoon salt
4 egg whites

Beat egg yolks; add skim milk, cheese, nutmeg and salt. Fold in stiffly beaten egg whites. Pour into a 10-inch *shallow* casserole or pie plate. Bake at 350 degrees for 30 minutes or until custard is set. Serves 8. 110 calories per serving. Delicious.

MRS. WILLIAM (MARCIA) MOSS

LOW CALORIE SECRETS

MENU
(272 or 345, depending upon entrée)

CRAB DIVAN
(165)

OR

CURRIED OYSTERS
(92)

BOSTON LETTUCE
(5)
WITH FOUR SEASONS DRESSING
(175)

CRAB DIVAN

- 3 6-ounce packages fresh or frozen crabmeat or 3 6½ or 7½-ounce cans crabmeat
- 2 10-ounce packages frozen broccoli spears
- 2 tablespoons flour
- 1 teaspoon salt
- ¼ teaspoon pepper
- 1 tablespoon diet margarine, melted
- ½ cup skim milk
- ¼ cup grated American cheese
- 1 1-pound can tomatoes, well drained
- 2 tablespoons crushed corn flakes

Thaw frozen crabmeat and drain. Remove any shell. Cut into pieces if necessary. Cook broccoli one half the time specified on the package. Drain and place in greased baking pan, 8 x 8 x 2 inches. Spread crabmeat over top of broccoli. Blend flour and seasonings into margarine. Add milk gradually and cook until thick and smooth, stirring constantly. Add cheese and stir until melted. Stir in tomatoes. Pour cheese sauce over crabmeat. Sprinkle with crushed corn flakes. Bake at 400 degrees for 20 to 25 minutes. Makes 6 servings. Approximately 165 calories per serving.

MRS. WILLIAM (DELORIA) HAYNES

CURRIED OYSTERS

2 dozen oysters, drained
1 tablespoon butter
1 cup liquefied instant nonfat dry milk
1 tablespoon flour
1 tablespoon curry powder
½ teaspoon salt
½ teaspoon onion powder

Pour liquefied milk into top of double boiler. Sprinkle flour, curry powder, salt and onion powder over surface. Beat until just blended. Cook over hot water, stirring constantly until mixture thickens. Melt butter in large skillet. Put in drained oysters and simmer until edges curl (3 to 5 minutes). Put into sauce. Serves 4. 92 calories per serving.

FOUR SEASONS DRESSING

1 egg yolk
½ teaspoon garlic powder
½ teaspoon dry mustard
½ teaspoon seasoned salt
¼ cup lemon juice
1 teaspoon dehydrated horseradish
¾ cup vegetable oil
1 teaspoon Worcestershire sauce

Put all ingredients, except oil, in blender. Blend until smooth. Add oil slowly with blender still running. Stop blender; blend again if necessary to have smooth dressing. Makes 1 cup. Serves 8. 175 calories per 1 ounce.

MRS. WILLIAM (LU) MOSS

LOW CALORIE SECRETS

LOW CALORIE SECRETS

MENU (375)

OVEN "BROILED" CHICKEN
(150)

MARINATED BROCCOLI SUPREME
(130)

FRESH BABY CARROTS, STEAMED
(8 ounces 45)

FRESH PEAR HALF
(50)

OVEN "BROILED" CHICKEN

1 small broiler, split
Salt and pepper
Oil

Flour
1 small onion, sliced

Place chicken pieces cut side down on rack in roasting pan. Brush with oil; sprinkle with salt and pepper and dredge lightly with flour. Place thin slices of onion over chicken. Put a little water in the bottom of the pan and place in a 400-degree oven. Baste frequently. Cook 45 to 55 minutes. If not sufficiently browned, run briefly under broiler. Serves 2. 150 calories per serving.

MRS. WILLIAM (MARCIA) MOSS

MARINATED BROCCOLI SUPREME

2/3 cup diet Italian dressing
2 10-ounce packages frozen
   broccoli

2 hard-boiled eggs, chopped
Lemon slices
Parsley

Cook broccoli until just tender in boiling, salted water. Drain. Place in an 8-inch square dish. Pour dressing over broccoli. Cover container and refrigerate several hours or overnight. Before serving, drain off marinade. Place broccoli in serving dish and sprinkle with chopped eggs. Garnish with lemon slices and parsley. Serves 6. 130 calories per serving.

MRS. WILLIAM (MARCIA) MOSS

MENU
(180 or 356, depending upon entrée)

**EGGS BENEDICT
WITH LOW CALORIE HOLLANDAISE SAUCE
(331)**

OR

**EGGS PARMESAN
(155)**

**SLICED TOMATOES SPRINKLED WITH FRESH DILL
(25)**

EGGS BENEDICT

½ English muffin   4 tablespoons Hollandaise sauce
1 poached egg

Broil muffin. Place egg on top and cover with sauce. Broil for 1 minute. Serve immediately. Serves 1. 331 calories per serving.

LOW CALORIE HOLLANDAISE SAUCE:
1 cup skim milk   ½ teaspoon butter-flavored salt
2 tablespoons lemon juice   4 egg yolks
Dash red pepper   1½ teaspoons cornstarch

Heat milk in saucepan until bubbles form around edge. Combine egg yolks, salt, pepper, lemon juice, butter-flavored salt and cornstarch in blender. Cover and blend until smooth. Slowly add hot milk to mixture with blender on medium speed. Pour mixture into saucepan in which milk was heated. Heat over medium heat until it reaches boiling, stirring often. Serves 6. 181 calories per 4 tablespoons.

MRS. WILLIAM (LU) MOSS

LOW CALORIE SECRETS

EGGS PARMESAN

4 eggs
Salt and pepper
2 thin slices lean ham, cut in slivers
2 tablespoons grated Parmesan cheese
2 teaspoons diet margarine, melted

Break eggs into greased shallow casserole (about 8 x 8). Season with salt and pepper. Sprinkle ham slivers and grated cheese over eggs and pour melted butter over all. Bake in 400-degree oven 15 minutes for hard set or 10 minutes for soft set. Serves 4. 155 calories per serving.

MENU (445)

BROILED CLUB STEAK
(3½ ounces 190)

SWEET AND SOUR RED CABBAGE
(95)

**WATERCRESS AND MUSHROOM SALAD
WITH DIET BOTTLED DRESSING**
(100)

MELON BALLS, FRESH OR FROZEN
(8 ounces 60)

LOW CALORIE SECRETS

SWEET AND SOUR RED CABBAGE

1 medium onion, sliced
2 tablespoons diet margarine
1 small head red cabbage, shredded
1 tablespoon brown sugar
½ cup dry red wine (½ cup vinegar for fewer calories)
Salt and pepper to taste

Sauté onion in margarine until tender. Add the remaining ingredients and simmer until cabbage is tender. Serves 6 with approximately 95 calories per serving.

MRS. EDWARD (GAYLE) CROCKER

LOW CALORIE SECRETS

MENU (765)

CHINESE PEPPER STEAK
(606)

ASPARAGUS
(8 ounces 35)

FRESH CAULIFLOWERETS
(4 ounces 12)

APRICOT SHERBET
(½ cup 34)

CHINESE PEPPER STEAK

3 pounds boneless round steak, cut ½ inch thick
¼ cup soy sauce
1 beef bouillon cube
½ teaspoon ginger
½ teaspoon garlic salt
2 tablespoons shortening
5 large green peppers, cut into thin strips
3 tablespoons cornstarch
3 cups cooked rice

On the day before serving trim any fat from meat and cut into strips ¼-inch wide. In medium bowl, combine soy sauce, bouillon cube, ginger, garlic powder and 1 cup boiling water. Add meat; cover and refrigerate. About 1 hour and 15 minutes before serving drain meat; reserve ½ cup marinade. Add shortening to a large skillet and cook meat until it loses red color. Add reserved marinade and 1 cup water; reduce heat and simmer covered 1 hour. Add green pepper and cook 15 minutes or until meat is tender.

GRAVY:
Combine ¼ cup cold water with cornstarch. Gradually stir into hot pan liquid; cook, stirring until mixture thickens slightly. Serve over ½ cup rice per serving. Serves 6. 606 calories per serving.

MRS. WILLIAM (MARCIA) MOSS

APRICOT SHERBET

4 cups apricot nectar
1 cup water-packed apricots, chopped
1 3-ounce package lemon gelatin
Juice of one lemon

Mix all ingredients and freeze in ice cream freezer, 6 parts ice to 1 part ice cream salt, *or* freeze in deep freeze and whip with electric mixer when mixture is partially frozen. Return to freezer. Be careful not to freeze too long. Makes 1½ quarts. ½ cup contains 34 calories.

MRS. WILLIAM (MARCIA) MOSS

LOW CALORIE SECRETS

LOW CALORIE SECRETS

MENU (293)

TACO SALAD
(233)

LOW CALORIE "JELL-O"
(25)

FRESH PEACH
(35)

TACO SALAD

1 pound lean ground chuck
1 1¼-ounce package Old El Paso taco seasoning
2 cups lettuce, chopped
1 large tomato, chopped
½ medium bell pepper, chopped
½ medium onion, chopped
1 tablespoon Cheddar cheese, grated

Broil meat; then crumble in saucepan. Add packaged seasoning and prepare as directions state. At serving time place on each plate a layer of lettuce, pepper, onion, tomato, meat and cheese. Serve immediately. Serves 4. 233 calories per serving. NOTE: Add a layer of crushed Fritos corn chips if you can afford the extra calories.

MRS. LINDA RICE FORBES

LOW CALORIE "JELL-O"

2 0.4-ounce packages unflavored gelatin
1 0.24-ounce package pre-sweetened Kool-Aid
2 cups boiling water
1 cup cool water

Dissolve gelatin and Kool-Aid in 1 cup of cool water. Add 2 cups of boiling water and mix well. Chill until set. Yields six ½-cup servings. 25 calories per serving.

MRS. DAVID (ARLENE) JOSLIN

COOK'S GUIDE
COOKING TERMS

Boil—Cooking in water, or liquid at boiling temperature. Bubbles will rise continually and break on the surface.
Broil—Cooking uncovered by direct heat, placing rack under the source of heat.
Pan-boil—Cooking in lightly greased pan on top of stove. Pour fat off as it accumulates so food does not fry.
Baste—Moistening food while cooking by pouring melted fat, drippings or other liquid over it.
Cream—Mashing or mixing foods together until creamy.
Pan-fry—Cooking in small amount of fat in fry pan.
Knead—Pressing, stretching and folding dough mixture to make it smooth. Bread dough will become elastic.
Parboil—Boiling until partly cooked.
Scald—Heating liquid to just below boiling point.
Simmer—Cooking in liquid just below boiling point. Bubbles will form slowly and break below surface.
Stew—Boiling or simmering in small amount of liquid.
Braise—Cooking slowly in fat and little moisture in closed pot.

HANDY HERB GUIDE

BASIL—Potatoes, cheese, eggs, fish, lamb, tomatoes, peas, squash, duck.
BAY LEAF—Soups, meat stews, tomato sauces and juice.
CHERVIL—Chicken, peas, egg and cheese dishes, spinach, green salads.
CHIVES—Eggs, potatoes, salads, garnish for meats and fish.
DILL—Fish, potatoes, pickles, tomatoes, cream and cottage cheese, fish and vegetable salads.
GARLIC—Meats, vegetables, salads, egg, cheese.
MARJORAM—Vegetable soups, eggs, cheese dishes, beef, lamb, stuffings.
MINT—Beverages, cakes, pies, ice cream, candies, jellies, potatoes.
OREGANO—Tomato sauces, pizza, vegetable salads, chili, pork and veal.
PARSLEY—Meat, vegetables, eggs, cheese, soup.
ROSEMARY—Potatoes, cauliflower, fish, duck, veal, poultry stuffing.
SAGE—Sausages, poultry, hamburgers, pork, stuffings.
SAVORY—Meat, eggs, salads, chicken, soups.
TARRAGON—Vinegar, pickles, chicken, tomatoes, sauces for vegetables and meats, egg and cheese dishes, fish, salads.
THYME—Soups, beef, lamb, veal, pork, oysters, fish, eggs, cheese, stuffings.

COOK'S GUIDE

TABLE OF EQUIVALENTS

Standard Equivalents:
A few grains .... less than ⅛ teaspoon
1 coffee spoon .... 1 teaspoon
60 drops .... 1 teaspoon
3 teaspoons .... 1 tablespoon
2 tablespoons .... 1 fluid ounce
16 fluid ounces .... 1 pint
16 ounces .... 1 pound
16 tablespoons .... 1 cup
1 cup .... ½ pint
2 pints .... 1 quart
4 cups .... 1 quart
4 quarts .... 1 gallon
8 quarts .... 1 peck
4 pecks .... 1 bushel

METRIC CONVERSIONS

COMMON UNITS OF WEIGHT

1 pound .... 454 grams
1 kilogram .... 1000 grams or 2.2. pounds
100 grams .... 3⅓ ounces
1 gram .... 1/1000 kilogram or
                               .001 kilogram or
                               1000 milligrams
1 milligram .... 1/1000 gram or .001 gram or
                               1000 micrograms

COMMON UNITS OF VOLUME

1 quart, 2 pints or 4 cups .... 947 milliliters
1 cup, 8 fluid ounces or
    16 tablespoons .... 237 milliliters
1 fluid ounce .... 29.57 milliliters
1 teaspoon .... 5 milliliters
1 liter .... 1000 milliliters or
                               1.06 quarts
100 milliliters .... 3⅓ fluid ounces
1 milliliter .... 1 cubic centimeter

COMMON UNITS OF LENGTH

1 inch . . . . 2.54 centimeters

COMMON UNITS OF TEMPERATURE

250 degrees fahrenheit . . . . 106 degrees centigrade
350 degrees fahrenheit . . . . 162 degrees centigrade
450 degrees fahrenheit . . . . 218 degrees centigrade

CAKE TROUBLESHOOTING

PROBLEM	POSSIBLE CAUSE
Cake is bready and solid.	Too much flour used.
Cake falls	Insufficient quantity of flour or rising ingredients OR excess temperature OR moving cake in the oven before the cell walls have become firm by the heat after the cake has risen.
Uneven surface	Too much heat used.
Crusting over the top before mixture has risen to full height	Too much heat used.
Bursting at weakest point	Too much heat used.
Coarse-grained cakes	Too much leavening ingredients OR too slow an oven OR insufficient creaming of shortening and sugar OR insufficient beating of batter before adding egg whites.
Heavy cakes	Too slow an oven OR too much sugar or shortening.

TABLE OF EQUIVALENTS

FOOD EQUIVALENTS

Apples	3 pounds	= about 2 quarts, sliced
Baking Powder	1 t. single-acting	= ¾ t. double-acting
Cheese	1 pound	= 4½ cups
Cottage Cheese	1 pound	= 2 cups
Chocolate, unsweetened	1 square (1 oz.)	= 3-4 T. grated chocolate
Cornstarch	1 T.	= 2 T. flour
Crackers, graham	3 cups crumbs	= 30-36 crackers
Crackers, salted	1 cups fine crumbs	= 20 crackers
Dates, pitted	1 pound	= 2 cups
Eggs		
Whole	1 egg	= about 3 T.
	1 cup	= 5-6 eggs
Whites	1 white	= about 2 T.
	1 cup	= 8-10 whites
Yolks	1 yolk	= about 1 T.
	1 cup	= 14-16 yolks
Figs, chopped	1 pound	= 3 cups
Flour, unsifted	1 pound	= 3 cups
All-purpose, sifted once	1 pound	= 3¾ cups
Cake, sifted once	1 pound	= 2 cups
Gelatin, unflavored	1 envelope (Knox)	= 1 T.
Lemon	1 average size	= 2-3 T. juice, 3 T. rind
Lentils	1 cup dry	= 2 cups cooked
Macaroni	1-1¼ cups dry (4 oz.)	= 2¼ cups cooked
Marshmallows	½ pound	= 30 standard size
	1 standard size	= 10 miniature
Noodles	1½-2 cups dry (4 oz.)	= 2¼ cups cooked
Prunes, dried	1 pound, dried	= 2½ cups
	1 pound, cooked	= 4 cups
Punch	1 gallon	= serves approx. 20
	12 quarts	= 96 punch glasses
Raisins	1 pound seeded	= 2½ cups
	1 pound seedless	= 3 cups
Rice	1 cup raw	= 3-3½ cups cooked
	1 cup pre-cooked	= 2 cups
Shortening, Butter	1 pound	= 2 cups
	½ pound	= 2 sticks
	1 stick	= ½ cup or 8 T.
Spaghetti	1-1¼ cups raw (4 oz.)	= 2½ cups cooked
Sugar		
Brown, sieved and packed	1 pound	= 2⅛ cups
Confectioners' sifted	1 pound	= about 4 cups
Granulated	1 pound	= 2⅛ cups
Yeast	1 cake yeast	= 1 level T. active dry
	1 pkg. dry yeast	= 1 level T. active dry
Vanilla Wafers	1 cup crumbs	= about 22 wafers
Zweibach	1 cup crumbs	= 8-9 slices

COOKING FOR 25

Beef	10 pounds
Ham	10 pounds
Pork	10 pounds
Hamburger	8½-9 pounds
Weiners	6-7 pounds
Meat Loaf	6 pounds
Potatoes	8½ pounds
Vegetables	1 No. 10 can
Baked Beans	1¼ gallons
Cabbage for Slaw	5 pounds
Bread	3 loaves
Rolls	50
Pie	5
Cakes	2
Ice Cream	1 gallon
Pickles	½ quart
Olives	⅜ pound
Fruit Salad	5 quarts
Potato Salad	3 quarts
Vegetable Salad	5 quarts
Lettuce	5 heads
Salad Dressing	¾ quart
Milk	1½ gallons
Coffee	¾ pound
Sugar	¾ pound
Cream	¾ quart

To serve 50 people, multiply by 2
To serve 100 people, multiply by 4

COOK'S GUIDE

Type of Meat	Cooking Temp.	Internal Temp.	Approximate Time
POULTRY			
Chicken	325°F.	185°F.	35-40 minutes per pound (4-5 pounds)
	325°F.	185°F.	20-25 minutes per pound (over 5 lbs.)
Turkeys	325°F.	185°F.	20-25 minutes per pound (6-10 lbs.)
			18-20 minutes per pound (10-16 lbs.)
Goose	Same as turkey of equivalent weight		
Duck	Same as chicken of equivalent weight		
PORK			
Loin	350°F.	185°F.	30-35 minutes per pound
Shoulder (Butt)	350°F.	185°F.	45-50 minutes per pound
Fresh Ham	350°F.	185°F.	30-35 minutes per pound
Spare Ribs (1 side)	350°F.	185°F.	1-1½ hours total
Picnic Ham	325°F.	170°F.	33-35 minutes per pound
BEEF			
Rolled Rib	325°F		
Rare		140°F.	28-30 minutes per pound
Medium		160°F.	32-34 minutes per pound
Well Done		170°F.	37-40 minutes per pound
Rib (Standing)	325°F.		
Rare		140°F.	16-18 minutes per pound
Medium		160°F.	20-22 minutes per pound
Well Done		170°F.	25-30 minutes per pound
Rump (Boneless)	325°F.	170°F.	30 minutes per pound
VEAL			
Leg (center cut)	325°F.	170°F.	25 minutes per pound
Loin	325°F.	170°F.	30-35 minutes per pound
Shoulder (Boneless)	325°F.	170°F.	35-40 minutes per pound
Shoulder (Bone-in)	325°F.	170°F.	25 minutes per pound
LAMB			
Leg	325°F.	175°F.	30-35 minutes per pound
Shoulder (Boneless)	325°F.	175°F.	40-45 minutes per pound
Shoulder (Bone-in)	325°F.	175°F.	30-35 minutes per pound

A

Acorn Squash	221
Alaskan Clam-Corn Chowder	115
Almond Bars	37
Almond Cookies, Chinese	194
Almond Spread, Chicken	49
Almondine, Chicken	67
Amazing Pie	185
Angel Biscuits, Quick and Easy	42
Angel Delight	190
Angel Food Cake, Tipsy	83

APPETIZERS

CANAPES

Broiled Cheese Appetizer	93
Burgundy Cheese Ring	97
Carrot and Cucumber Sandwiches	57
Cheese Pastry Appetizer	91
Cheese Puffs	50
Cheese Triangles (Tiropetes)	55
Chicken Puffs	90
Chicken Salad	61
Crabbies	48
Fried Wontons	35
Hot Cheese Puffs	59
Mushroom Crescents	52
Olive Cheese Puffs	89
Puffs with Shrimp Salad	205
Swiss Olive Canapes	66
Toasted Mushroom Rolls	89

CHAFING DISH

Cocktail Meat Balls	100
Drunken Franks	100
Gullah Hot Crab Dip	95
Hot Clam Dip	41
Low Country Oysters	45
Mock Oysters Rockefeller	50
Mushroom Crescents	52
Mushrooms Divine	46
Prairie Fire	94
Spiced Pineapple	100
Spinach Madeleine	46
Spinach Oriental	55

DIPS

Cheese Dip	66
Clam Cheese Dip	94
Crab Dip	66
Creamy Dipping Sauce	97
Delicious Low Calorie Snack	202
Dill Dip	12
Fantastic Shrimp Dip	66
Hot Clam Dip	41
Shrimp Dip	65
Shrimp Dip	94
Spinach Dip	95
Texas Dip	93
Tropical Fruit Fluff	58
Water Chestnut Dip	95
Zippy Beef Dip	96

PICK UP FOOD

Mushroom Strudels	93
Pickled Shrimp	53
Rolled Ham Surprise	92
Sausage Balls	92
Spiced Pineapple Chunks	49
Spinach Stuffed Mushrooms	92
Stuffed Mushrooms	43
Sugared Pecans	40
Sugared Pecans	98
Vegetable Bouquet	149

SPREADS, MOLDS

Avocado Mousse	108
Beef and Cheese Spread	12
Cheese Ball	87
Chicken Almond Spread	49
Easy Cheese Ball	53
Ham Mousse	99
Martha's Individual Cheese Balls	23
Mock Paté	98
"Our Favorite" Cheese Ball	88
Pineapple Cheese Ball	47
Seafood Mold	55
Shrimp Ball	87
Shrimp Mold	58
Swiss Almond Cheese Mold	88
Tuna Paté	108

APPLE

Fresh Apple Cake	177
Tuna Apple Mold	204

APRICOT

Apricot Sherbet	231
Apricot Sunrise Salad	107
Baked Apricots	42
Ginger Apricot Sauce	56

ARTICHOKE

Artichoke Velvet	151
Oyster Artichoke Soup	114

ASPARAGUS

Asparagus Casserole	78
Asparagus-Egg Mold	109
Asparagus with Cheese Sauce	79
Baked Asparagus Dish	33

ASPIC

Orange Aspic	15
Tart Aspic	10
Tomato Soup Aspic	111

AVOCADO
- Avocado Mousse 108
- Avocado Soup 14
- Chicken and Avocado Soup 115

B
Bacon and Egg Bake 209
Bacon Corn Bread 167
Baked Apricots 42
Baked Asparagus Dish 33
Baked Crabmeat Salad 10
Baked Scrambled Eggs 76
Baked Tomatoes 215
Baklava 31
Barbecue Sauce, Family-Style ... 203
Barbecue Sauce 121
Barbecued Chicken 137
Barbecue, Ham 67
Barbecued Pork Chops 70
Bars, Almond 37
Bars, Caramel 21
Basic Muffins 157

BEANS
- Carol's Baked Beans 146
- Ellen Smith's Bean Casserole .. 145
- Spiced Bean Salad 109
- String Beans in Foil 217
- Sweet and Sour Beans I 144
- Sweet and Sour Green Beans II 144

Béarnaise Sauce 120

BEEF (Also See Main Dishes)
- Chicken and Beef Cacciatore .. 140
- Chinese Pepper Steak 230
- Country Fried Steak 74
- Flank Steak Sandwiches 124
- Marguerite's Sukiyaki 122
- Round Steak Casserole 69
- Round Steak Royale 69
- Sauerbraten 123
- Sirloin and Roquefort 125
- Stifado 125
- Zippy Beef Dip 96

BEEF, GROUND
(Also See Main Dishes)
- Chili 13
- Cocktail Meat Balls 100
- Hamburger-Cheese Casserole 72
- Husband's Delight 71
- Jiffy Hamburger Stew 130
- Lasagna 132
- Little Lambless Loaves 72
- Quick-Good Sloppy Joes 73
- Seven Layer Casserole 73
- Spanish Delight 131
- Texas Dip 93

Beef and Cheese Spread 12
Beef Filling for crepes 26
Beer Bread 81
Berries on a Cloud, Cherry 28

BEVERAGES
- French Mint Tea 87
- Fruit Whizz 203
- Hot Cinnamon Mocha 17
- Hot Spiced Cocoa Mix 204
- Hot Mulled Wine 39
- Quantity Fruit Punch 61
- Easy Easy Boiled Custard 65
- Super Eggnog 65

Bisque, Lemon 188
Blum's Coffee-Toffee Pie 182
Boneless Chicken Cacciatore 220
Braised Celery 152
Bran Buds Refrigerator Rolls ... 172
Bran Flakes Muffins 157
Bran Muffins 16

BREADS
- Beer Bread 81
- Buttermilk White Bread 160
- Cheese Bread 161
- Cream Cheese Braids 164
- English Muffin Bread 156
- Fiesta Bread 166
- French Bread 40
- Loaf Bread 160
- Navajo Fry Bread 163
- Oatmeal Bread 161
- Shugfeter Light Bread 165
- Sourdough Bread 159
- Whole Wheat Bread 166
- Whole Wheat Oatmeal Bread 24

BATTERS
- Crepes 26
- Fried Crepe Tidbits 91
- Pancakes 156
- Timbales 170

BISCUITS
- Quick and Easy Angel Biscuits . 42

COFFEE CAKES
- Bucket Bread 158
- Butter Braid Coffee Cake 173
- Cream Cheese Braids 164
- Navajo Fry Bread 163
- Pumpkin Bread 169
- Shugfeter Light Bread 165

CORN BREAD
- Bacon Corn Bread 167
- Corn Light Bread 167
- Corn Meal Cakes 168
- Corn Meal Light Bread 167

Easy Corn Bread	81
Hush Puppies	168
Mexican Corn Bread	21
Sour Cream Corn Bread	168

MUFFINS
Basic Muffins	157
Bran Flakes Muffins	157
Bran Muffins	16
Miracle Muffins	81
Six Weeks Bran Muffins	157

ROLLS
Bran Buds Refrigerator Rolls	172
Easy Quick Rolls	10
Homemade Rolls	18
Icebox Rolls	34
Light Rolls	171
Refrigerator Rolls	27

SWEET BREADS
Bucket Bread	158
Filled Bread	162
Pumpkin Bread	169
Whole Wheat Oatmeal Bread	24

BROCCOLI
Blanche's Broccoli	39
Broccoli Casserole	154
Cold Broccoli Spears	155
Holiday Broccoli	80
Marinated Broccoli Supreme	226
Swiss Vegetable Custard	150

Broiled Cheese Appetizer	93
Broiled Tomatoes	222
Brown Sugar Crust	186
Brown Sugar Fluff	179
Brown Sugar Pecan Pie	183
Brunswick Stew	118
Bucket Bread	158
Burgundy Cheese Ring	97
Butter Braid Coffee Cake	173
Butter Pecan Torte	175
Butter, Strawberry	24
Buttermilk White Bread	160
Butterscotch Brownies	49

C

CABBAGE
German Sauerkraut Salad	111
Overnight Slaw	111
Oriental Cabbage	151
Sweet and Sour Red Cabbage	229

CAKES
Angel Delight	190
Butter Pecan Torte	175
Fresh Apple Cake	177
German Cheese Cake	83
Individual Cheese Cakes	56
Maw's Jam Cake	179
Mother's Orange Slice Cake	175
Pat's Pumpkin Cake	177
Perfect Prune Cake	178
Pineapple Supreme Cake	176
Sherry Cake	190
Sugar Plum Pudding	187
Tipsy Angel Food Cake	83
Truly Different Cupcakes	174
Ugly Duckling Cake	189
Whipping Cream Pound Cake	176

CANDY
Chocolate Bark	197
Chocolate Millionaires	196
Chocolate Truffles	194
Fudge for Memories	195
Granny Taylor's Caramel Candy	195
Magnificent Pralines	196
Marzipan	196
Silver Tip Blossoms	59

Caramel Bars	21
Caramel Candy, Granny Taylor's	195
Caramel Grahams	82
Carmelitos, Oatmeal	13
Carol's Baked Beans	146

CARROT
Carrot and Cucumber Sandwiches	57
Marinated Carrots	79

CAULIFLOWER
Cauliflower Soup	113

CELERY
Braised Celery	152
Far East Celery	153
Supreme Water Chestnuts and Celery	215

CHEESE
Beef and Cheese Spread	12
Broiled Cheese Appetizers	93
Cheese Ball	87
Cheese Bread	161
Cheese Cakes, Individual	56
Cheese Custard	223
Cheese Dip	66
Cheese Grits Casserole	42
Cheese Grits Casserole	77
Cheese Pastry Appetizer	91
Cheese Puffs	50
Cheese Sticks, Parmesan	25
Cheese Sandwiches	143
Cheese Triangles (Tiropetes)	55
Easy Cheese Ball	53
Hot Cheese Puffs	59

Martha's Individual Cheese Balls . 23
"Our Favorite" Cheese Ball 88
Olive, Cheese Puffs 89
Parmesan Cheese Sticks 25
Pineapple Cheese Ball 47
Special Macaroni Cheese 142
Swiss Almond Cheese Mold 88
CHERRY
Cherry Berries on a Cloud 28
Cherry Freeze Salad 112
Cherry Surprise 187
Chess Squares 54
CHICKEN
Barbecued Chicken 137
Boneless Chicken Cacciatore 220
Cherokee Chicken 68
Chicken Almondine 67
Chicken Almond Spread 49
Chicken and Avocado Soup 115
Chicken and Beef Cacciatore 140
Chicken and Dressing 137
Chicken Bienville 141
Chicken Breasts in Wine Sauce .. 138
Chicken Casserole with Rice 136
Chicken Curry 30
Chicken Excelsior 68
Chicken in Cheese Shell 139
Chicken Kabobs 213
Chicken Las Vegas 141
Chicken Monterrey 135
Chicken Pineapple Mold 223
Chicken Puffs 90
Chicken Salad 61
Chicken Salad with a Difference .. 104
Chicken Spectacular 135
Chicken to Lose Weight By 218
Chicken Tetrazzini 133
Glorious Fried Chicken 23
Hot Chicken Salad I 105
Hot Chicken Salad II 105
Hot Chicken Salad III 105
Hot Chicken Salad Casserole 15
Milky-way Chicken 134
Oven "Broiled" Chicken 226
Pressed Chicken 137
Savory Chicken Casserole 134
Sweet and Sour Chicken 68
Williamsburg chicken 136
Chili 13
Chinese Almond Cookies 194
Chinese Pepper Steak 230
CHOCOLATE
Chocolate Bark 197
Chocolate Chip Pie 180

Chocolate Icebox Tarts.......... 16
Chocolate Millionaires 196
Chocolate Truffles 194
My Sinfully Easy Chocolate
  Mousse 180
Versatile Chocolate Pie 185
Chop Suey 36
Christmas Pudding 188
CLAMS
Alaskan Clam-Corn Chowder 115
Clam Cheese Dip 94
Hot Clam Dip 41
Skinny Clam Chowder 212
Cocktail Meat Balls 100
Cocoa Mix, Hot Spiced 204
Coconut Cream Pie 82
Coconut Pie, Crustless 82
Coffee Toffee Pie, Blum's 182
Cold Broccoli Spears 155
Cold Red Snapper 129
COOKIES
Chinese Almond Cookies 194
Marvelous Meringue Cookies 191
Old-Fashioned Tea Cakes 192
Orange Slice Cookies 191
Pringle Cookies 193
Silver Tip Blossoms 59
Sour Cream Cashew Drops 192
Coquilles St. Jacques 128
CORN
Alaskan Clam-Corn Chowder 115
Corn Pudding 33
Cream of Corn Soup 114
Corn Light Bread 167
CORN BREAD
Bacon Corn Bread 167
Corn Light Bread 167
Corn Meal Cakes 168
Corn Meal Light Bread 167
Easy Corn Bread 81
Hush Puppies 168
Mexican Corn Bread 21
Sour Cream Corn Bread 168
Country Fried Steak 74
CRAB
Baked Crabmeat Salad 10
Crab Casserole 73
Crab Dip 66
Crab Divan 224
Crabbies 48
Crabmeat Casserole 130
Gullah Hot Crab Dip 95
Cream Cheese Braids 164
Cream of Corn Soup 114

Cream of Watercress Soup	113
Cream of Wild Rice Soup	116
Creamed Mushrooms on Toast	210
Creamed Shrimp in Sour Cream	126
Creamy Dipping Sauce	97
Creole Egg Casserole	143

CREPES
Crepes	26
Beef Filling for Crepes	26
Fried Crepe Tidbits	91
Sausage Filling for Crepes	75
Crescents, Mushroom	52
Crustless Coconut Pie	82
Crust, Brown Sugar	186

CUCUMBER
Carrot and Cucumber Sandwiches	57
"Secret" Dilled Cucumbers	110
Curried Oysters	225
Curried Tomatoes	145
Curry, Chicken	30

CUSTARD
Cheese Custard	223
Easy Easy Boiled Custard	65

D

Delicious Low Calorie Snack	202

DESSERTS

CAKES, TORTES
Angel Delight	190
Butter Pecan Torte	175
Christmas Pudding	188
Fresh Apple Cake	177
German Cheese Cake	83
Individual Cheese Cakes	56
Maw's Jam Cake	179
Mother's Orange Slice Cake	175
Pat's Pumpkin Cake	177
Perfect Prune Cake	178
Pineapple Supreme Cake	176
Raspberry Pecan Torte	189
Sherry Cake	190
Strawberry Torte	11
Sugar Plum Pudding	187
Tipsy Angel Food Cake	83
Truly Different Cupcakes	174
Ugly Duckling Cake	189
Whipping Cream Pound Cake	176

CANDY
Chocolate Bark	197
Chocolate Millionaires	196
Chocolate Truffles	194
Fudge for Memories	195
Granny Taylor's Caramel Candy	195
Magnificent Pralines	196

Marzipan	196

COOKIES
Chinese Almond Cookies	194
Marvelous Meringue Cookies	191
Orange Slice Cookies	191
Pringle Cookies	193
Old-Fashioned Tea Cakes	192
Silver Tip Blossoms	59
Sour Cream Cashew Drops	192

FROZEN DESSERTS
Apricot Sherbet	231
Chocolate Icebox Tarts	16
Easy Ice Cream Balls	40
French Mint Frango Pies	19
Strawberry Sherbet	34

PASTRY
Brown Sugar Crust	186
Navajo Fry Bread	163
Timbales	170

PICK UP
Almond Bars	37
Baklava	31
Butterscotch Brownies	49
Caramel Bars	21
Caramel Grahams	82
Chess Squares	54
Chocolate Truffles	194
Individual Cheese Cakes	56
Luscious Squares	60
Oatmeal-Carmelitos	13
Pecan Tarts	43
Pecan Tassies	193
Silver Tip Blossoms	59

PIES
Amazing Pie	185
Blum's Coffee-Toffee Pie	182
Brown Sugar Pecan Pie	183
Chocolate Chip Pie	180
Coconut Cream Pie	82
Crustless Coconut Pie	82
Easy Fruit Cobbler	180
Japanese Fruit Pie	184
Lemon Ribbon Pie	184
Lemon Sponge Pie	25
Pineapple Pie	181
Quick and Easy Lemon or Lime Pie	83
Toffee Ice Cream Pie and Sauce	186
Versatile Chocolate Pie	185

REFRIGERATOR DESSERTS
Angel Delight	190
Brown Sugar Fluff	179
Cherry Surprise	187

Cherry Berries on a Cloud 28
  Ginger Apricot Sauce 56
  Lemon Bisque 188
  Low Calorie "Jell-o" 232
  My Sinfully Easy Chocolate
    Mousse 180
  Pineapple Mint Dessert 208
  Raspberry Pecan Torte 189
  Sherry Cake 190
  Strawberry Torte 11
Deviled English Pea Casserole 152
Diet Poppy Seed Dressing 213
Diet Quiche 222
Dill Dip 12
Dip, Hot Clam 41
Dirty Rice 79
Dressing, Diet Poppy Seed 213
Dressing, Four Seasons 225
Dressing for Pear Salad 101
Dressing for Spinach or Lettuce
  Salad 27
Dressing, Poppy Seed 18
Drunken Franks 100
DUCK
  Delicious Ducks 32
  Jo's Roast Duck and Wild Rice ... 133
Duckling Cake, Ugly 189

E

Easy Cheese Ball 53
Easy Corn Bread 81
Easy Easy Boiled Custard 65
Easy Fruit Cobbler 180
Easy Ice Cream Balls 40
Easy Quick Rolls 10
EGG DISHES (Also See Quiche)
  Bacon and Egg Bake 209
  Baked Scrambled Eggs 76
  Creole Egg Casserole 143
  Diet Quiche 222
  Florida Brunch Casserole 76
  Eggs Benedict 227
  Eggs Parmesan 228
  Old Fashioned Farm Fry 77
Eggnog, Super Duper 65
Eggplant and Shrimp Casserole 18
Ellen Smith's Bean Casserole 145
English Muffin Bread 156
English Pea Casserole, Deviled 152

F

Family-Style Barbecue Sauce 203
Fantastic Fruit Salad 106
Fantastic Shrimp Dip 66
Far East Celery 153

Fiesta Bread 166
Filet of Sole, Normandy 216
Filled Bread 162
Filling for Crepes, Beef 26
FISH
  Cold Red Snapper 129
  Filet of Sole, Normandy 216
  Fish Fantastic 214
  Salmon Cakes with Topping ... 74
  Salmon Soufflé 74
  Tuna Apple Mold 204
Flank Steak Sandwiches 124
Florida Brunch Casserole 76
Four Seasons Dressing 225
French Bread 40
French Mint Frango Pies 19
French Mint Tea 87
French Onion Soup 117
Fresh Apple Cake 177
Fried Crepe Tidbits 91
Fried Chicken, Glorious 23
Fried Wontons 35
Frosted Grapes 54
FRUIT
  Fantastic Fruit Salad 106
  Frozen Fruit Cups 112
  Fruit Salad Dressing 101
  Fruit Whizz 203
  Hot Fruit Casserole 102
  Hot Fruit Salad 102
  Quantity Fruit Punch 61
  Quick and Easy Fruit 206
  Tropical Fruit Fluff 58
Fudge for Memories 195

G

GARNISHES
  Frosted Grapes 54
German Cheese Cake 83
German Sauerkraut Salad 111
Ginger Apricot Sauce 56
Glorious Fried Chicken 23
Gourmet Onions 80
GRAINS
  Cheese Grits Casserole 42
  Cheese Grits Casserole 77
  Dirty Rice 79
  Rice Casserole 147
Granny Taylor's Caramel Candy 195
GRAPES
  Frosted Grapes 54
Green Vegetable Casserole 149
GRITS
  Cheese Grits Casserole 42
  Cheese Grits Casserole 77

Gullah Hot Crab Dip 95

H

HAM
    Ham 44
    Ham Barbecue 67
    Ham Mousse 99
    Rolled Ham Surprise 92
    Spearcarrier 122
Hamburger-Cheese Casserole 72
Heaven, St. Paul's 39
Henry Bain Sauce 120
Holiday Broccoli 80
Homemade Rolls 18
Horseradish Cheese Mousse 202
Horseradish Cream 120
Horseradish Sauce 51
Hot Cheese Puffs 59
Hot Chicken Salad I 105
Hot Chicken Salad II 105
Hot Chicken Salad III 105
Hot Chicken Salad Casserole 15
Hot Cinnamon Mocha 17
Hot Clam Dip 41
Hot Fruit Casserole 102
Hot Fruit Salad 102
Hot Mulled Wine 39
Hot Pineapple Casserole 101
Hot Spiced Cocoa Mix 204
Hot Tangy Shrimp 128
Hush Puppies 168
Husband's Delight 71

I

ICE CREAM
    Easy Ice Cream Balls 40
    Toffee Ice Cream Pie and Sauce . 186
Icebox Rolls 34
Icebox Tarts, Chocolate 16
Individual Cheese Cakes 56
Italian Zucchini Casserole 146

J

Japanese Fruit Pie 184
Jezebel Sauce 99
Jiffy Hamburger Stew 130
Jo's Roast Duck and Wild Rice 133

L

Lasagna 132
Lemon Bisque 188
Lemon Ribbon Pie 184

Lemon Sponge Pie 25
Lemon or Lime Pie, Quick and
    Easy 83
Lettuce Salad, Dressing for
    Spinach or 27
Light Rolls 171
Lima Bean and Onion Casserole ... 147
Lime Marinade for Baked Chicken .. 119
Little Lambless Loaves 72
Loaf Bread 160
Lorraine, Quiche 29
Low Calorie Hollandaise Sauce 227
Low Calorie "Jello-o" 232
Low Calorie Salad 202
Low Calorie Spinach Casserole 221
Low Calorie Whipped Topping 215
Low Country Oysters 45
Luscious Squares 60

M

Macaroni Cheese, Special 142
Magnificent Pralines 196
MAIN DISHES (BEEF)
    Brunswick Stew 118
    Chicken and Beef Cacciatore 140
    Chinese Pepper Steak 230
    Country Fried Steak 74
    Flank Steak Sandwiches 124
    French Onion Soup 117
    Marguerite's Sukiyaki 122
    Round Steak Casserole 69
    Round Steak Royale 69
    Sauerbraten 123
    Sirloin and Roquefort 125
    Stifado 125
MAIN DISHES (GROUND BEEF)
    Beef Filling for Crepes 26
    Chili 13
    Fiesta Bread 166
    Hamburger-Cheese Casserole ... 72
    Husband's Delight 71
    Jiffy Hamburger Stew 130
    Lasagna 132
    Little Lambless Loaves 72
    Quick-Good Sloppy Joes 73
    Seven Layer Casserole 73
    Spanish Delight 131
    Taco Salad 232
MAIN DISHES (CHEESE)
    (See Cheese)
MAIN DISHES (CHICKEN)
    Barbecued Chicken 137
    Boneless Chicken Cacciatore 220
    Brunswick Stew 118

Cherokee Chicken	68
Chicken Almondine	67
Chicken and Beef Cacciatore	140
Chicken and Dressing	137
Chicken Bienville	141
Chicken Breasts in Wine Sauce	138
Chicken Casserole (With Rice)	136
Chicken Curry	30
Chicken Excelsior	68
Chicken in Cheese Shell	139
Chicken Kabobs	213
Chicken Las Vegas	141
Chicken Monterrey	135
Chicken Puffs	90
Chicken Salad with a Difference	104
Chicken Spectacular	135
Chicken Tetrazzini	133
Chicken to Lose Weight By	218
Glorious Fried Chicken	23
Hot Chicken Salad I	105
Hot Chicken Salad II	105
Hot Chicken Salad III	105
Hot Chicken Salad Casserole	15
Milky-Way Chicken	134
Oven Broiled Chicken	226
Pressed Chicken	137
Savory Chicken Casserole	134
Sweet and Sour Chicken	68
Williamsburg Chicken	136

MAIN DISHES (EGGS)

Bacon and Egg Bake	209
Baked Scrambled Eggs	76
Cheese Custard	223
Creole Egg Casserole	143
Diet Quiche	222
Egg and Sausage Quiche	76
Eggs Benedict	227
Eggs Parmesan	228
Florida Brunch Casserole (Crustless Quiche)	76
Old-Fashioned Farm Fry	77
Quiche	142
Quiche Lorraine	29
Special Macaroni Cheese	142

MAIN DISHES (SEAFOOD)

COMBINATION

Mid-America Gumbo	118
Seafood Casserole	129

CRABMEAT

Baked Crabmeat Salad	10
Crab Casserole	73
Crab Divan	224
Crabmeat Casserole	130
Gullah Hot Crab Dip	95

FISH

Cold Red Snapper	129
Filet of Sole, Normandy	216
Fish Fantastic	214
Salmon Cakes with Topping	74
Salmon Soufflé	74
Tuna Apple Mold	204

OYSTERS

Curried Oysters	225
Low Country Oysters	45

SCALLOPS

Coquilles St. Jacques	128

SHRIMP

Creamed Shrimp in Sour Cream	126
Eggplant and Shrimp Casserole	18
Hot Tangy Shrimp	128
Puffs with Shrimp Salad	205
Shrimp Casserole	127
Shrimp Jambalaya	127
Shrimp Spaghetti	126

MAIN DISHES (GAME)

Delicious Ducks	32
Joe's Roast Duck and Wild Rice	133

MAIN DISHES (LAMB)

Little Lambless Loaves	72
Shish Kabobs with Peppers, Onions and Mushrooms	207

MAIN DISHES (MUSHROOMS)

Creamed Mushrooms on Toast	210

MAIN DISHES (PEPPERONI)

Pizza Casserole	131

MAIN DISHES (PORK)

Barbecued Pork Chops	70
Chop Suey	36
Ham	44
Ham Barbecue	67
Old Faithful	70
Old-Fashioned Farm Fry	77
Parmesan Bake	132
Pozole with Pork	75
St. Paul's Heaven	39
Sausage Filling for Crepes	75
Spearcarrier	122
Sweet 'n Sour Chops	71

MAIN DISHES (QUICHE)

(See Quiche)	
Mandarin Orange and Onion Salad with Poppy Seed Dressing	110
Marguerite's Sukiyaki	122

MARINADES

Lime Marinade for Baked Chicken	119
Marinade for Pork Chops	119

Marinade for Shish Kabobs	119
Marinated Broccoli Supreme	226
Marinated Carrots	79
Martha's Individual Cheese Balls	23
Marvelous Meringue Cookies	191
Marzipan	196
Maw's Jam Cake	179
Mexican Corn Bread	21
Mid-America Gumbo	118
Milky-Way Chicken	134
Millionaires	196
Mint Frango Pies, French	19
Mint Tea, French	87
Miracle Muffins	81
Mixed Diet Vegetable Salad	219
Mocha, Hot Cinnamon	17
Mock Oysters Rockefeller	50
Mock Paté	98
Mock Sour Cream	208
Mother's Orance Slice Cake	175
Mousse, Horseradish Cheese	202
Mousse, My Sinfully Easy Chocolate	180

MUSHROOMS

Creamed Mushrooms on Toast	210
Mushroom Crescents	52
Mushroom Strudels	93
Mushrooms Divine	46
Spinach Stuffed Mushrooms	92
Stuffed Mushrooms	43
Toasted Mushroom Rolls	89
Mustard Sauce	45
My Sinfully Easy Chocolate Mousse	180

N

Navajo Fry Bread	163

O

OATMEAL

Oatmeal Bread	161
Oatmeal-Carmelitos	13
Whole Wheat Oatmeal Bread	24
Old Faithful	70
Old-Fashioned Farm Fry	77
Old-Fashioned Soup Pot	20
Old-Fashioned Tea Cakes	192

OLIVES

Olive Cheese Puffs	89
Swiss Olive Canapes	66

ONION

French Onion Soup	117
Gourmet Onions	80
Mandarin Orange and Onion Salad with Poppy Seed Dressing	110

ORANGE

Mandarin Orange and Onion Salad with Poppy Seed Dressing	110
Mother's Orange Slice Cake	175
Orange Aspic	15
Orange Slice Cookies	191
Oriental Cabbage	151
Oriental Salad	109
"Our Favorite" Cheese Ball	88
Oven "Broiled" Chicken	226
Overnight Slaw	111

OYSTERS

Curried Oysters	225
Low-Country Oysters	45
Mock Oysters Rockefeller	50
Oyster Artichoke Soup	114

P

Pancakes	156
Parmesan Bake	132
Parmesan Cheese Sticks	25
Parmesan, Eggs	228

PASTRY

Chicken in Cheese Shell	139
Timbales	170
Pat's Pumpkin Cake	177

PEACHES

Peach Bavarian Salad	107
Spiced Peach Salad	108

PECANS

Pecan Tarts	43
Pecan Torte Raspberry	189
Pecan Tassies	193
Sugared Pecans	40
Sugared Pecans	98
Pepper Steak, Chinese	230
Perfect Prune Cake	178
Pickled Shrimp	53

PIE

Amazing Pie	185
Blum's Coffee-Toffee Pie	182
Brown Sugar Pecan Pie	183
Chocolate Chip Pie	180
Christmas Pie	183
Coconut Cream Pie	82
Crustless Coconut Pie	82
Easy Fruit Cobbler	180
French Mint Frango Pies	19
Japanese Fruit Pie	184
Lemon Ribbon Pie	184
Lemon Sponge Pie	25
Pineapple Pie	181
Quick and Easy Lemon or Lime Pie	83

Toffee Ice Cream Pie and Sauce	186
Versatile Chocolate Pie	185

PINEAPPLE
Chicken Pineapple Mold	223
Hot Pineapple Casserole	101
Pineapple Cheese Ball	47
Pineapple Mint Dessert	208
Pineapple Pie	181
Pineapple Supreme Cake	176
Spiced Pineapple	100
Spiced Pineapple Chunks	49
Pizza Casserole	131

PLUM
Plum Congealed Salad	106
Sugar Plum Pudding	187
Poppy Seed Dressing	18
Poppy Seed Dressing, Diet	213

PORK
Barbecued Pork Chops	70
Chop Suey	36
Old Faithful	70
Posole with Pork	75
Sweet 'n Sour Chops	71

POTATOES
Potatoes Anne	77
Super-Duper Potatoes	148
Sweet Potato Surprise	80
Vichyssoise	9
Pot, Old-Fashioned Soup	20
Prairie Fire	94
Pralines, Magnificent	196
Pressed Chicken	137
Pringle Cookies	193

PRUNE
Perfect Prune Cake	178
Pudding, Corn	33
Pudding, Sugar Plum	187
Pudding, Christmas	188
Puffs, Cheese	50
Puffs with Shrimp Salad	205

PUMPKIN
Pat's Pumpkin Cake	177
Pumpkin Bread	169
Punch, Quantity Fruit	61

Q
Quantity Fruit Punch	61

QUICHE
Diet Quiche	222
Egg and Sausage Quiche	76
Florida Brunch Casserole (Crustless Quiche)	76
Quiche	142
Quiche Lorraine	29
Quick and Easy Angel Biscuits	42
Quick and Easy Fruit	206
Quick and Easy Lemon or Lime Pie	83
Quick-Good Sloppy Joes	73
Quick Rolls, Easy	10

R

RASPBERRY
Raspberry Pecan Torte	189
Refrigerator Rolls	27

RICE
Cream of Wild Rice Soup	116
Dirty Rice	79
Rice Casserole	147
Rockefeller, Mock Oysters	50
Rolled Ham Surprise	92

ROLLS
Bran Buds Refrigerator Rolls	172
Easy Quick Rolls	10
Easy Yeast Rolls	170
Homemade Rolls	18
Icebox Rolls	34
Light Rolls	171
Refrigerator Rolls	27

ROUND STEAK
Round Steak Casserole	69
Round Steak Royale	69

S
St. Paul's Heaven	39

SALAD DRESSINGS
Diet Poppy Seed Dressing	213
Dressing for Pear Salad	101
Dressing for Spinach or Lettuce Salad	27
Four Seasons Dressing	225
Fruit Salad Dressing	101
Ginger Apricot Sauce	56
Mandarin Orange and Onion Salad with Poppy Seed Dressing	110
Poppy Seed Dressing	18
Yogurt Garlic Dressing	211

SALADS (CONGEALED)
Apricot Sunrise Salad	107
Asparagus-Egg Mold	109
Avocado Mousse	108
Chicken Pineapple Mold	223
Horseradish Cheese Mousse	202
Low Calorie "Jell-o"	232
Low Calorie Salad	202
Orange Aspic	15
Peach Bavarian Salad	107
Plum Congealed Salad	106
Pressed Chicken	137
Quick and Easy Fruit	206

Spiced Peach Salad	108
Tart Aspic	10
Tomato Soup Aspic	111
Tuna Apple Mold	204
Tuna Paté	108

SALADS (FROZEN)
Cherry Freeze Salad	112
Frozen Fruit Cups	112

SALADS (FRUIT)
Baked Apricots	42
Fantastic Fruit Salad	106
Hot Fruit Casserole	102
Hot Fruit Salad	102
Hot Pineapple Casserole	101

SALADS (GREEN)
Layered Green Salad I	103
Layered Green Salad II	103
Layered Green Salad III	104
Mandarin Orange and Onion Salad with Poppy Seed Dressing	110
Mixed Diet Vegetable Salad	219
"Secret" Dilled Cucumbers	110
Spiced Bean Salad	109
Spinach Salad	217

SALADS (HOT)
Baked Apricots	42
Baked Crabmeat Salad	10
Hot Chicken Salad I	105
Hot Chicken Salad II	105
Hot Chicken Salad III	105
Hot Chicken Salad Casserole	15
Hot Fruit Casserole	102
Hot Fruit Salad	102

SALADS (MEAT)
Baked Crabmeat Salad	10
Chicken Salad	61
Chicken Salad with a Difference	104
Puffs with Shrimp Salad	205
Taco Salad	232

SALADS (VEGETABLE)
Cold Broccoli Spears	155
German Sauerkraut Salad	111
Oriental Salad	109
Overnight Slaw	111
Vegetable Bouquet	149

SALMON
Salmon Cakes with Topping	74
Salmon Soufflé	74
Seafood Mold	55

SANDWICHES
Carrot and Cucumber Sandwiches	57
Cheese Sandwiches	143
Chicken Almond Spread	49
Chicken Salad	61
Fiesta Bread	166
Flank Steak Sandwiches	124
Spearcarrier	122

SAUCES
Barbecue Sauce	121
Béarnaise Sauce	120
Family-Style Barbecue Sauce	203
Ginger Apricot Sauce	56
Henry Bain Sauce	120
Horseradish Cream	120
Horseradish Sauce	51
Jezebel Sauce	99
Low Calorie Hollandaise Sauce	227
Low Calorie Whipped Topping	215
Mock Sour Cream	208
Mustard Sauce	45
Sauce for Wonton or Egg Rolls	36
Sweet and Sour Sauce	36
Sauerbraten	123

SAUERKRAUT
German Sauerkraut Salad	111

SAUSAGE
Egg and Sausage Quiche	76
Lasagna	132
St. Paul's Heaven	39
Sausage Balls	92
Sausage Filling for Crepes	75
Savory Chicken Casserole	134

SCALLOPS
Coquilles St. Jacques	128

SEAFOOD
Seafood Casserole	129
Seafood Mold	55
"Secret" Dilled Cucumbers	110
Seven Layer Casserole	73
Sherbet, Apricot	231
Sherbet, Strawberry	34
Sherry Cake	190
Shish Kabobs with Peppers, Onions and Mushrooms	207

SHRIMP
Creamed Shrimp in Sour Cream	126
Eggplant and Shrimp Casserole	18
Fantastic Shrimp Dip	66
Hot Tangy Shrimp	128
Pickled Shrimp	53
Puffs with Shrimp Salad	205
Shrimp Ball	87
Shrimp Casserole	127
Shrimp Dip	65
Shrimp Dip	94
Shrimp Jambalaya	127
Shrimp Mold	58

Shrimp Spaghetti	126
Shugfeter Light Bread	165
Silver Tip Blossoms	59
"Simply Delicious" Squash Casserole	153
Sirloin and Roquefort	125
Six Weeks Bran Muffins	157
Skinny Clam Chowder	212

SLAW
Overnight Slaw	111
Sloppy Joes, Quick-Good	73
Snack, Delicious Low Calorie	202

SNAPPER
Cold Red Snapper	129

SOLE
Filet of Sole, Normandy	216

SOUPS
Alaskan Clam-Corn chowder	115
Avocado Soup	14
Brunswick Stew	118
Cauliflower Soup	113
Chicken and Avocado Soup	115
Cream of Corn Soup	114
Cream of Watercress Soup	113
Cream of Wild Rice Soups	116
French Onion Soup	117
Mid-America Gumbo	118
Old-Fashioned Soup Pot	20
Oyster Artichoke Soup	114
Skinny Clam Chowder	212
Spring Tonic Soup	116
Vichyssoise	9
Sour Cream Cashew Drops	192
Sour Cream Corn Bread	168
Sour Cream, Mock	208
Sourdough Bread	159
Spanish Delight	131
Spearcarrier	122
Special Macaroni Cheese	142
Spiced Bean Salad	109
Spiced Peach Salad	108
Spiced Pineapple	100
Spiced Pineapple Chunks	49

SPINACH
Dressing for Spinach or Lettuce Salad	27
Low Calorie Spinach Casserole	221
Spinach Dip	95
Spinach Madeleine	46
Spinach Oriental	55
Spinach Salad	217
Spinach Stuffed Mushrooms	92
Spinach Stuffed Tomatoes	208
Superb Spinach	78

Sponge Pie, Lemon	25
Spread, Beef and Cheese	12
Spring Tonic Soup	116

SQUASH
Acorn Squash	221
"Simply Delicious" Squash Casserole	153
Squash Casserole	154
Swiss Vegetable Custard	150
St. Paul's Heaven	39
Stringed Beans in Foil	217

STEAK
(See Beef)

STEW
Brunswick Stew	118
Jiffy Hamburger Stew	130
Stifado	125
Stir Fry Vegetables	150
Stuffed Mushrooms	43

STRAWBERRY
Strawberry Butter	24
Strawberry Sherbet	34
Strawberry Torte	11
String Beans in Foil	217
Stuffed Mushrooms	43
Sugar Plum Pudding	187
Sugared Pecans	40
Sugared Pecans	98
Super-Duper Potatoes	148
Super Eggnog	65
Superb Spinach	78
Supreme Water Chestnuts and Celery	215
Surprise, Cherry	187
Sweet and Sour Beans I	144
Sweet and Sour Chicken	68
Sweet and Sour Green Beans II	144
Sweet and Sour Red Cabbage	229
Sweet and Sour Sauce	36
Sweet 'n Sour Chops	71
Sweet Potato Surprise	80
Swiss Almond Cheese Mold	88
Swiss Olive Canapés	66
Swiss Vegetable Custard	150

T
Taco Salad	232
Tart Aspic	10
Tarts, Chocolate Icebox	16
Tarts, Pecan	43
Tassies, Pecan	193

TEA
French Mint Tea	87
Tea Cakes, Old-Fashioned	192

Texas Dip	93
Three Vegetable Casserole	148
Timbales	170
Tipsy Angel Food Cake	83
Tiropetes, Cheese Triangles	55
Toasted Mushroom Rolls	89
Toffee Ice Cream Pie and Sauce	186
Tomato Soup Aspic	11
TOMATOES	
Baked Tomatoes	215
Broiled Tomatoes	222
Curried Tomatoes	145
Spinach Stuffed Tomatoes	208
Torte, Raspberry Pecan	189
Tropical Fruit Fluff	58
Truffles, Chocolate	194
Tuna Apple Mold	204
Tuna Paté	108

U

Ugly Duckling Cake	189

V

Vegetable Bouquet	149
VEGETABLES (ARTICHOKES)	
Artichoke Velvet	151
VEGETABLES (ASPARAGUS)	
Asparagus Casserole	78
Asparagus with Cheese Sauce	79
Baked Asparagus Dish	33
Green Vegetable Casserole	149
VEGETABLES (BEANS)	
Carol's Baked Beans	146
Ellen Smith's Bean Casserole	145
Green Vegetable Casserole	149
Lima Bean and Onion Casserole	147
String Beans in Foil	217
Sweet and Sour Beans I	144
Sweet and Sour Green Beans II	144
VEGETABLES (BROCCOLI)	
Blanche's Broccoli	39
Broccoli Casserole	154
Cold Broccoli Spears	155
Holiday Broccoli	80
Marinated Broccoli Supreme	226
Swiss Vegetable Custard	150
Three Vegetable Casserole	148
VEGETABLES (CABBAGE)	
German Sauerkraut Salad	111
Oriental Cabbage	151
Overnight Slaw	111
Sweet and Sour Red Cabbage	229
VEGETABLES (CARROTS)	
Marinated Carrots	79
VEGETABLES (CAULIFLOWER)	
Three Vegetable Casserole	148
VEGETABLES (CELERY)	
Braised Celery	152
Far East Celery	153
Supreme Water Chestnuts and Celery	215
VEGETABLES (COMBINATION)	
Green Vegetable Casserole	149
Stir Fry Vegetables	150
VEGETABLES (CORN)	
Corn Pudding	33
VEGETABLES (MUSHROOMS)	
Creamed Mushrooms on Toast	210
Mushroom Crescents	52
Mushrooms Divine	46
Stuffed Mushrooms	43
VEGETABLES (ONIONS)	
Gourmet Onions	80
VEGETABLES (PEAS)	
Deviled English Pea Casserole	152
Green Vegetable Casserole	149
VEGETABLES (POTATOES)	
Parmesan Cheese Sticks	25
Potatoes Anne	77
Super-Duper Potatoes	148
Sweet Potato Surprise	80
VEGETABLES (SPINACH)	
Low Calorie Spinach Casserole	221
Spinach Madeleine	46
Spinach Oriental	55
Spinach Stuffed tomatoes	208
Superb Spinach	78
Three Vegetable Casserole	148
VEGETABLES (SQUASH)	
Acorn Squash	221
Italian Zucchini Casserole	146
"Simply Delicious" Squash Casserole	153
Squash Casserole	154
Swiss Vegetable Custard	150
VEGETABLES (TOMATOES)	
Baked Tomatoes	215
Broiled Tomatoes	222
Curried Tomatoes	145
Spinach Stuffed Tomatoes	208
VEGETABLES (WATER CHESTNUTS)	
Supreme Water Chestnuts and Celery	215
VEGETABLES (ZUCCHINI)	
Zucchini Creole	219
Versatile Chocolate Pie	185
Vichyssoise	9

W

WATER CHESTNUTS
    Supreme Water Chestnuts and
        Celery 215
    Water Chestnut Dip 95

WATERCRESS
    Cream of Watercress Soup 113
    Whipped Topping, Low Calorie 215
    Whipping Cream Pound Cake 176
    Whole Wheat Bread 166
    Whole Wheat Oatmeal Bread 24
    Williamsburg Chicken 136

WINE
    Hot Mulled Wine 39

WONTONS
    Fried Wontons 35

X-Y-Z

Yogurt Garlic Dressing   211
Zippy Beef Dip 96

ZUCCHINI
    Italian Zucchini Casserole 146
    Zucchini Creole 219

Re-Order Additional Copies

SOUTHERN SECRETS
University School of Jackson
232 McCellan Road
Jackson, Tennessee 38305

Please send me _____ copies of SOUTHERN SECRETS at $20.00 plus $3.00 each to cover postage and handling. (Tennessee residents add $1.95 Sales Tax per book.)

NAME _____

ADDRESS_____

CITY_____STATE _____ZIP _____

Make checks payable to SOUTHERN SECRETS.

SOUTHERN SECRETS
University School of Jackson
232 McCellan Road
Jackson, Tennessee 38305

Please send me _____ copies of SOUTHERN SECRETS at $20.00 plus $3.00 each to cover postage and handling. (Tennessee residents add $1.95 Sales Tax per book.)

NAME _____

ADDRESS_____

CITY_____STATE _____ZIP _____

Make checks payable to SOUTHERN SECRETS.

SOUTHERN SECRETS
University School of Jackson
232 McCellan Road
Jackson, Tennessee 38305

Please send me _____ copies of SOUTHERN SECRETS at $20.00 plus $3.00 each to cover postage and handling. (Tennessee residents add $1.95 Sales Tax per book.)

NAME _____

ADDRESS_____

CITY_____STATE _____ZIP _____

Make checks payable to SOUTHERN SECRETS.

Names and addresses of bookstores, gift shops, etc. in your area would be appreciated. _____
_____
_____
_____
_____
_____
_____

- -

Names and addresses of bookstores, gift shops, etc. in your area would be appreciated. _____
_____
_____
_____
_____
_____
_____

- -

Names and addresses of bookstores, gift shops, etc. in your area would be appreciated. _____
_____
_____
_____
_____
_____
_____

SOUTHERN SECRETS
University School of Jackson
232 McCellan Road
Jackson, Tennessee 38305

Please send me _____ copies of SOUTHERN SECRETS at $20.00 plus $3.00 each to cover postage and handling. (Tennessee residents add $1.95 Sales Tax per book.)

NAME _____

ADDRESS _____

CITY _____ STATE _____ ZIP _____

Make checks payable to SOUTHERN SECRETS.

SOUTHERN SECRETS
University School of Jackson
232 McCellan Road
Jackson, Tennessee 38305

Please send me _____ copies of SOUTHERN SECRETS at $20.00 plus $3.00 each to cover postage and handling. (Tennessee residents add $1.95 Sales Tax per book.)

NAME _____

ADDRESS _____

CITY _____ STATE _____ ZIP _____

Make checks payable to SOUTHERN SECRETS.

SOUTHERN SECRETS
University School of Jackson
232 McCellan Road
Jackson, Tennessee 38305

Please send me _____ copies of SOUTHERN SECRETS at $20.00 plus $3.00 each to cover postage and handling. (Tennessee residents add $1.95 Sales Tax per book.)

NAME _____

ADDRESS _____

CITY _____ STATE _____ ZIP _____

Make checks payable to SOUTHERN SECRETS.

Names and addresses of bookstores, gift shops, etc. in your area would be appreciated. _____

_____

_____

_____

_____

_____

Names and addresses of bookstores, gift shops, etc. in your area would be appreciated. _____

_____

_____

_____

_____

_____

Names and addresses of bookstores, gift shops, etc. in your area would be appreciated. _____

_____

_____

_____

_____

_____